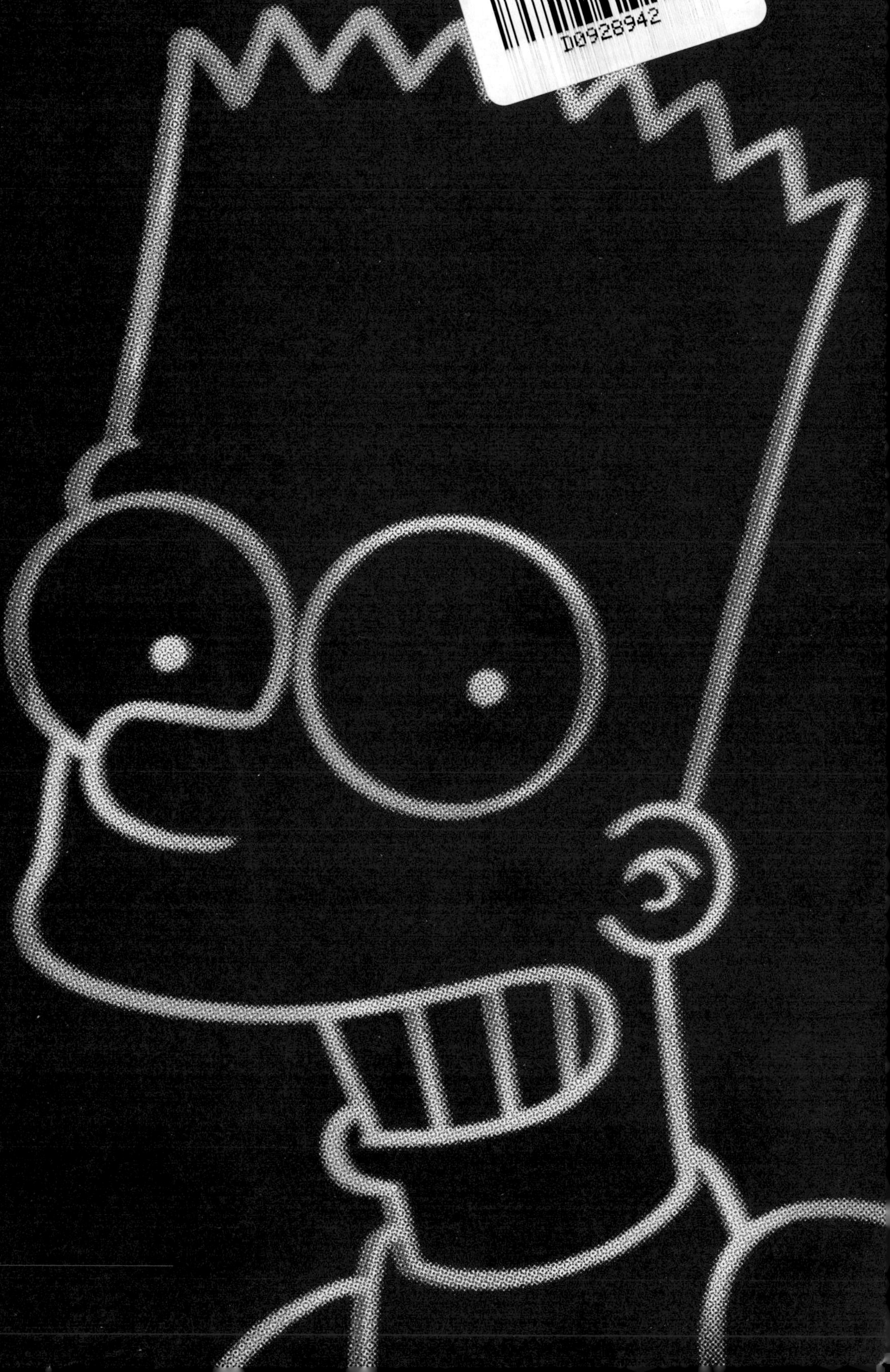

BIG BRATTY BOOK OF BART SIMPSON

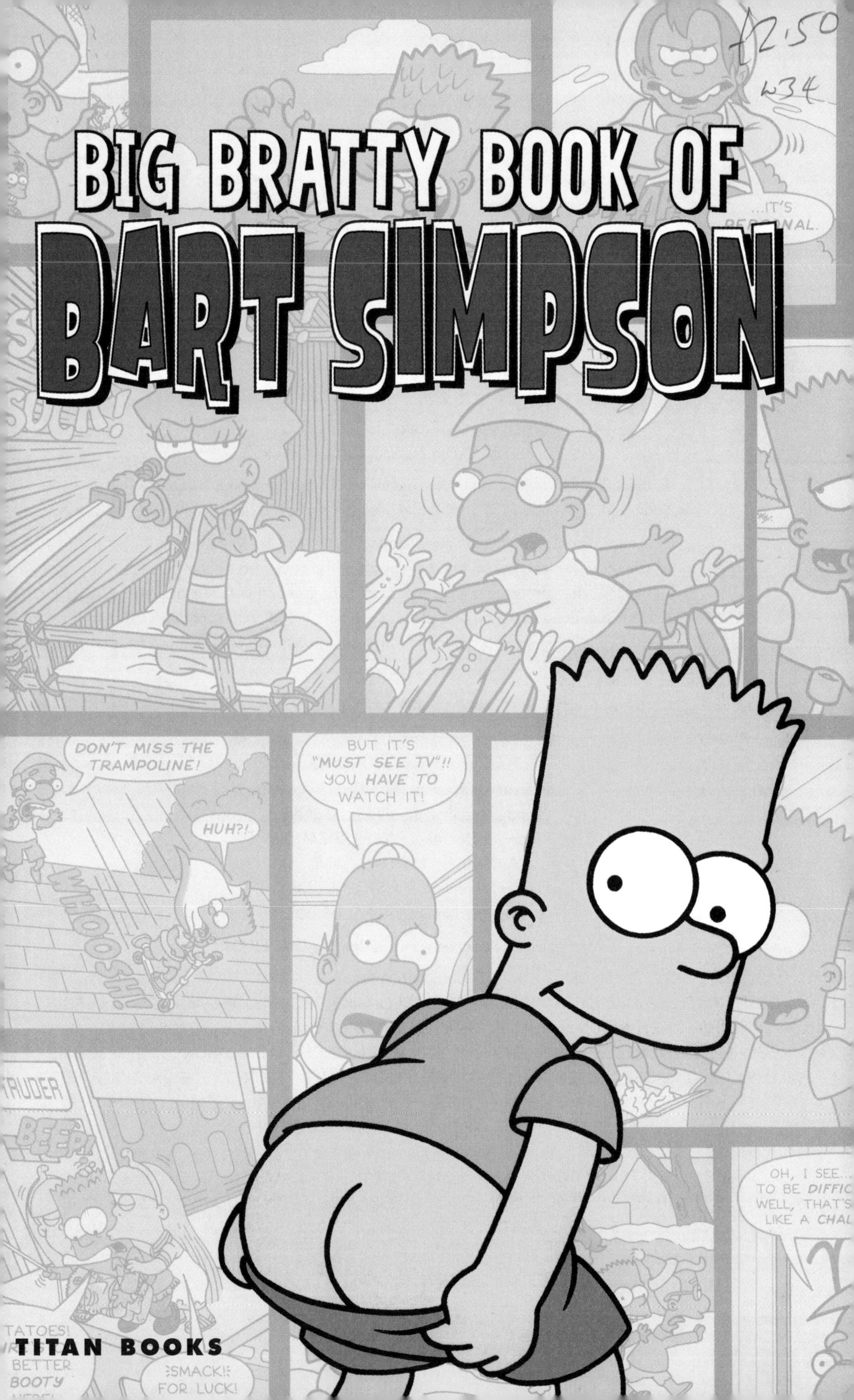
DON'T MISS THE TRAMPOLINE!
HUH?!
WHOOSH!
BUT IT'S "MUST SEE TV"!! YOU HAVE TO WATCH IT!
BEEP!
SMACK!
FOR LUCK!

TITAN BOOKS

BIG BRATTY BOOK OF BART SIMPSON

Bongo Comics Group c/o Titan Books
P.O. Box 1963, Santa Monica, CA 90406-1963

Published in the UK by Titan Books, a division of Titan Publishing Group,
144 Southwark St., London SE1 0UP, under licence from Bongo Entertainment, Inc.

FIRST EDITION: JUNE 2004

ISBN 1-84023-846-1
2 4 6 8 10 9 7 5 3 1

Publisher: MATT GROENING
Creative Director: BILL MORRISON
Managing Editor: TERRY DELEGEANE
Director of Operations: ROBERT ZAUGH
Art Director: NATHAN KANE
Production Manager: CHRISTOPHER UNGAR
Legal Guardian: SUSAN A. GRODE

Trade Paperback Concepts and Design: NATHAN KANE

Contributing Artists:
KAREN BATES, JOHN COSTANZA, DAN DECARLO, MIKE DECARLO, FRANCIS DINGLASAN,
CHIA-HSIEN JASON HO, JAMES HUANG, JASON LATOUR, KIM LE, JAMES LLOYD,
OSCAR GONZALEZ LOYO, NATHAN KANE, ISTVAN MAJOROS, JOEY MASON, SCOTT MCRAE,
BILL MORRISON, JOEY NILGES, PHYLLIS NOVIN, PHIL ORTIZ, PATRICK OWSLEY, ANDREW PEPOY,
RICK REESE, RYAN RIVETTE, MIKE ROTE, HORACIO SANDOVAL, STEVE STEERE, JR.,
CHRIS UNGAR, ART VILLANUEVA, MIKE WORLEY
Contributing Writers:
JAMES BATES, TRACY BERNA, ABBY DENSON, TONY DIGEROLAMO, GEORGE GLADIR,
ROBERT L. GRAFF, CLINT JOHNSON, EARL KRESS, JESSE LEON MCCANN, GAIL SIMONE,
SHERRI L. SMITH, PATRIC VERRONE, CHRIS YAMBAR

PRINTED IN CANADA

TABLE OF CONTENTS

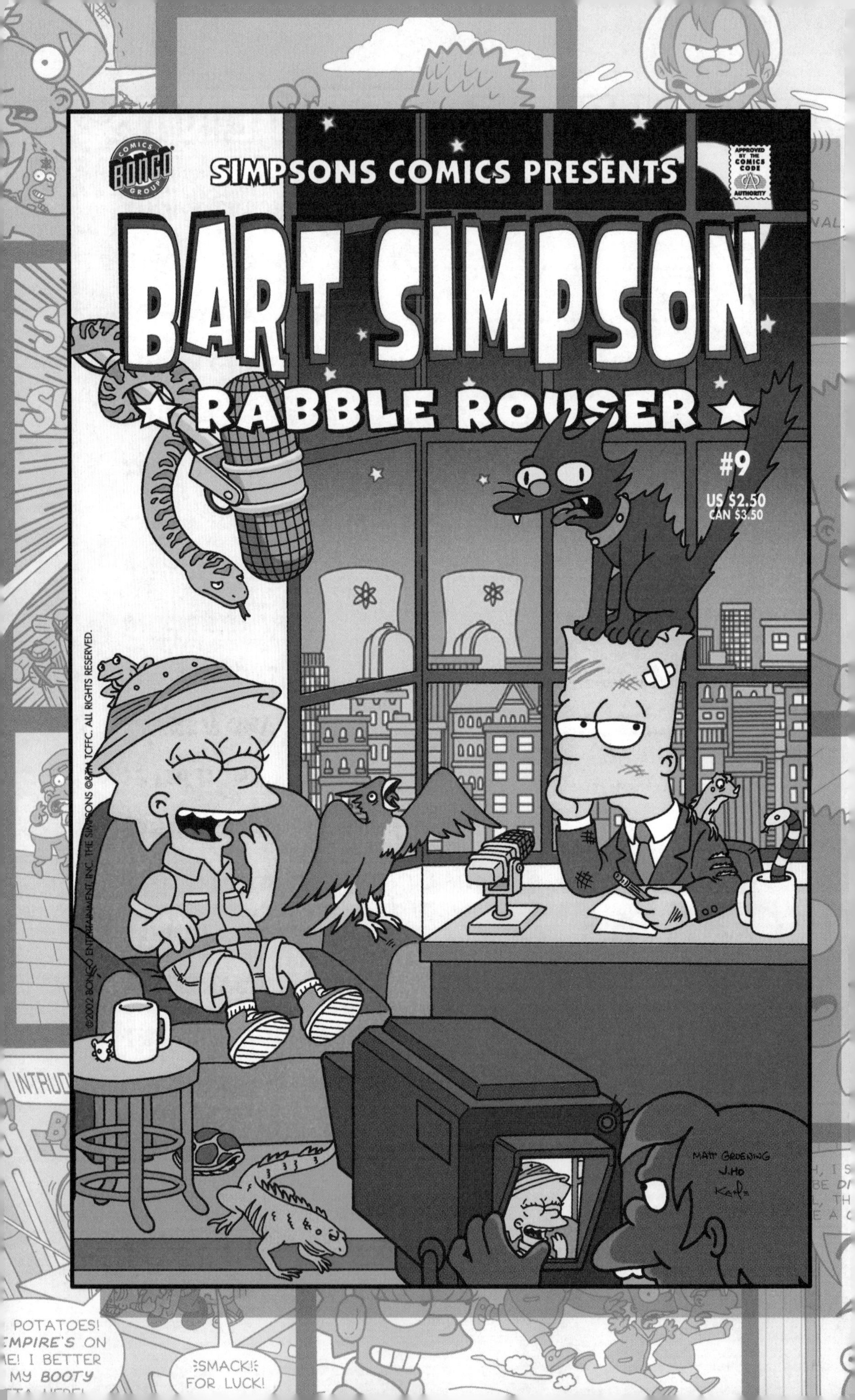

BONGO COMICS GROUP
APPROVED BY THE COMICS CODE AUTHORITY
SIMPSONS COMICS PRESENTS
BART SIMPSON
★ RABBLE ROUSER ★
#9
US $2.50
CAN $3.50
©2002 BONGO ENTERTAINMENT, INC. THE SIMPSONS ©&™ TCFFC. ALL RIGHTS RESERVED.
MATT GROENING
J.HO
POTATOES!
SMACK! FOR LUCK!

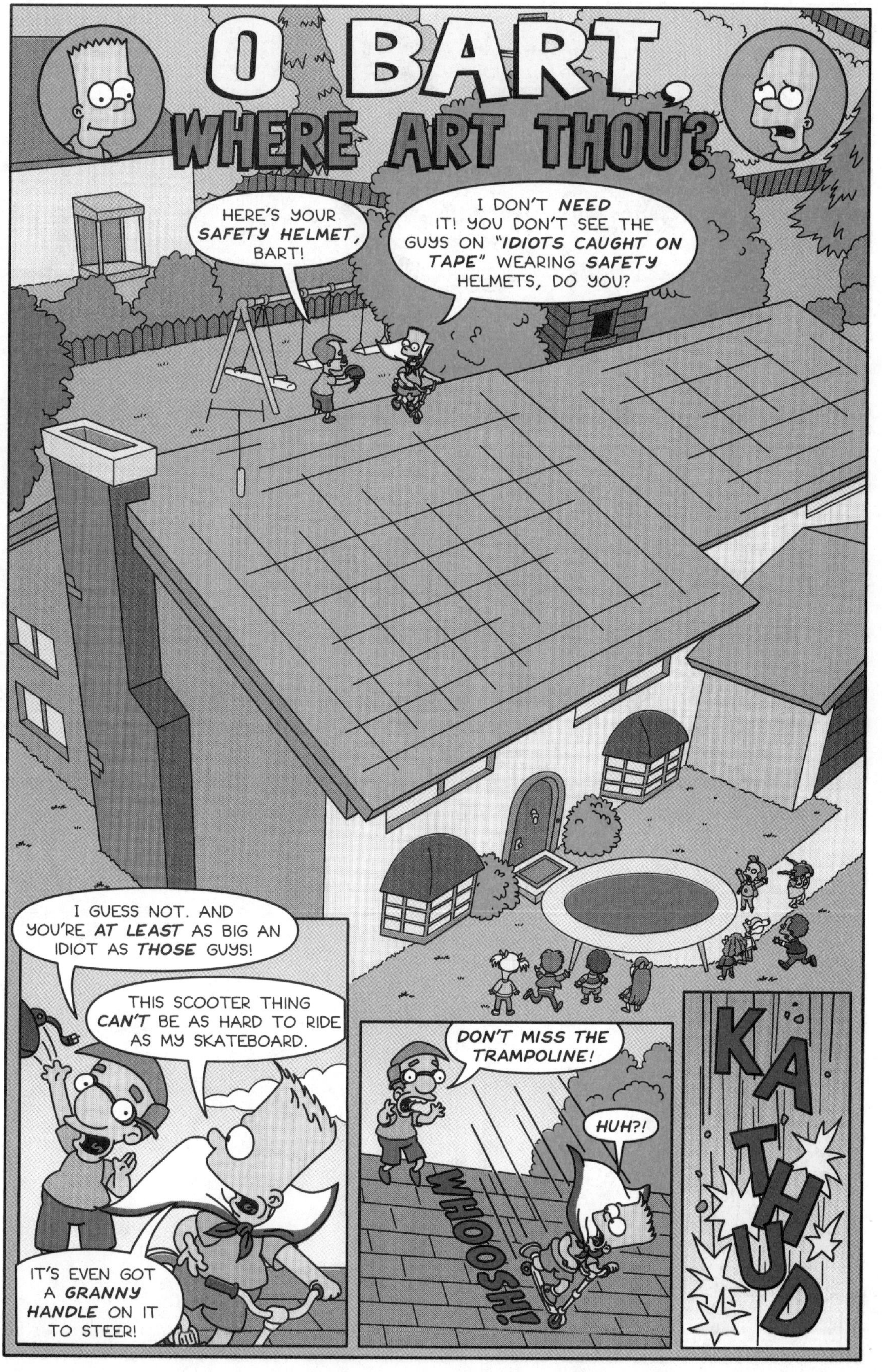
O BART, WHERE ART THOU?
HERE'S YOUR SAFETY HELMET, BART!
I DON'T NEED IT! YOU DON'T SEE THE GUYS ON "IDIOTS CAUGHT ON TAPE" WEARING SAFETY HELMETS, DO YOU?
I GUESS NOT. AND YOU'RE AT LEAST AS BIG AN IDIOT AS THOSE GUYS!
THIS SCOOTER THING CAN'T BE AS HARD TO RIDE AS MY SKATEBOARD.
IT'S EVEN GOT A GRANNY HANDLE ON IT TO STEER!
DON'T MISS THE TRAMPOLINE!
HUH?!
WHOOOSH!
KA THUD

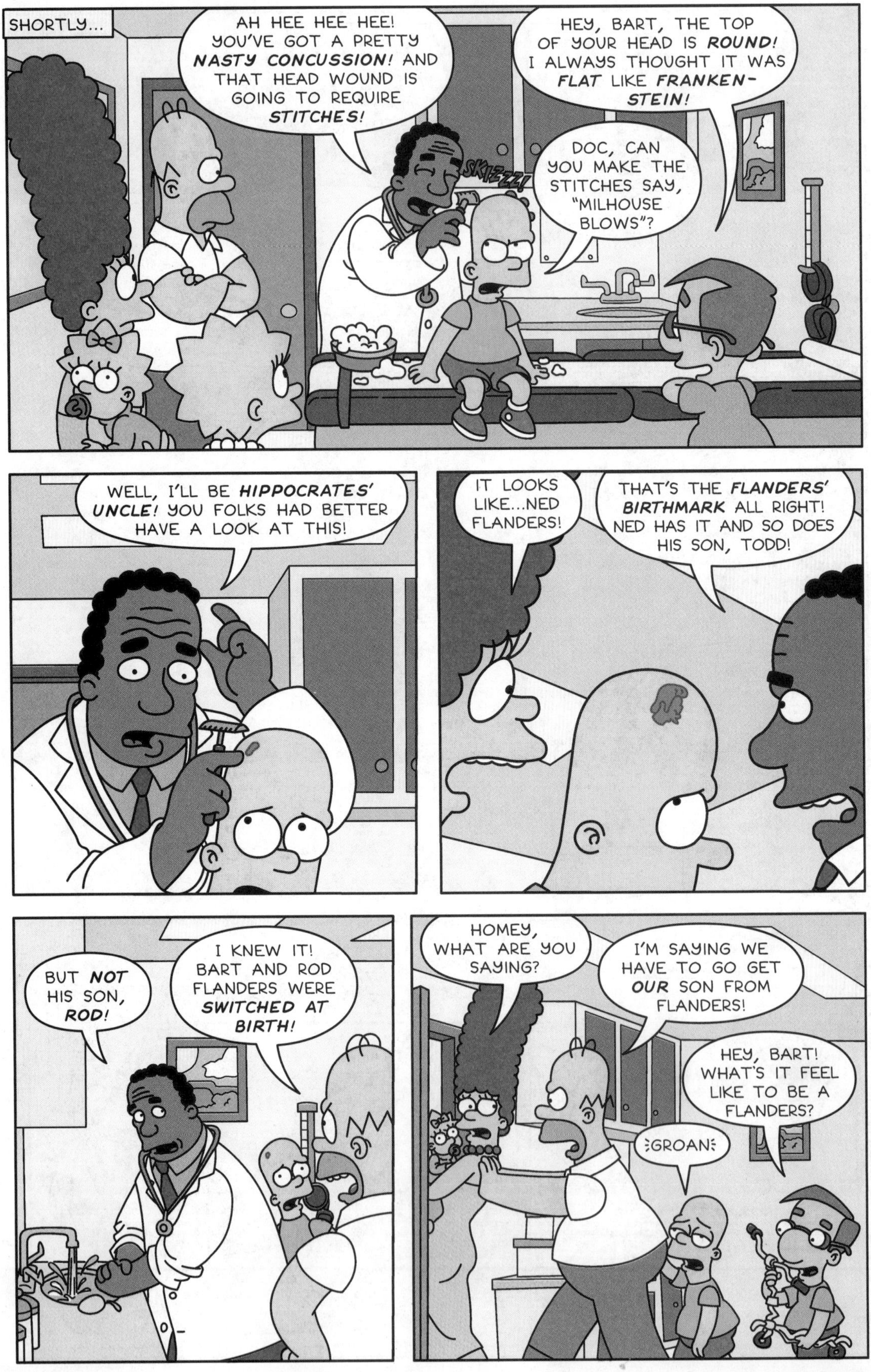
SHORTLY...
AH HEE HEE HEE! YOU'VE GOT A PRETTY NASTY CONCUSSION! AND THAT HEAD WOUND IS GOING TO REQUIRE STITCHES!
HEY, BART, THE TOP OF YOUR HEAD IS ROUND! I ALWAYS THOUGHT IT WAS FLAT LIKE FRANKEN-STEIN!
SKIZZZ!
DOC, CAN YOU MAKE THE STITCHES SAY, "MILHOUSE BLOWS"?
WELL, I'LL BE HIPPOCRATES' UNCLE! YOU FOLKS HAD BETTER HAVE A LOOK AT THIS!
IT LOOKS LIKE...NED FLANDERS!
THAT'S THE FLANDERS' BIRTHMARK ALL RIGHT! NED HAS IT AND SO DOES HIS SON, TODD!
BUT NOT HIS SON, ROD!
I KNEW IT! BART AND ROD FLANDERS WERE SWITCHED AT BIRTH!
HOMEY, WHAT ARE YOU SAYING?
I'M SAYING WE HAVE TO GO GET OUR SON FROM FLANDERS!
HEY, BART! WHAT'S IT FEEL LIKE TO BE A FLANDERS?
GROAN

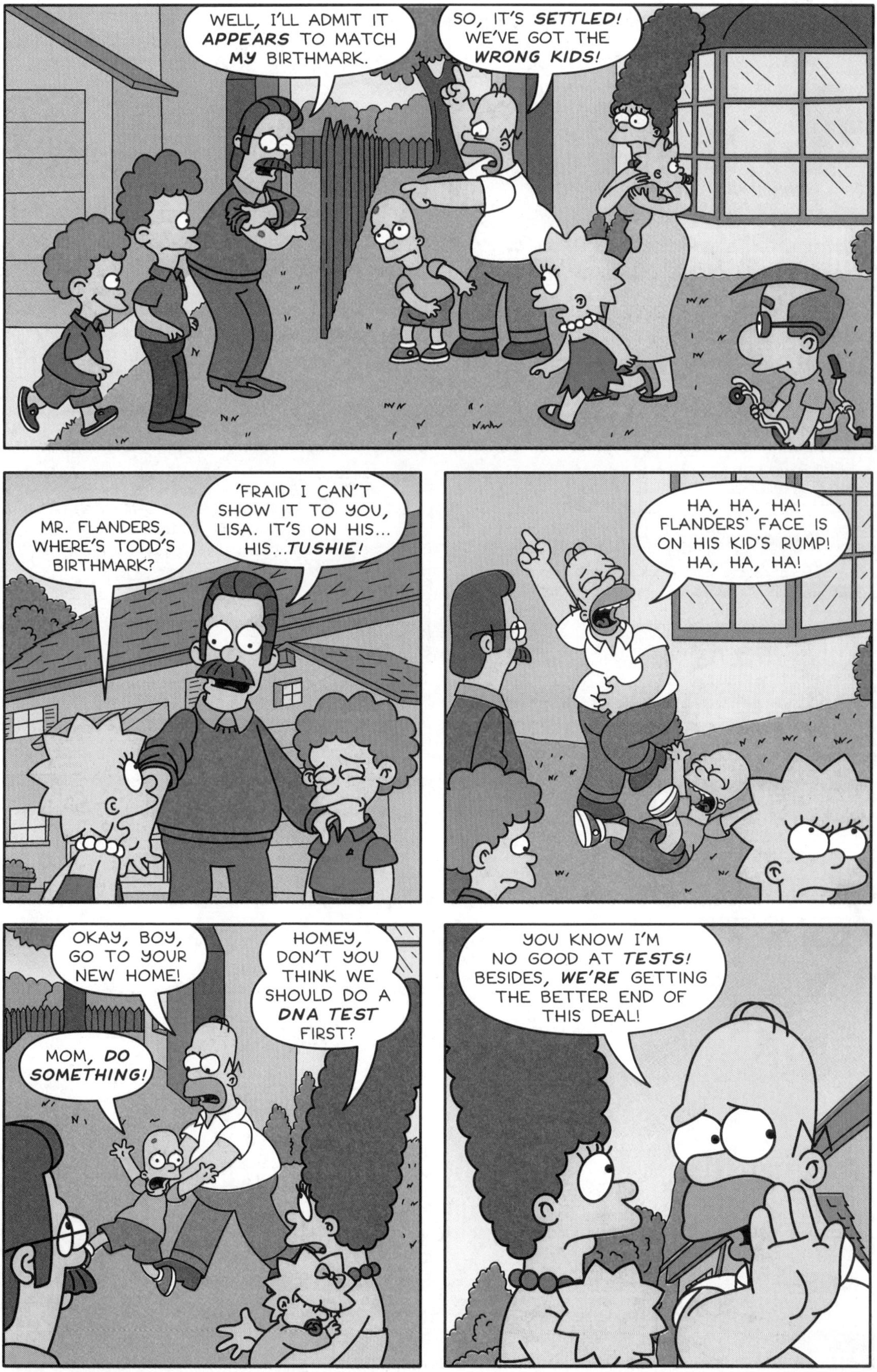
WELL, I'LL ADMIT IT APPEARS TO MATCH MY BIRTHMARK.
SO, IT'S SETTLED! WE'VE GOT THE WRONG KIDS!
MR. FLANDERS, WHERE'S TODD'S BIRTHMARK?
'FRAID I CAN'T SHOW IT TO YOU, LISA. IT'S ON HIS... HIS...TUSHIE!
HA, HA, HA! FLANDERS' FACE IS ON HIS KID'S RUMP! HA, HA, HA!
OKAY, BOY, GO TO YOUR NEW HOME!
HOMEY, DON'T YOU THINK WE SHOULD DO A DNA TEST FIRST?
MOM, DO SOMETHING!
YOU KNOW I'M NO GOOD AT TESTS! BESIDES, WE'RE GETTING THE BETTER END OF THIS DEAL!

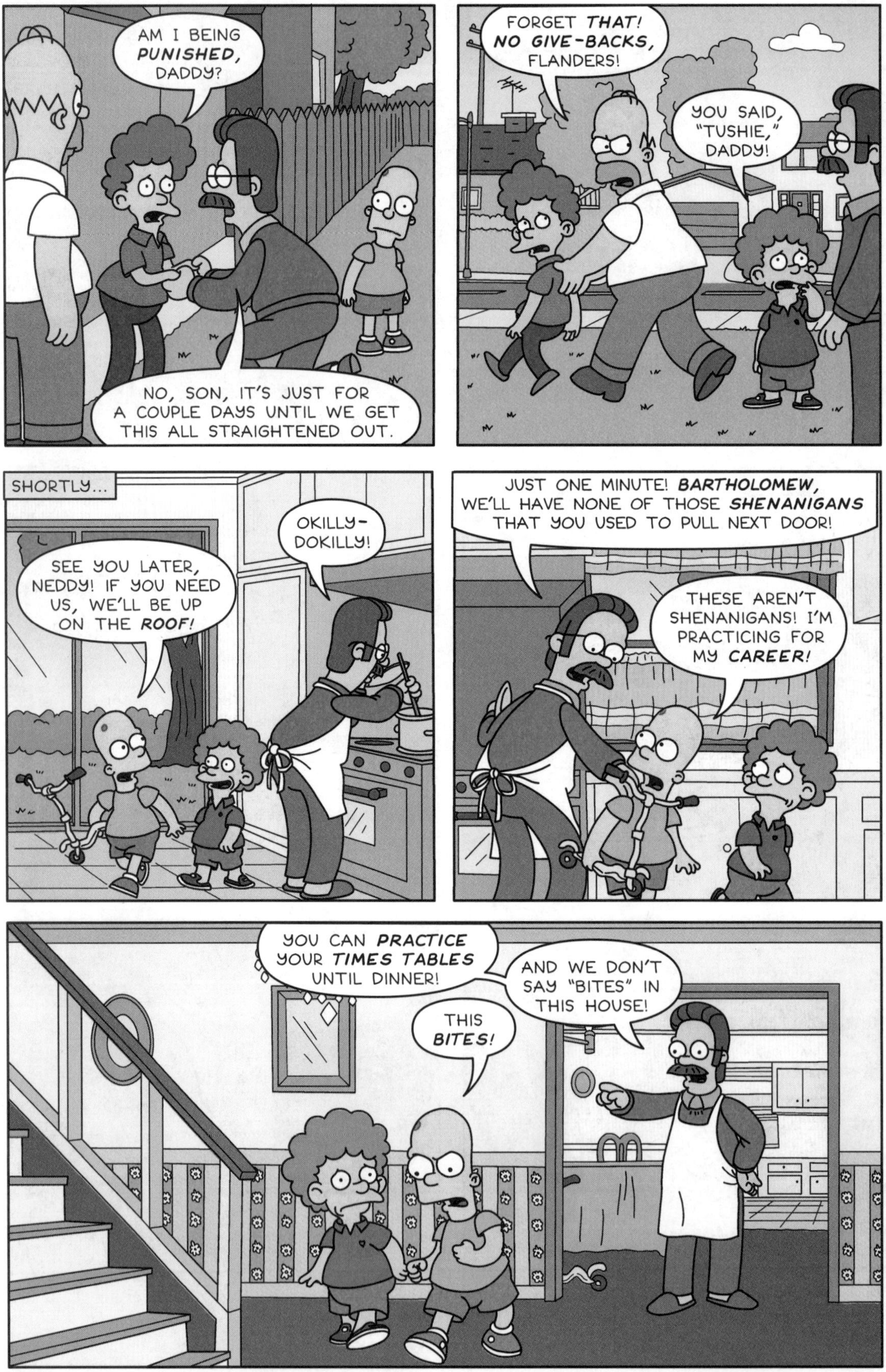
AM I BEING *PUNISHED,* DADDY?
NO, SON, IT'S JUST FOR A COUPLE DAYS UNTIL WE GET THIS ALL STRAIGHTENED OUT.
FORGET *THAT!* *NO GIVE-BACKS,* FLANDERS!
YOU SAID, "TUSHIE," DADDY!
SHORTLY...
SEE YOU LATER, NEDDY! IF YOU NEED US, WE'LL BE UP ON THE *ROOF!*
OKILLY-DOKILLY!
JUST ONE MINUTE! *BARTHOLOMEW,* WE'LL HAVE NONE OF THOSE *SHENANIGANS* THAT YOU USED TO PULL NEXT DOOR!
THESE AREN'T SHENANIGANS! I'M PRACTICING FOR MY *CAREER!*
YOU CAN *PRACTICE* YOUR *TIMES TABLES* UNTIL DINNER!
THIS *BITES!*
AND WE DON'T SAY "BITES" IN THIS HOUSE!

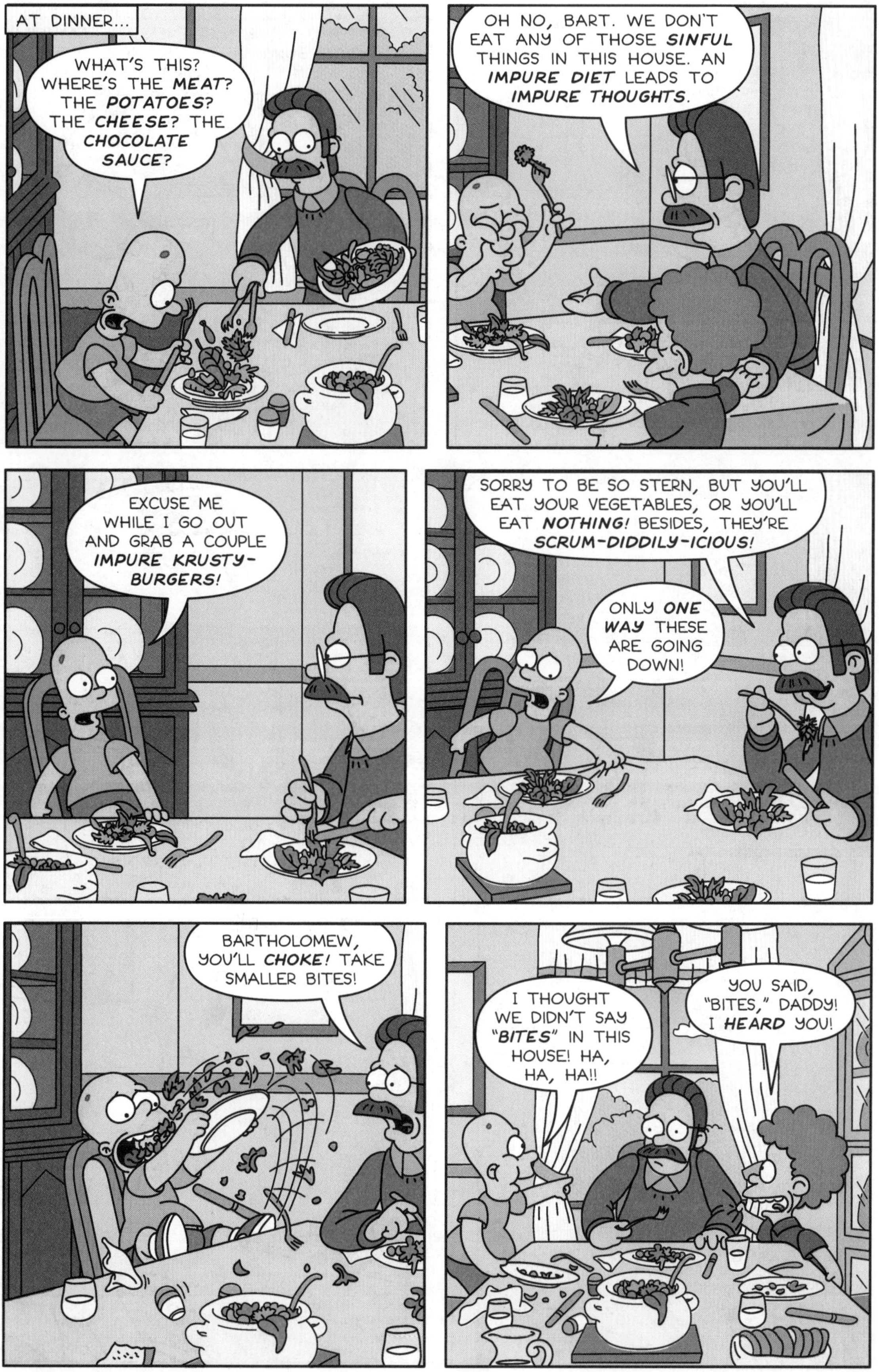
AT DINNER...
WHAT'S THIS? WHERE'S THE MEAT? THE POTATOES? THE CHEESE? THE CHOCOLATE SAUCE?
OH NO, BART. WE DON'T EAT ANY OF THOSE SINFUL THINGS IN THIS HOUSE. AN IMPURE DIET LEADS TO IMPURE THOUGHTS.
EXCUSE ME WHILE I GO OUT AND GRAB A COUPLE IMPURE KRUSTY-BURGERS!
SORRY TO BE SO STERN, BUT YOU'LL EAT YOUR VEGETABLES, OR YOU'LL EAT NOTHING! BESIDES, THEY'RE SCRUM-DIDDILY-ICIOUS!
ONLY ONE WAY THESE ARE GOING DOWN!
BARTHOLOMEW, YOU'LL CHOKE! TAKE SMALLER BITES!
I THOUGHT WE DIDN'T SAY "BITES" IN THIS HOUSE! HA, HA, HA!!
YOU SAID, "BITES," DADDY! I HEARD YOU!

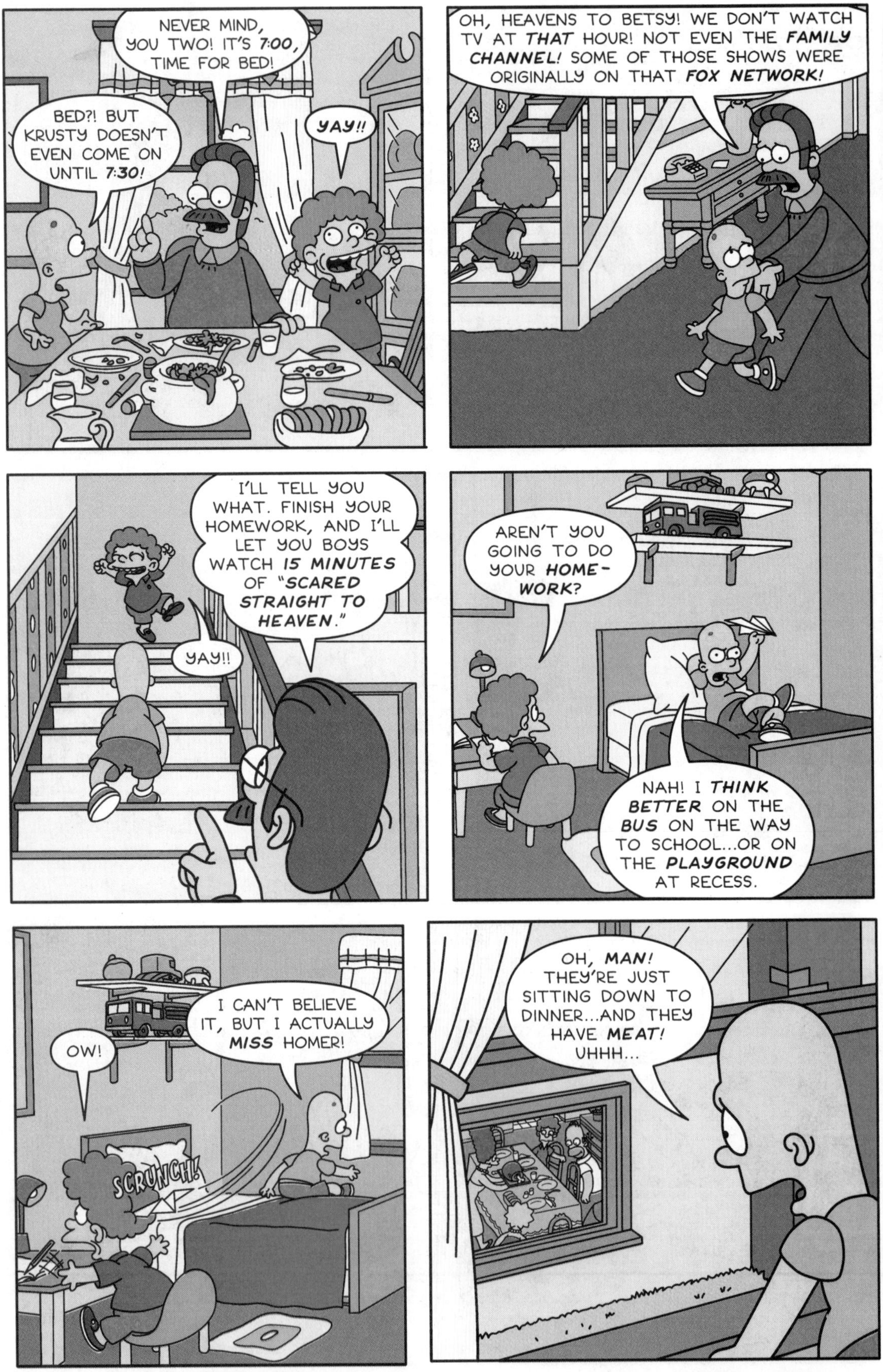
NEVER MIND, YOU TWO! IT'S 7:00, TIME FOR BED!
BED?! BUT KRUSTY DOESN'T EVEN COME ON UNTIL 7:30!
YAY!!
OH, HEAVENS TO BETSY! WE DON'T WATCH TV AT THAT HOUR! NOT EVEN THE FAMILY CHANNEL! SOME OF THOSE SHOWS WERE ORIGINALLY ON THAT FOX NETWORK!
I'LL TELL YOU WHAT. FINISH YOUR HOMEWORK, AND I'LL LET YOU BOYS WATCH 15 MINUTES OF "SCARED STRAIGHT TO HEAVEN."
YAY!!
AREN'T YOU GOING TO DO YOUR HOME-WORK?
NAH! I THINK BETTER ON THE BUS ON THE WAY TO SCHOOL...OR ON THE PLAYGROUND AT RECESS.
OW!
I CAN'T BELIEVE IT, BUT I ACTUALLY MISS HOMER!
SCRUNCH!
OH, MAN! THEY'RE JUST SITTING DOWN TO DINNER...AND THEY HAVE MEAT! UHHH...

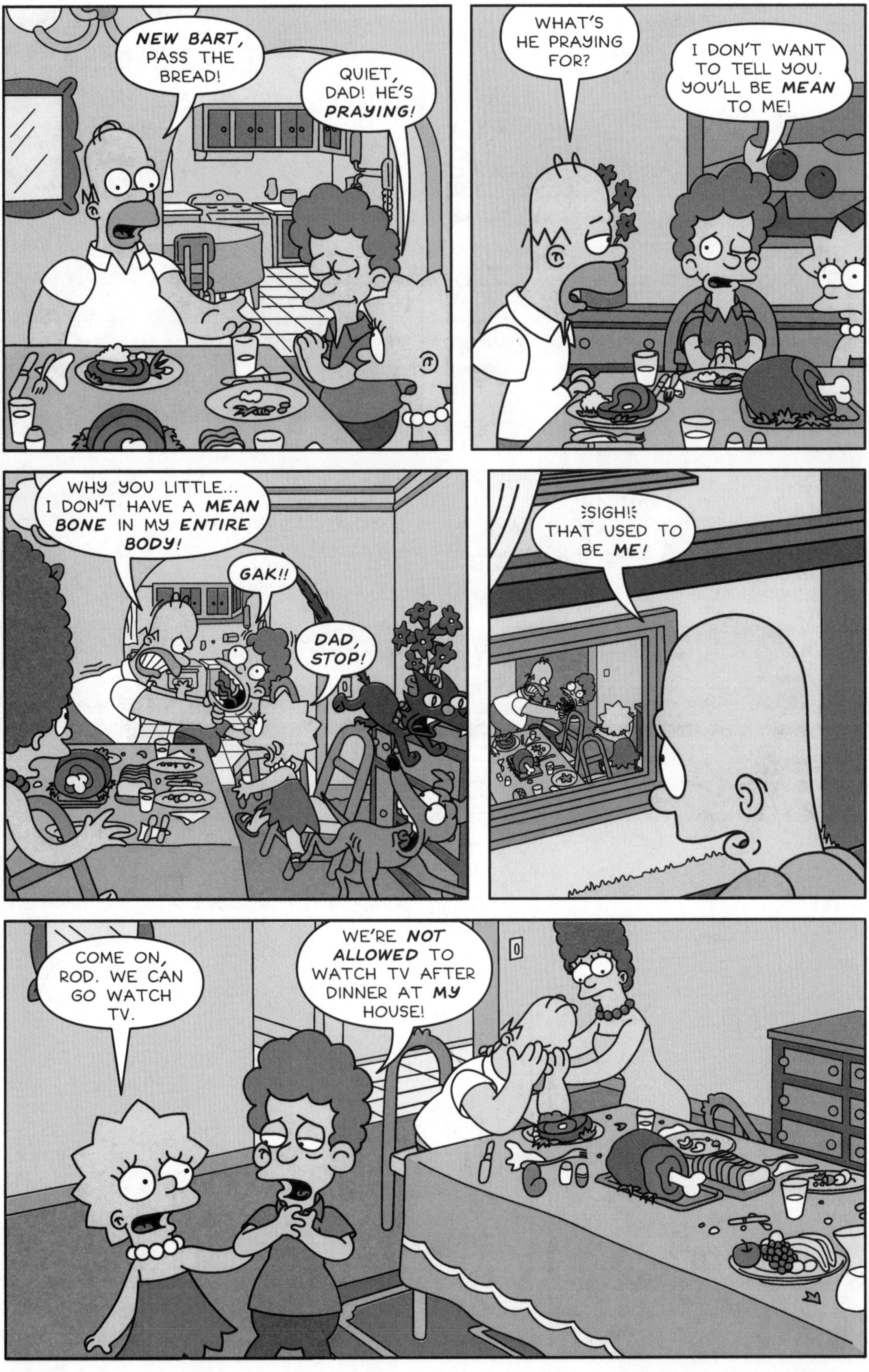

NEW BART, PASS THE BREAD!
QUIET, DAD! HE'S PRAYING!
WHAT'S HE PRAYING FOR?
I DON'T WANT TO TELL YOU. YOU'LL BE MEAN TO ME!
WHY YOU LITTLE... I DON'T HAVE A MEAN BONE IN MY ENTIRE BODY!
GAK!!
DAD, STOP!
SIGH! THAT USED TO BE ME!
COME ON, ROD. WE CAN GO WATCH TV.
WE'RE NOT ALLOWED TO WATCH TV AFTER DINNER AT MY HOUSE!

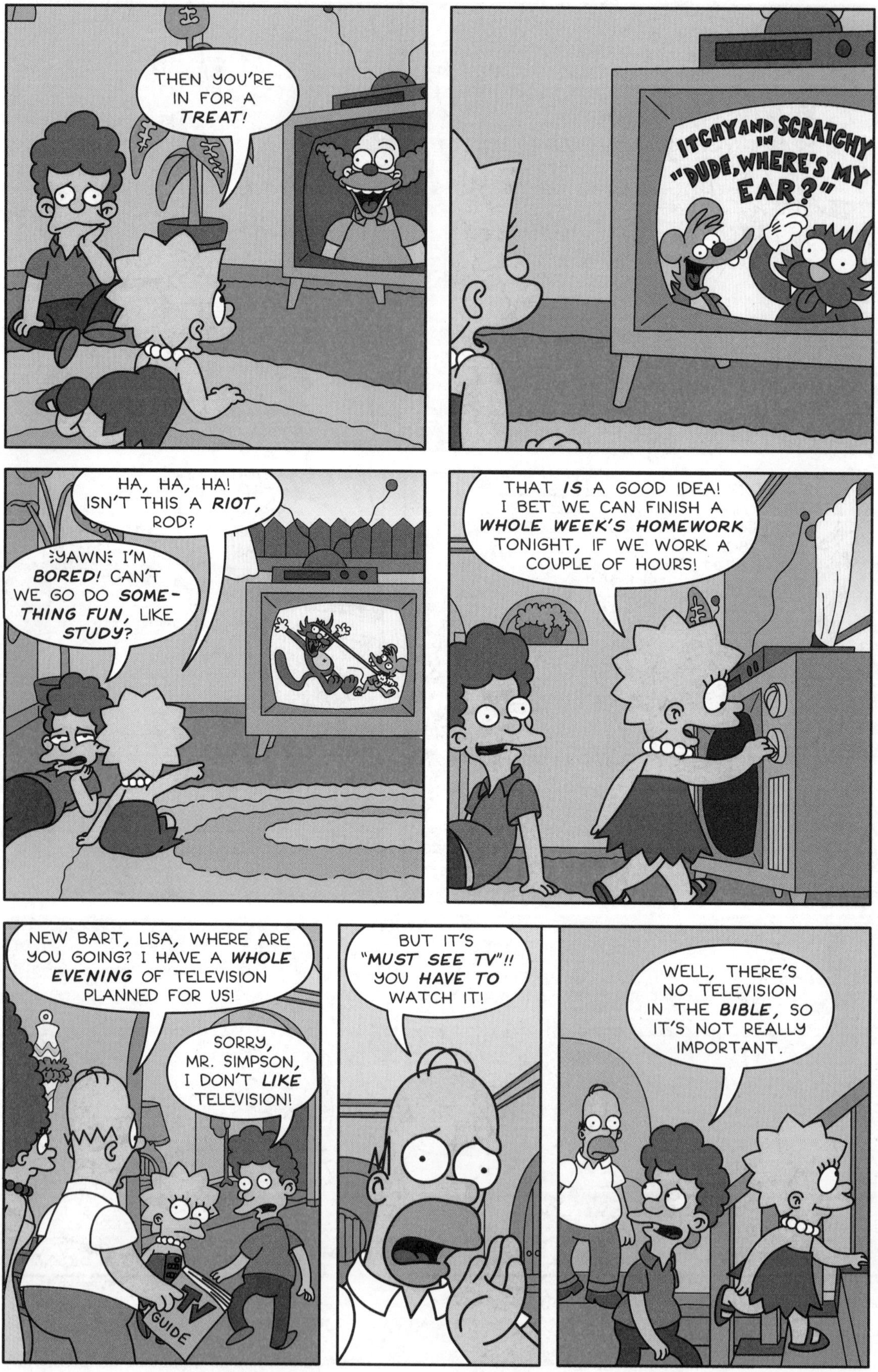
THEN YOU'RE IN FOR A TREAT!
ITCHY AND SCRATCHY IN "DUDE, WHERE'S MY EAR?"
HA, HA, HA! ISN'T THIS A RIOT, ROD?
YAWN I'M BORED! CAN'T WE GO DO SOMETHING FUN, LIKE STUDY?
THAT IS A GOOD IDEA! I BET WE CAN FINISH A WHOLE WEEK'S HOMEWORK TONIGHT, IF WE WORK A COUPLE OF HOURS!
NEW BART, LISA, WHERE ARE YOU GOING? I HAVE A WHOLE EVENING OF TELEVISION PLANNED FOR US!
SORRY, MR. SIMPSON, I DON'T LIKE TELEVISION!
TV GUIDE
BUT IT'S "MUST SEE TV"!! YOU HAVE TO WATCH IT!
WELL, THERE'S NO TELEVISION IN THE BIBLE, SO IT'S NOT REALLY IMPORTANT.

THEY DIDN'T WEAR *CLOTHES* IN THE BIBLE, EITHER! YOU DON'T SEE *US* WALKING AROUND *NAKED!*

UH, HOMEY, *MOST* OF THE PEOPLE IN THE BIBLE WORE CLOTHES.

NOT IN THE PART *I* READ! AND THAT'S BESIDE THE POINT! *"OLD"* BART WOULD *NEVER* DESERT ME TO "STUDY"!

BART, DON'T YOU WANT TO WATCH THE ANGEL *REBUKE* THE *BAD MAN* FOR HIS *MISDEEDS?*

NOT UNLESS *MCBAIN* SHOWS UP AND *BLOWS HIM AWAY!*

THEN YOU MIGHT AS WELL TAKE YOUR BATH!

BATH!?

STUPID *BATH!* STUPID *FLANDERS!* STUPID *HOMER* FOR MAKING ME *LIVE* HERE!

RUB! RUB!

SPLORSH!

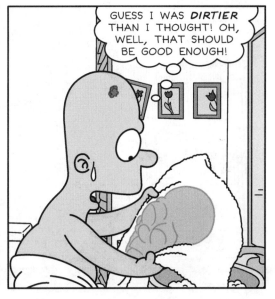

GUESS I WAS *DIRTIER* THAN I THOUGHT! OH, WELL, THAT SHOULD BE GOOD ENOUGH!

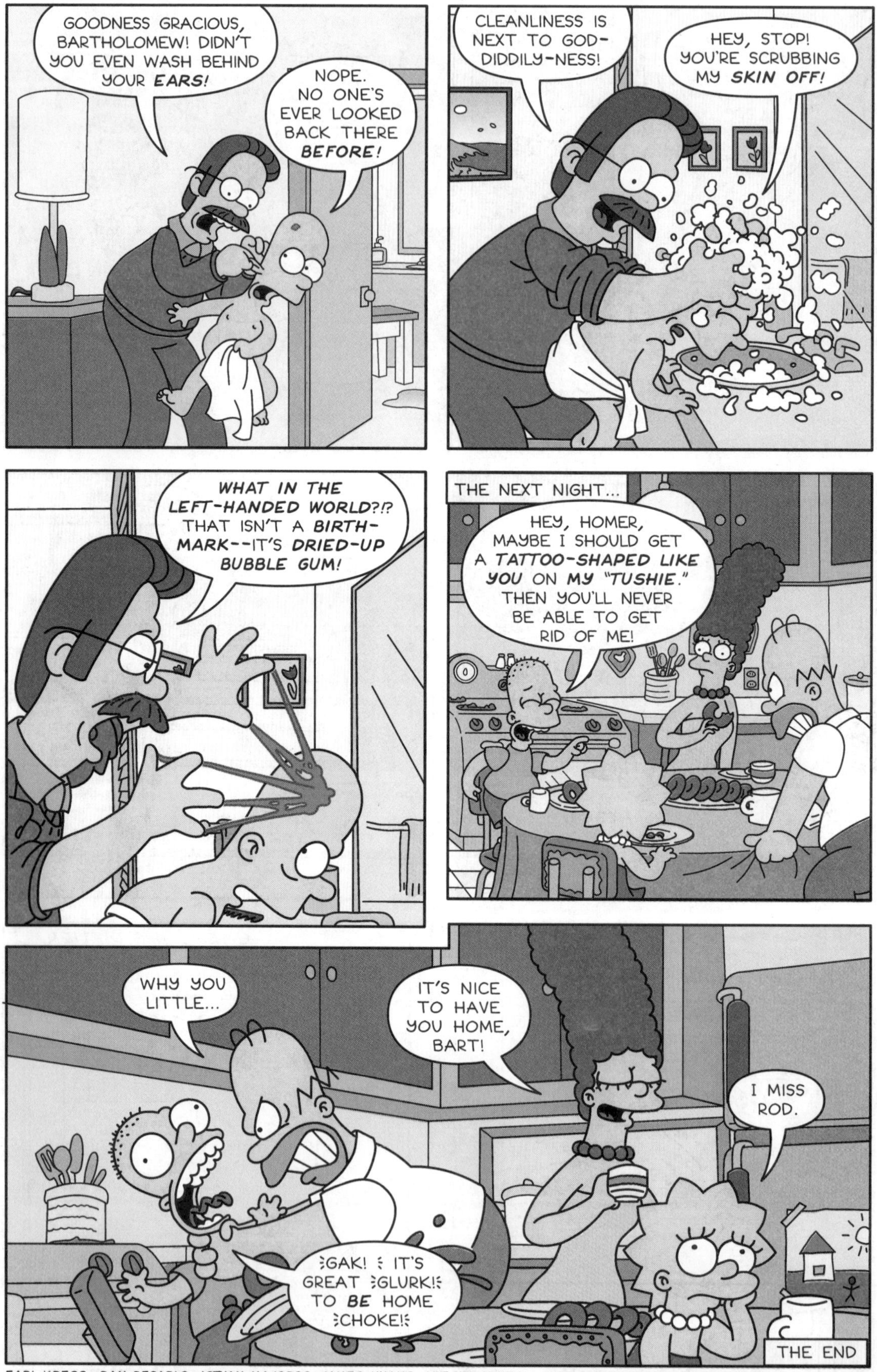
GOODNESS GRACIOUS, BARTHOLOMEW! DIDN'T YOU EVEN WASH BEHIND YOUR **EARS!**
NOPE. NO ONE'S EVER LOOKED BACK THERE **BEFORE!**
CLEANLINESS IS NEXT TO GOD-DIDDILY-NESS!
HEY, STOP! YOU'RE SCRUBBING MY **SKIN OFF!**
WHAT IN THE LEFT-HANDED WORLD?!? THAT ISN'T A **BIRTH-MARK**--IT'S **DRIED-UP BUBBLE GUM!**
THE NEXT NIGHT...
HEY, HOMER, MAYBE I SHOULD GET A **TATTOO-SHAPED LIKE YOU** ON **MY "TUSHIE."** THEN YOU'LL NEVER BE ABLE TO GET RID OF ME!
WHY YOU LITTLE...
IT'S NICE TO HAVE YOU HOME, BART!
I MISS ROD.
GAK! IT'S GREAT GLURK! TO **BE** HOME CHOKE!
THE END

EARL KRESS STORY ***DAN DECARLO*** LAYOUTS ***ISTVAN MAJOROS*** PENCILS ***JAMES HUANG*** INKS ***ART VILLANUEVA*** COLORS ***KAREN BATES*** LETTERS ***BILL MORRISON*** EDITOR ***MATT GROENING*** MARKED FOR LIFE

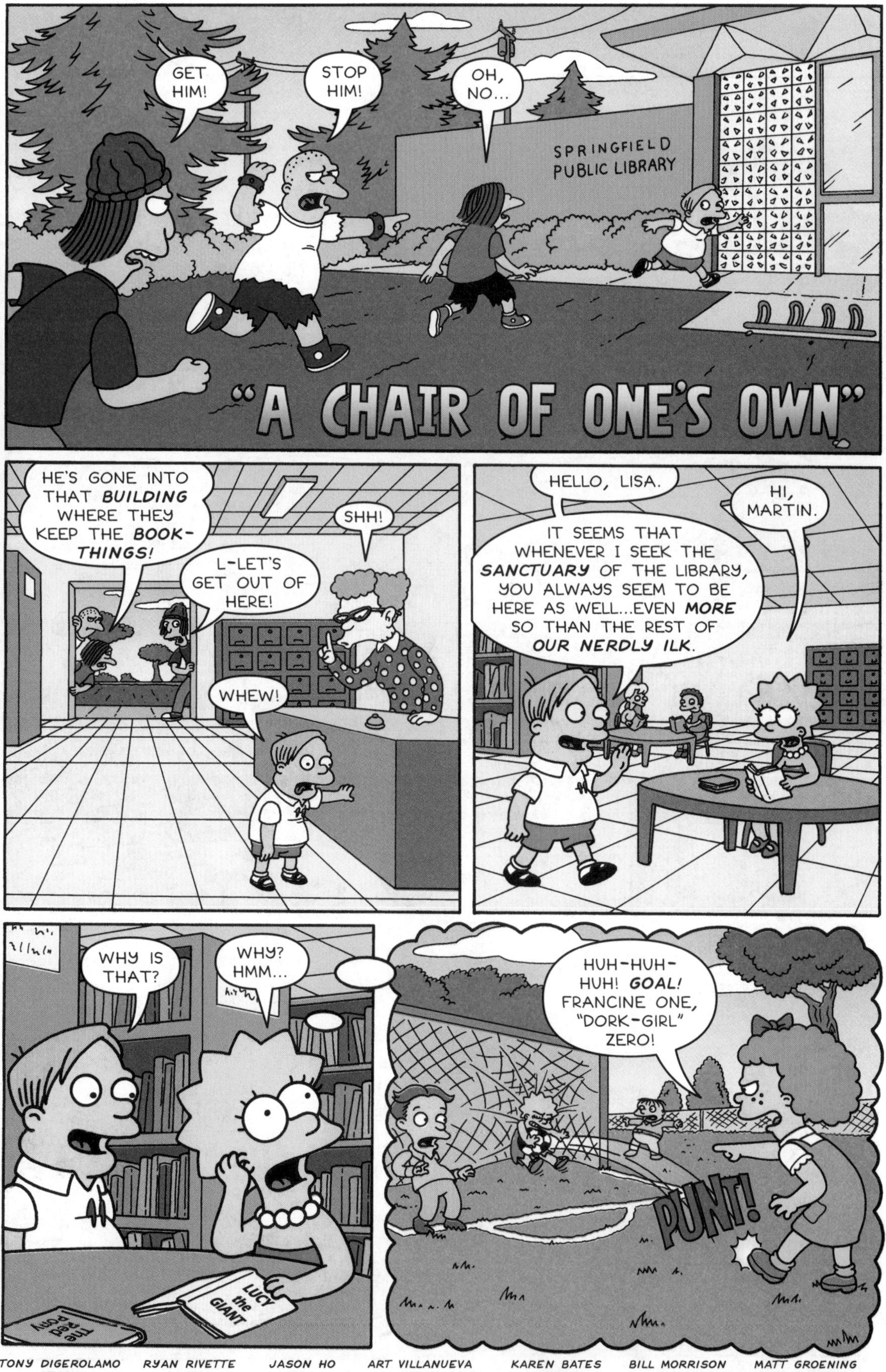
GET HIM!
STOP HIM!
OH, NO...
SPRINGFIELD PUBLIC LIBRARY
"A CHAIR OF ONE'S OWN"
HE'S GONE INTO THAT **BUILDING** WHERE THEY KEEP THE **BOOK-THINGS**!
L-LET'S GET OUT OF HERE!
SHH!
WHEW!
HELLO, LISA.
IT SEEMS THAT WHENEVER I SEEK THE **SANCTUARY** OF THE LIBRARY, YOU ALWAYS SEEM TO BE HERE AS WELL...EVEN **MORE** SO THAN THE REST OF **OUR NERDLY ILK**.
HI, MARTIN.
WHY IS THAT?
WHY? HMM...
LUCY the GIANT
HUH-HUH-HUH! **GOAL!** FRANCINE ONE, "DORK-GIRL" ZERO!
PUNT!

TONY DIGEROLAMO STORY · *RYAN RIVETTE* PENCILS · *JASON HO* INKS · *ART VILLANUEVA* COLORS · *KAREN BATES* LETTERS · *BILL MORRISON* EDITOR · *MATT GROENING* BOOKWORM

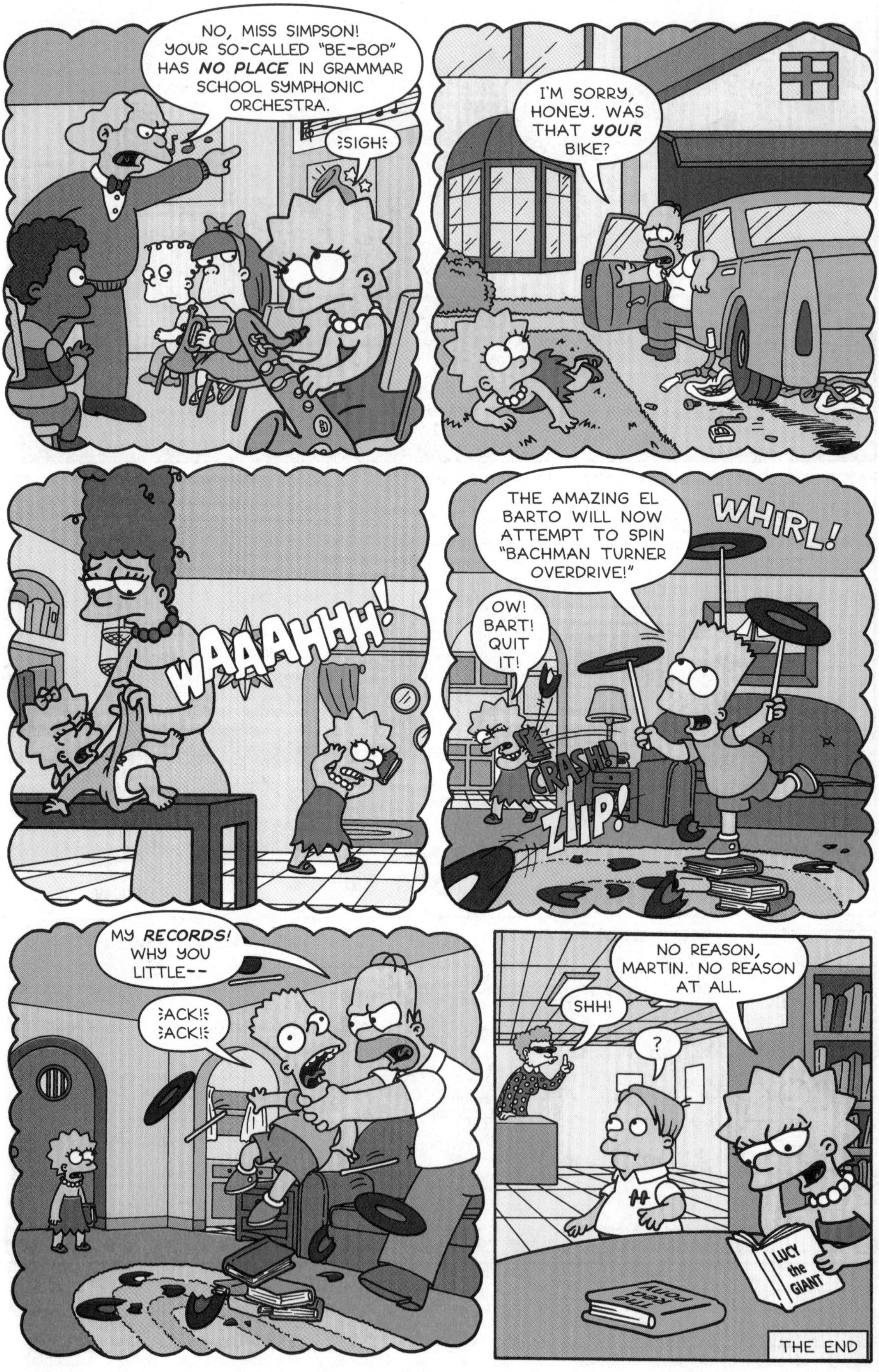
NO, MISS SIMPSON! YOUR SO-CALLED "BE-BOP" HAS NO PLACE IN GRAMMAR SCHOOL SYMPHONIC ORCHESTRA.
SIGH
I'M SORRY, HONEY. WAS THAT YOUR BIKE?
WAAAAHHH!
THE AMAZING EL BARTO WILL NOW ATTEMPT TO SPIN "BACHMAN TURNER OVERDRIVE!"
WHIRL!
OW! BART! QUIT IT!
CRASH!
ZIIP!
MY RECORDS! WHY YOU LITTLE--
ACK! ACK!
NO REASON, MARTIN. NO REASON AT ALL.
SHH!
?
LUCY the GIANT
THE RED PONY
THE END

BART'S NASTY SHIRT

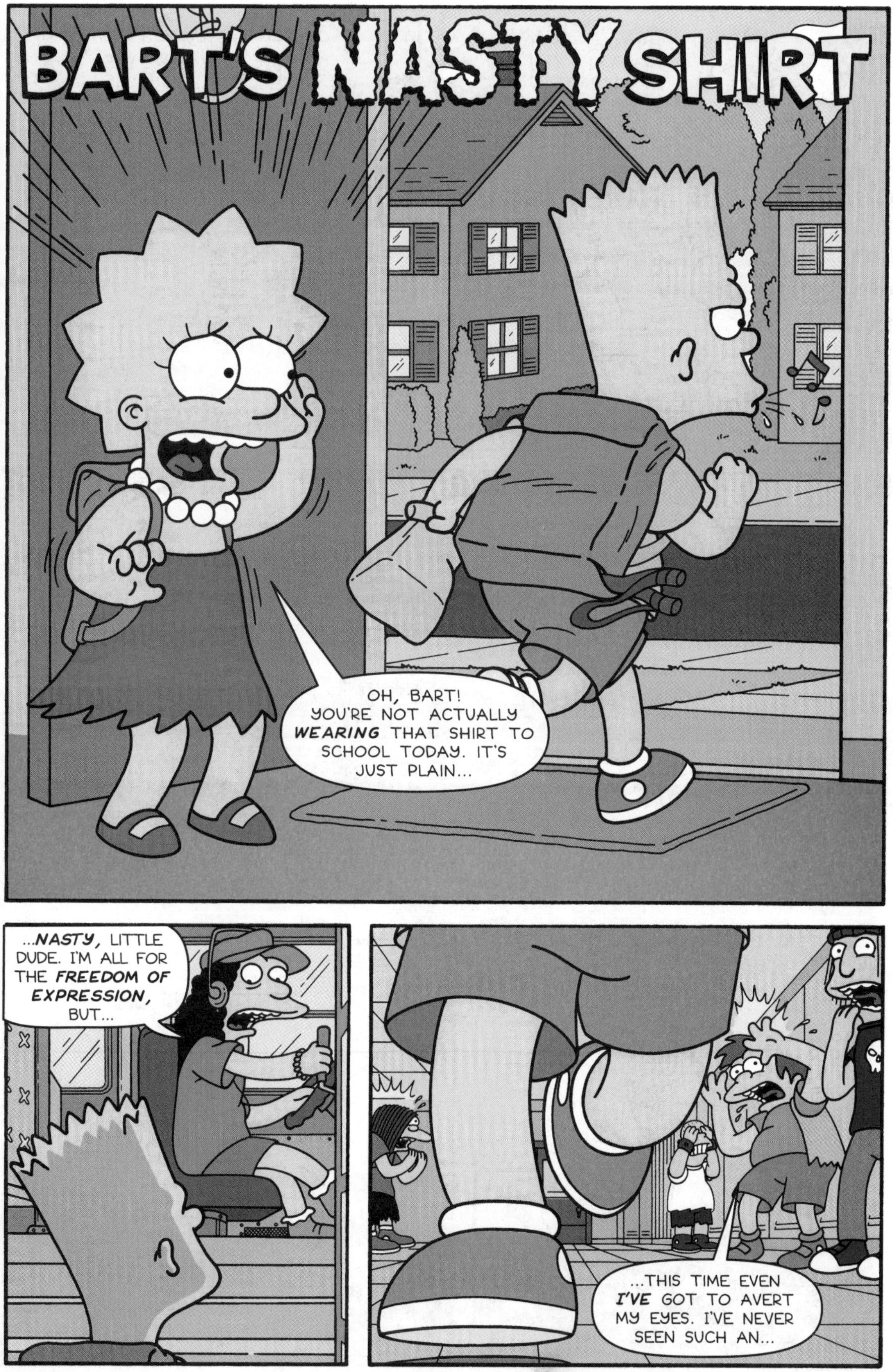
OH, BART! YOU'RE NOT ACTUALLY **WEARING** THAT SHIRT TO SCHOOL TODAY. IT'S JUST PLAIN...
...**NASTY,** LITTLE DUDE. I'M ALL FOR THE **FREEDOM OF EXPRESSION,** BUT...
...THIS TIME EVEN **I'VE** GOT TO AVERT MY EYES. I'VE NEVER SEEN SUCH AN...

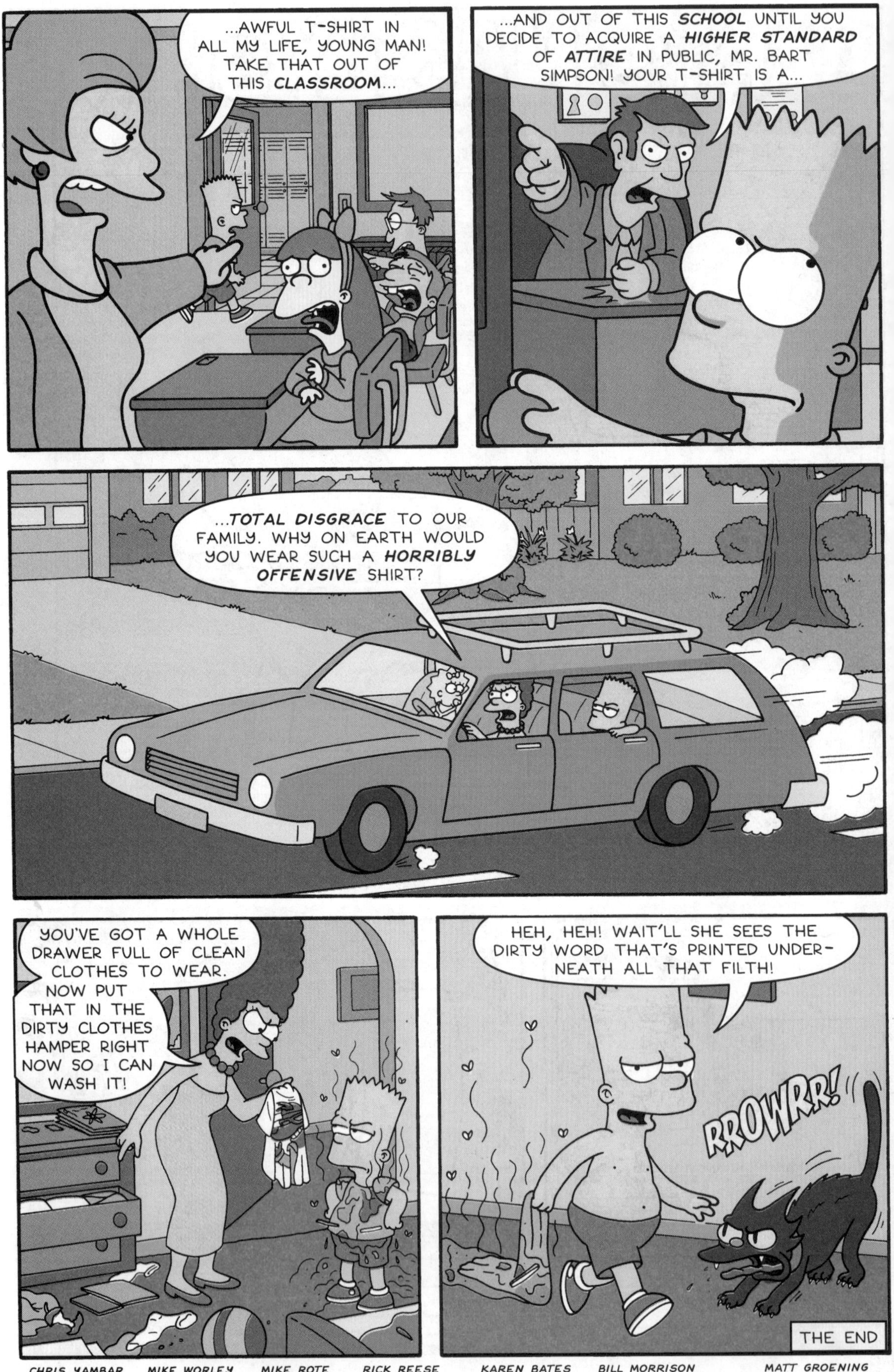
...AWFUL T-SHIRT IN ALL MY LIFE, YOUNG MAN! TAKE THAT OUT OF THIS CLASSROOM...
...AND OUT OF THIS SCHOOL UNTIL YOU DECIDE TO ACQUIRE A HIGHER STANDARD OF ATTIRE IN PUBLIC, MR. BART SIMPSON! YOUR T-SHIRT IS A...
...TOTAL DISGRACE TO OUR FAMILY. WHY ON EARTH WOULD YOU WEAR SUCH A HORRIBLY OFFENSIVE SHIRT?
YOU'VE GOT A WHOLE DRAWER FULL OF CLEAN CLOTHES TO WEAR.
NOW PUT THAT IN THE DIRTY CLOTHES HAMPER RIGHT NOW SO I CAN WASH IT!
HEH, HEH! WAIT'LL SHE SEES THE DIRTY WORD THAT'S PRINTED UNDER-NEATH ALL THAT FILTH!
RROWRR!
THE END

CHRIS YAMBAR STORY | **MIKE WORLEY** PENCILS | **MIKE ROTE** INKS | **RICK REESE** COLORS | **KAREN BATES** LETTERS | **BILL MORRISON** EDITOR | **MATT GROENING** FASHION POLICEMAN

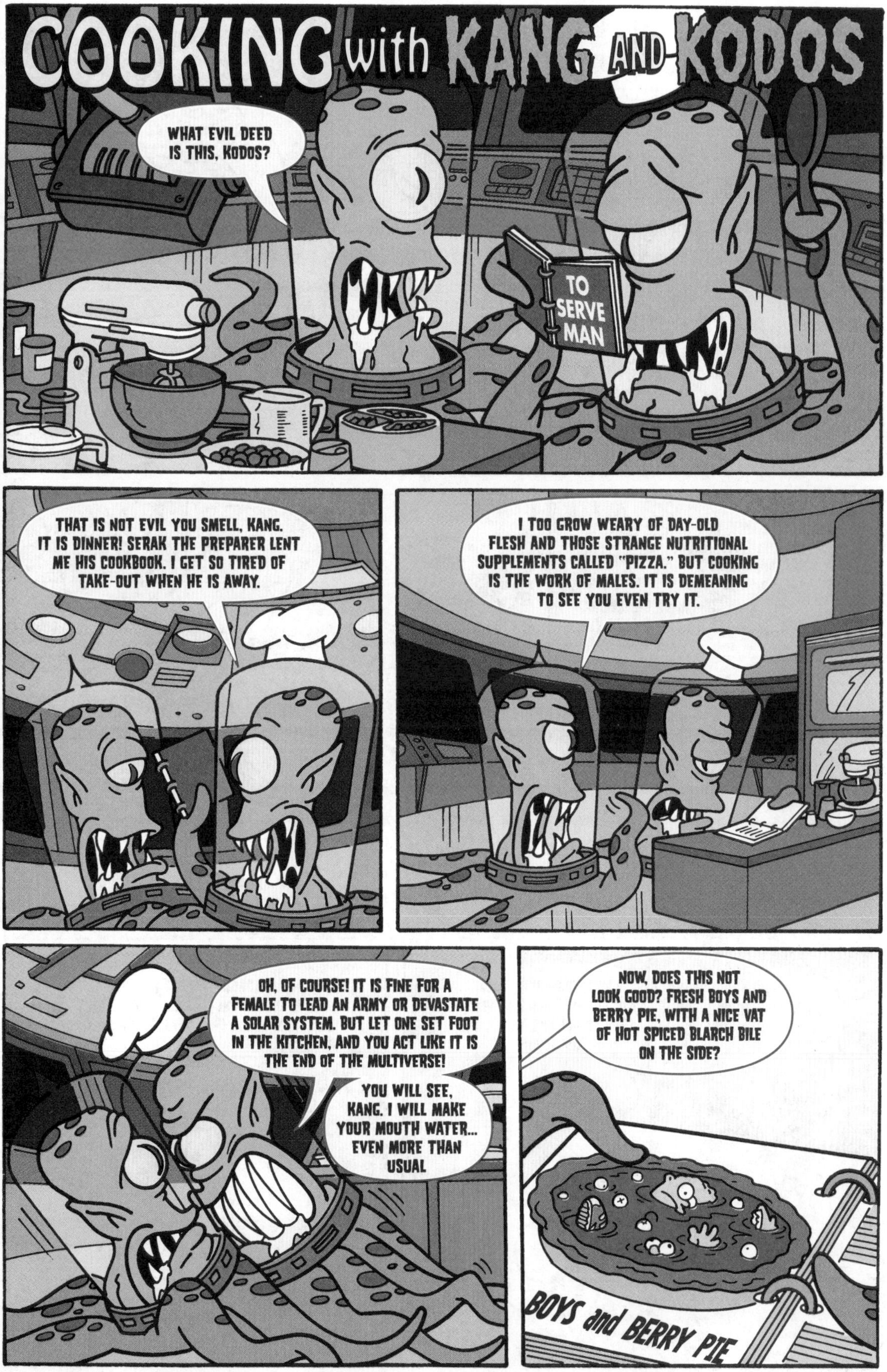
COOKING with KANG AND KODOS
WHAT EVIL DEED IS THIS, KODOS?
TO SERVE MAN
THAT IS NOT EVIL YOU SMELL, KANG. IT IS DINNER! SERAK THE PREPARER LENT ME HIS COOKBOOK. I GET SO TIRED OF TAKE-OUT WHEN HE IS AWAY.
I TOO GROW WEARY OF DAY-OLD FLESH AND THOSE STRANGE NUTRITIONAL SUPPLEMENTS CALLED "PIZZA." BUT COOKING IS THE WORK OF MALES. IT IS DEMEANING TO SEE YOU EVEN TRY IT.
OH, OF COURSE! IT IS FINE FOR A FEMALE TO LEAD AN ARMY OR DEVASTATE A SOLAR SYSTEM. BUT LET ONE SET FOOT IN THE KITCHEN, AND YOU ACT LIKE IT IS THE END OF THE MULTIVERSE!
YOU WILL SEE, KANG. I WILL MAKE YOUR MOUTH WATER... EVEN MORE THAN USUAL
NOW, DOES THIS NOT LOOK GOOD? FRESH BOYS AND BERRY PIE, WITH A NICE VAT OF HOT SPICED BLARCH BILE ON THE SIDE?
BOYS and BERRY PIE

SHERRI L. SMITH STORY | *JOHN COSTANZA* PENCILS & INKS | *CHRIS UNGAR* COLORS | *KAREN BATES* LETTERS | *BILL MORRISON* EDITOR | *MATT GROENING* TASTE TESTER

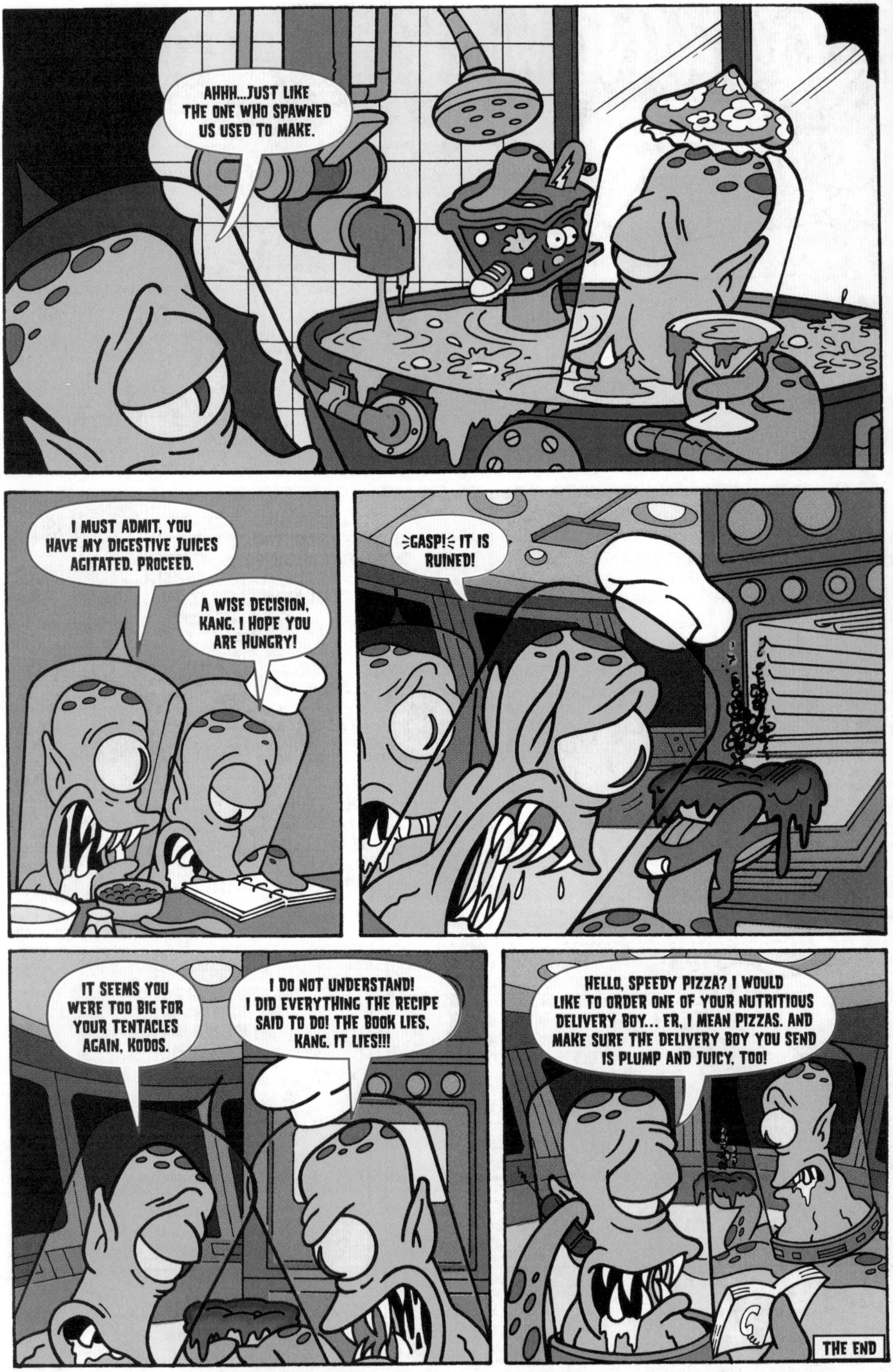
AHHH...JUST LIKE THE ONE WHO SPAWNED US USED TO MAKE.
I MUST ADMIT, YOU HAVE MY DIGESTIVE JUICES AGITATED. PROCEED.
A WISE DECISION, KANG. I HOPE YOU ARE HUNGRY!
GASP! IT IS RUINED!
IT SEEMS YOU WERE TOO BIG FOR YOUR TENTACLES AGAIN, KODOS.
I DO NOT UNDERSTAND! I DID EVERYTHING THE RECIPE SAID TO DO! THE BOOK LIES, KANG. IT LIES!!!
HELLO, SPEEDY PIZZA? I WOULD LIKE TO ORDER ONE OF YOUR NUTRITIOUS DELIVERY BOY... ER, I MEAN PIZZAS. AND MAKE SURE THE DELIVERY BOY YOU SEND IS PLUMP AND JUICY, TOO!
THE END

PRIZE POSSESSION

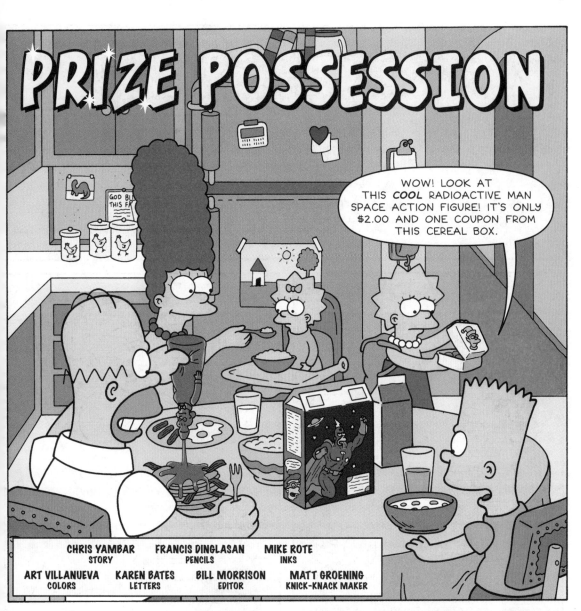

WOW! LOOK AT THIS **COOL** RADIOACTIVE MAN SPACE ACTION FIGURE! IT'S ONLY $2.00 AND ONE COUPON FROM THIS CEREAL BOX.

CHRIS YAMBAR	FRANCIS DINGLASAN	MIKE ROTE
STORY	PENCILS	INKS
ART VILLANUEVA	KAREN BATES	BILL MORRISON	MATT GROENING
COLORS	LETTERS	EDITOR	KNICK-KNACK MAKER

GIMME THE **LOOT**, HOMER!

NO.

C'MON, HOMER.

NO.

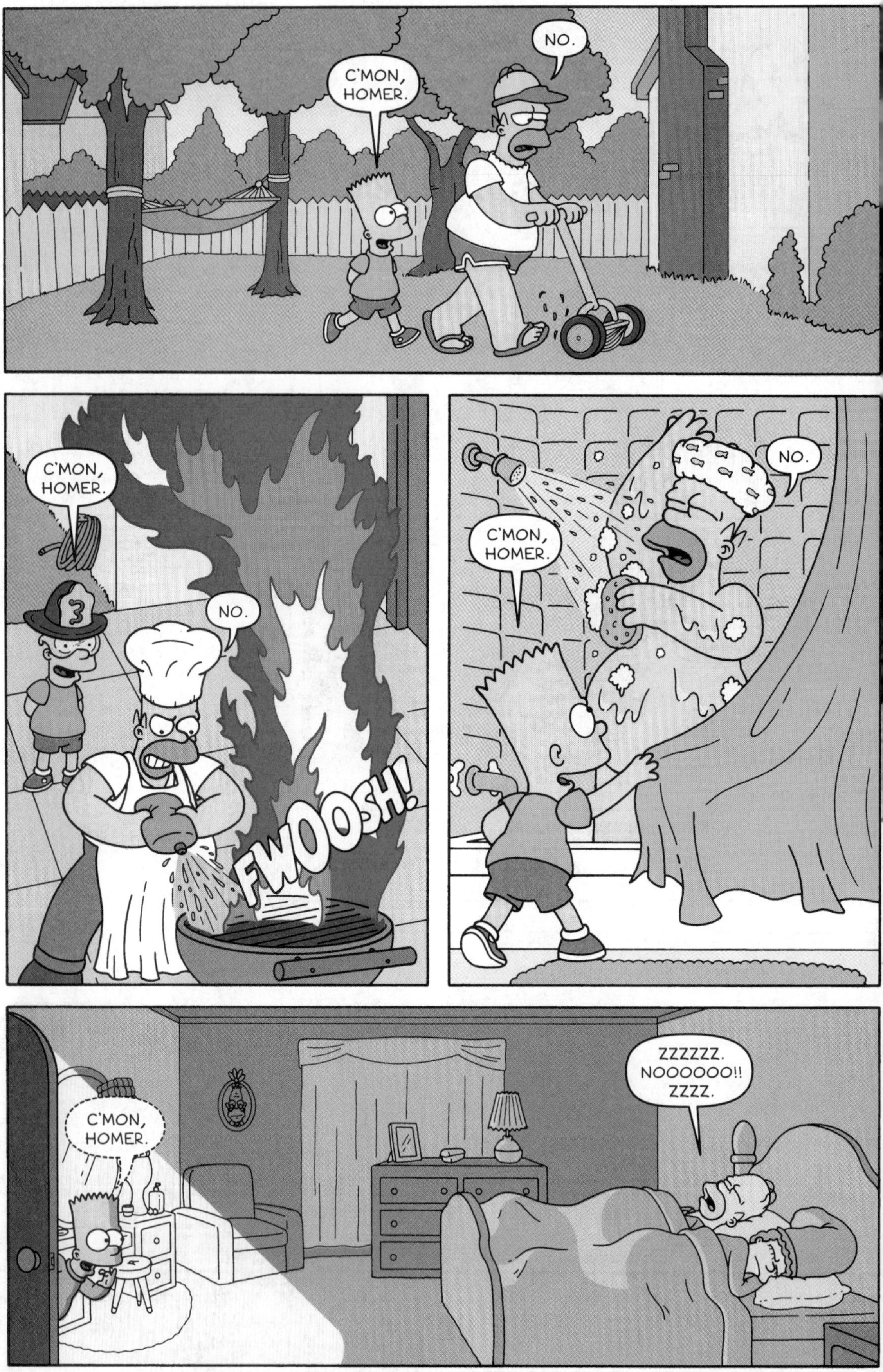
C'MON, HOMER.
NO.
C'MON, HOMER.
NO.
FWOOSH!
C'MON, HOMER.
NO.
C'MON, HOMER.
ZZZZZZ. NOOOOOO!! ZZZZ.

I KNOW I'VE *WEAKENED* HIS *DEFENSES!* HE'S PROBABLY ALREADY *FORGOTTEN* WHAT HE'S SAYING "NO" TO. TIME FOR ONE *FINAL ASSAULT.*

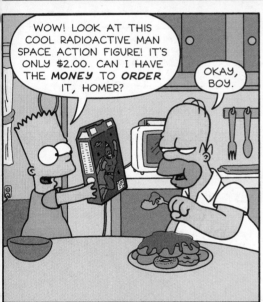

WOW! LOOK AT THIS COOL RADIOACTIVE MAN SPACE ACTION FIGURE! IT'S ONLY $2.00. CAN I HAVE THE *MONEY* TO *ORDER* IT, HOMER?

OKAY, BOY.

YOU THE MAN, HOMER!!

I DON'T KNOW, HOMER. HE'LL JUST GET *BORED* WITH IT AND *THROW IT AWAY.*

LIGHTEN UP, MARGE. WEREN'T *YOU* EVER YOUNG?

OH, YEAH! THE *PATENTED* BART SIMPSON *GENIUS* NEVER *FAILS!* OHHH, BABY!

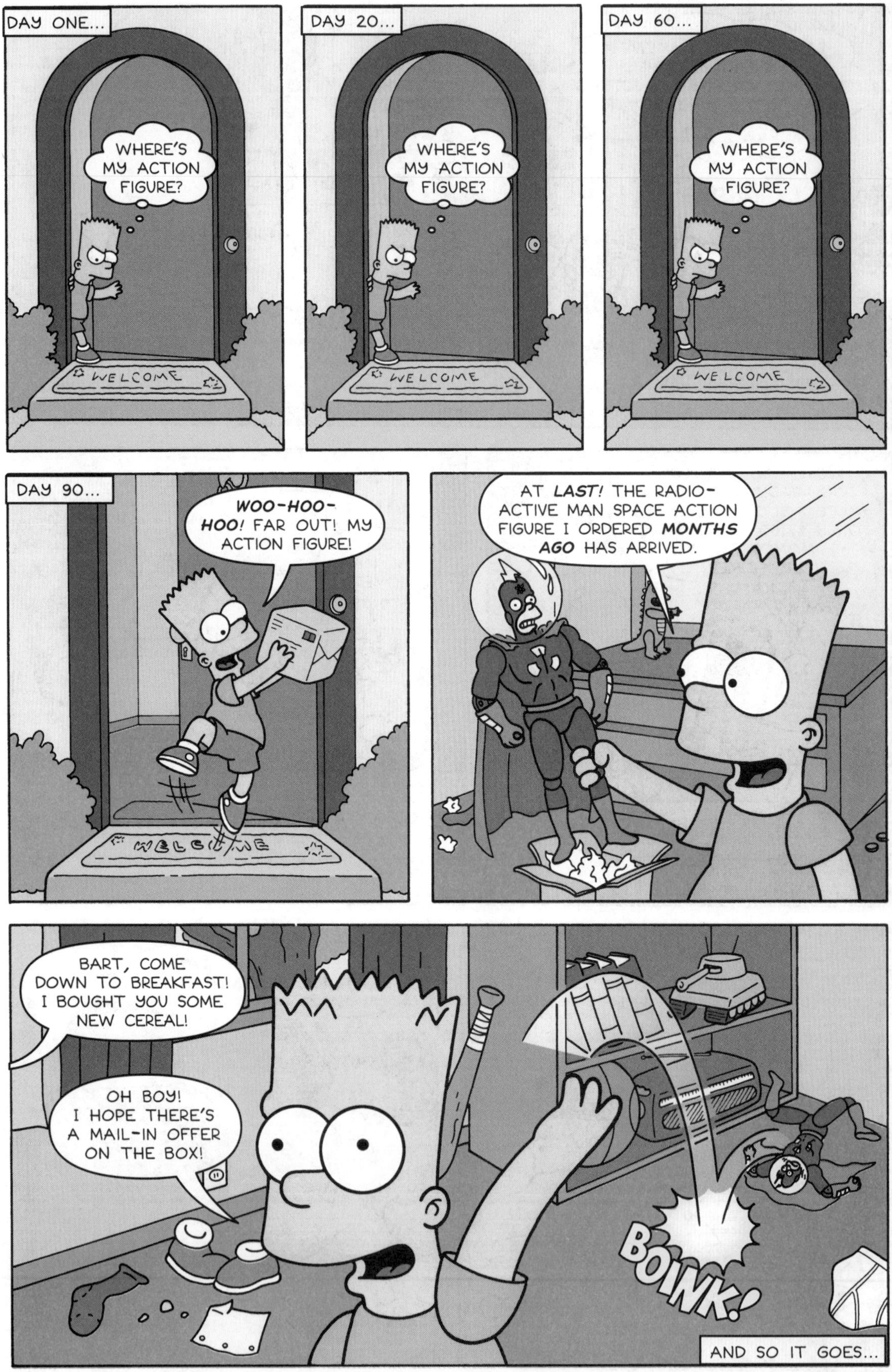

DAY ONE...
WHERE'S MY ACTION FIGURE?
WELCOME
DAY 20...
WHERE'S MY ACTION FIGURE?
WELCOME
DAY 60...
WHERE'S MY ACTION FIGURE?
WELCOME
DAY 90...
WOO-HOO-HOO! FAR OUT! MY ACTION FIGURE!
AT LAST! THE RADIO-ACTIVE MAN SPACE ACTION FIGURE I ORDERED MONTHS AGO HAS ARRIVED.
BART, COME DOWN TO BREAKFAST! I BOUGHT YOU SOME NEW CEREAL!
OH BOY! I HOPE THERE'S A MAIL-IN OFFER ON THE BOX!
BOINK!
AND SO IT GOES...

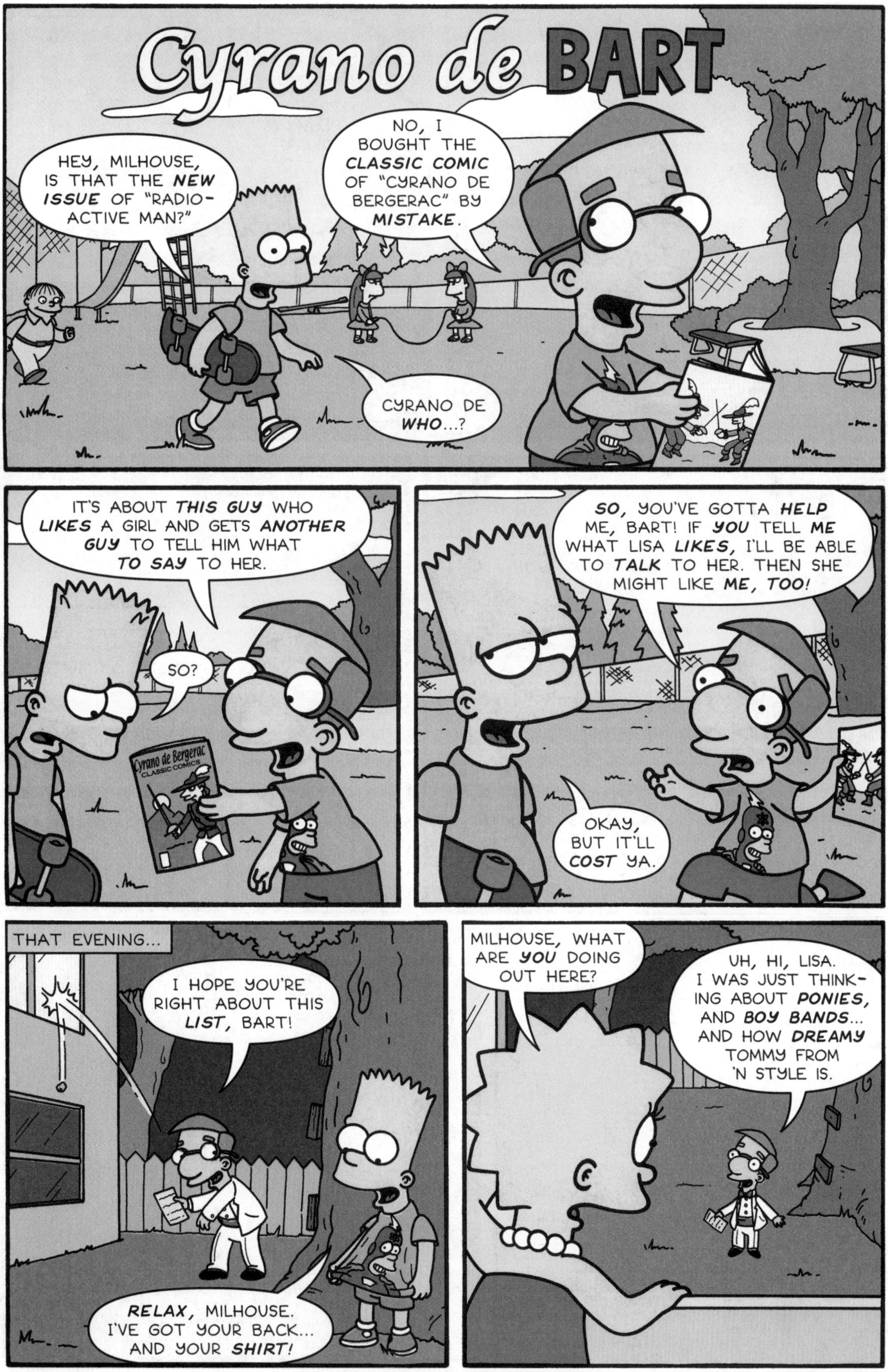
Cyrano de BART
HEY, MILHOUSE, IS THAT THE NEW ISSUE OF "RADIO-ACTIVE MAN?"
NO, I BOUGHT THE CLASSIC COMIC OF "CYRANO DE BERGERAC" BY MISTAKE.
CYRANO DE WHO...?
IT'S ABOUT THIS GUY WHO LIKES A GIRL AND GETS ANOTHER GUY TO TELL HIM WHAT TO SAY TO HER.
SO?
Cyrano de Bergerac
CLASSIC COMICS
SO, YOU'VE GOTTA HELP ME, BART! IF YOU TELL ME WHAT LISA LIKES, I'LL BE ABLE TO TALK TO HER. THEN SHE MIGHT LIKE ME, TOO!
OKAY, BUT IT'LL COST YA.
THAT EVENING...
I HOPE YOU'RE RIGHT ABOUT THIS LIST, BART!
RELAX, MILHOUSE. I'VE GOT YOUR BACK... AND YOUR SHIRT!
MILHOUSE, WHAT ARE YOU DOING OUT HERE?
UH, HI, LISA. I WAS JUST THINKING ABOUT PONIES, AND BOY BANDS... AND HOW DREAMY TOMMY FROM 'N STYLE IS.

SHERRI L. SMITH STORY | RYAN RIVETTE PENCILS | MIKE ROTE INKS | ART VILLANUEVA COLORS | KAREN BATES LETTERS | BILL MORRISON EDITOR | MATT GROENING POETIC MUSE

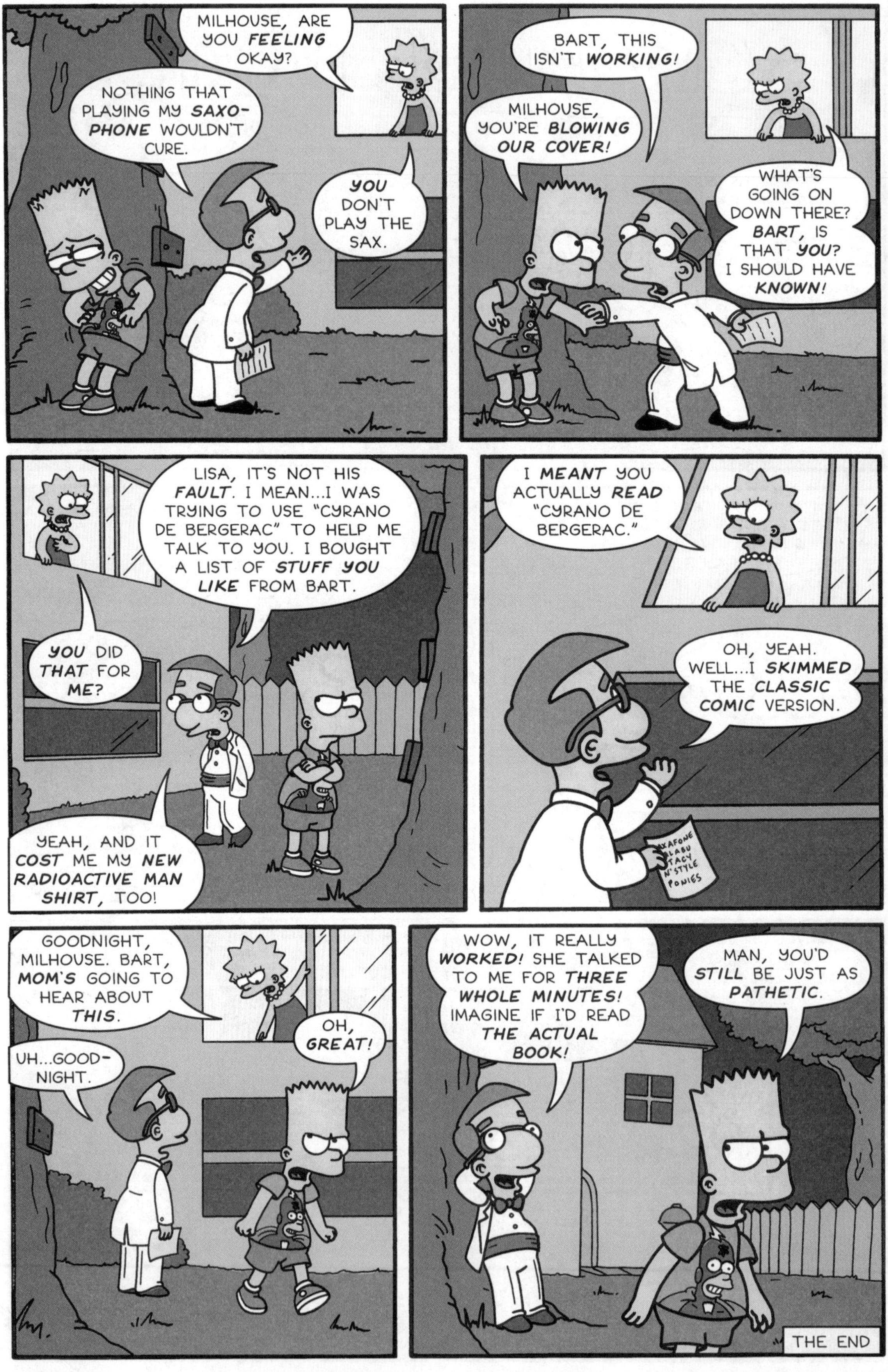
MILHOUSE, ARE YOU FEELING OKAY?
NOTHING THAT PLAYING MY SAXO-PHONE WOULDN'T CURE.
YOU DON'T PLAY THE SAX.
BART, THIS ISN'T WORKING!
MILHOUSE, YOU'RE BLOWING OUR COVER!
WHAT'S GOING ON DOWN THERE? BART, IS THAT YOU? I SHOULD HAVE KNOWN!
LISA, IT'S NOT HIS FAULT. I MEAN...I WAS TRYING TO USE "CYRANO DE BERGERAC" TO HELP ME TALK TO YOU. I BOUGHT A LIST OF STUFF YOU LIKE FROM BART.
YOU DID THAT FOR ME?
YEAH, AND IT COST ME MY NEW RADIOACTIVE MAN SHIRT, TOO!
I MEANT YOU ACTUALLY READ "CYRANO DE BERGERAC."
OH, YEAH. WELL...I SKIMMED THE CLASSIC COMIC VERSION.
GOODNIGHT, MILHOUSE. BART, MOM'S GOING TO HEAR ABOUT THIS.
UH...GOOD-NIGHT.
OH, GREAT!
WOW, IT REALLY WORKED! SHE TALKED TO ME FOR THREE WHOLE MINUTES! IMAGINE IF I'D READ THE ACTUAL BOOK!
MAN, YOU'D STILL BE JUST AS PATHETIC.
THE END

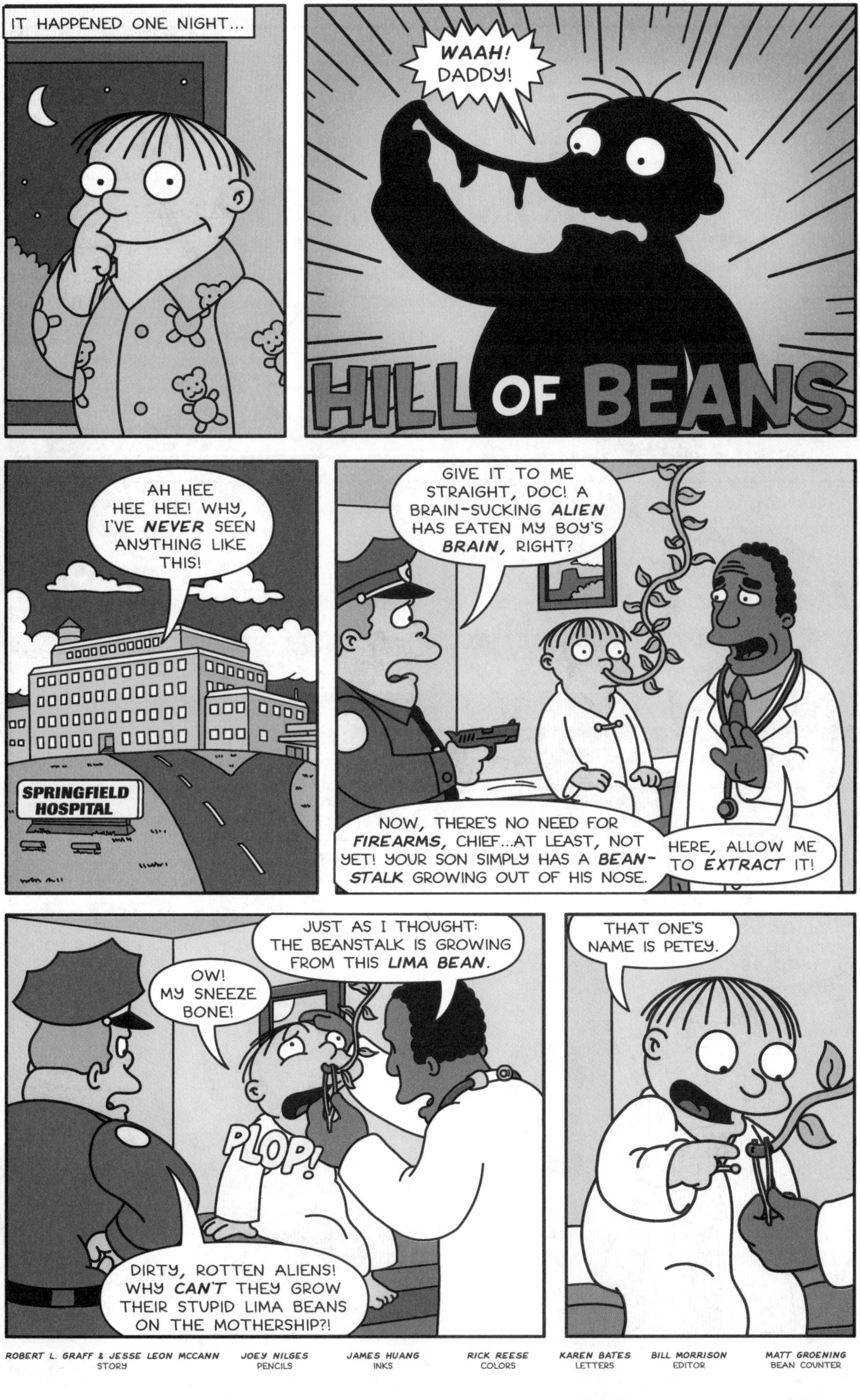
IT HAPPENED ONE NIGHT...
WAAH! DADDY!
HILL OF BEANS
AH HEE HEE HEE! WHY, I'VE NEVER SEEN ANYTHING LIKE THIS!
SPRINGFIELD HOSPITAL
GIVE IT TO ME STRAIGHT, DOC! A BRAIN-SUCKING ALIEN HAS EATEN MY BOY'S BRAIN, RIGHT?
NOW, THERE'S NO NEED FOR FIREARMS, CHIEF...AT LEAST, NOT YET! YOUR SON SIMPLY HAS A BEAN-STALK GROWING OUT OF HIS NOSE.
HERE, ALLOW ME TO EXTRACT IT!
JUST AS I THOUGHT: THE BEANSTALK IS GROWING FROM THIS LIMA BEAN.
OW! MY SNEEZE BONE!
PLOP!
DIRTY, ROTTEN ALIENS! WHY CAN'T THEY GROW THEIR STUPID LIMA BEANS ON THE MOTHERSHIP?!
THAT ONE'S NAME IS PETEY.

ROBERT L. GRAFF & JESSE LEON MCCANN STORY | JOEY NILGES PENCILS | JAMES HUANG INKS | RICK REESE COLORS | KAREN BATES LETTERS | BILL MORRISON EDITOR | MATT GROENING BEAN COUNTER

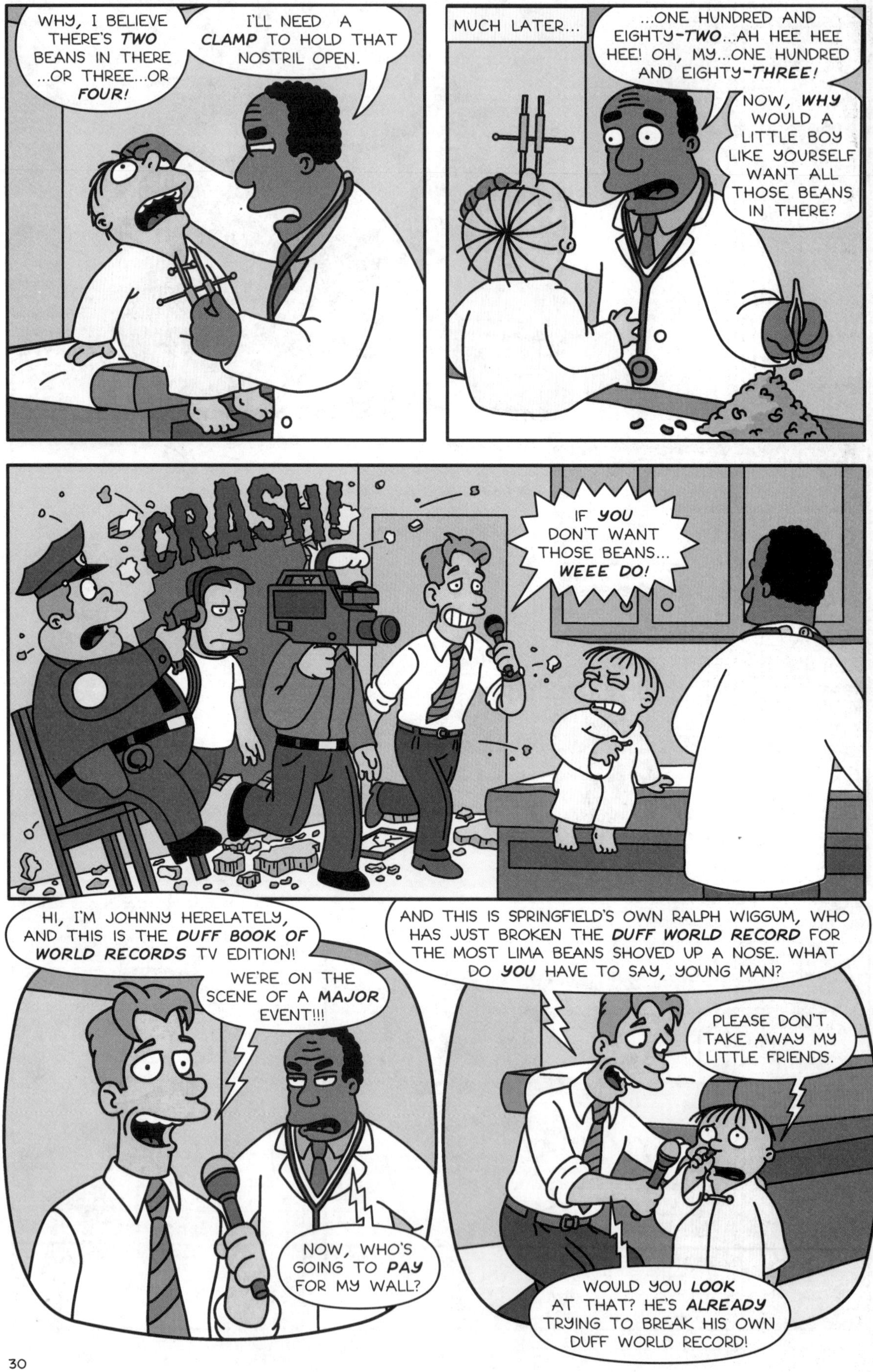
WHY, I BELIEVE THERE'S TWO BEANS IN THERE ...OR THREE...OR FOUR!
I'LL NEED A CLAMP TO HOLD THAT NOSTRIL OPEN.
MUCH LATER...
...ONE HUNDRED AND EIGHTY-TWO...AH HEE HEE HEE! OH, MY...ONE HUNDRED AND EIGHTY-THREE!
NOW, WHY WOULD A LITTLE BOY LIKE YOURSELF WANT ALL THOSE BEANS IN THERE?
CRASH!
IF YOU DON'T WANT THOSE BEANS... WEEE DO!
HI, I'M JOHNNY HERELATELY, AND THIS IS THE DUFF BOOK OF WORLD RECORDS TV EDITION!
WE'RE ON THE SCENE OF A MAJOR EVENT!!!
NOW, WHO'S GOING TO PAY FOR MY WALL?
AND THIS IS SPRINGFIELD'S OWN RALPH WIGGUM, WHO HAS JUST BROKEN THE DUFF WORLD RECORD FOR THE MOST LIMA BEANS SHOVED UP A NOSE. WHAT DO YOU HAVE TO SAY, YOUNG MAN?
PLEASE DON'T TAKE AWAY MY LITTLE FRIENDS.
WOULD YOU LOOK AT THAT? HE'S ALREADY TRYING TO BREAK HIS OWN DUFF WORLD RECORD!

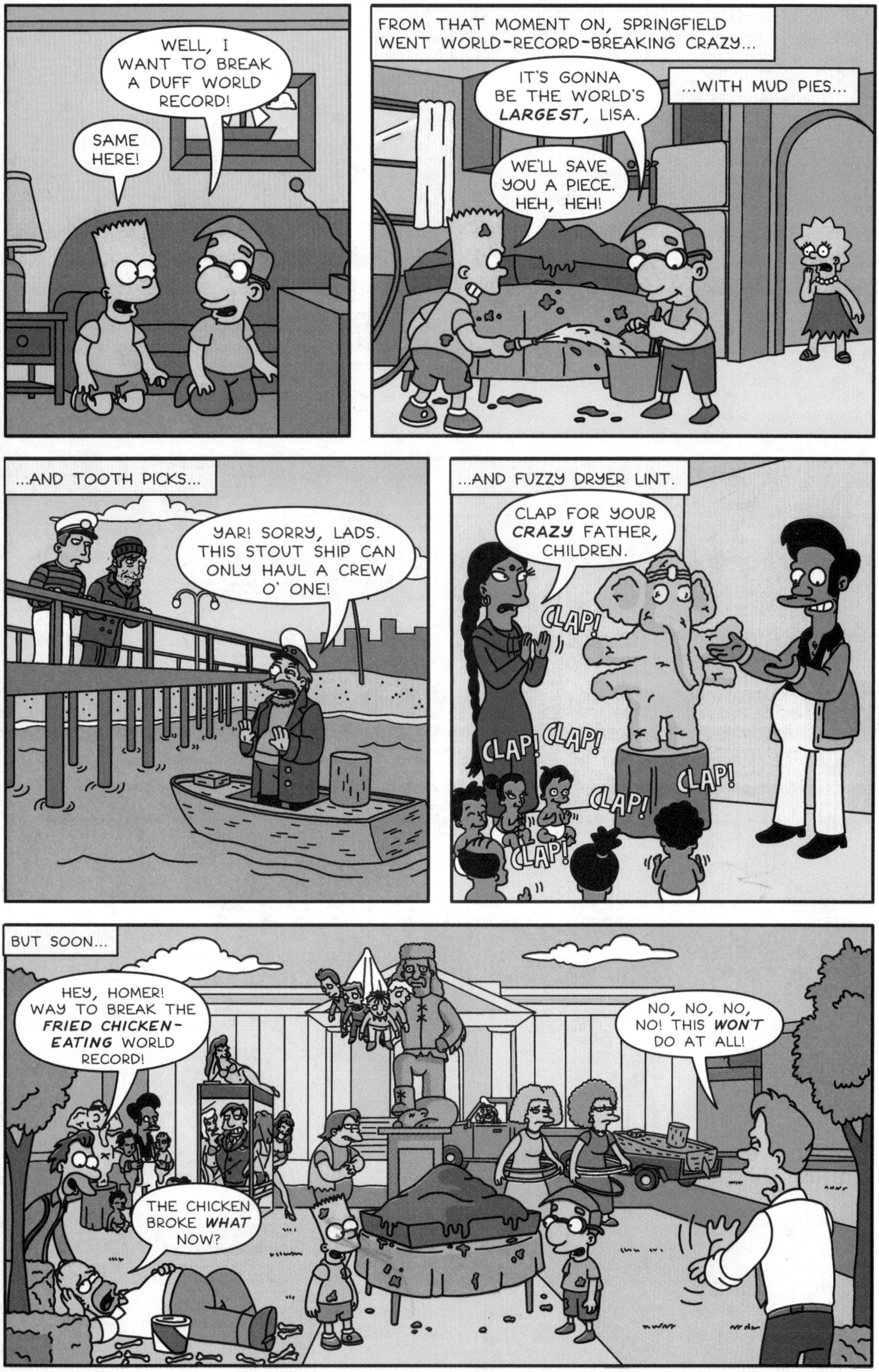

WELL, I WANT TO BREAK A DUFF WORLD RECORD!
SAME HERE!
FROM THAT MOMENT ON, SPRINGFIELD WENT WORLD-RECORD-BREAKING CRAZY...
...WITH MUD PIES...
IT'S GONNA BE THE WORLD'S LARGEST, LISA.
WE'LL SAVE YOU A PIECE. HEH, HEH!
...AND TOOTH PICKS...
YAR! SORRY, LADS. THIS STOUT SHIP CAN ONLY HAUL A CREW O' ONE!
...AND FUZZY DRYER LINT.
CLAP FOR YOUR CRAZY FATHER, CHILDREN.
CLAP!
CLAP!
CLAP!
CLAP!
CLAP!
CLAP!
BUT SOON...
HEY, HOMER! WAY TO BREAK THE FRIED CHICKEN-EATING WORLD RECORD!
THE CHICKEN BROKE WHAT NOW?
NO, NO, NO, NO! THIS WON'T DO AT ALL!

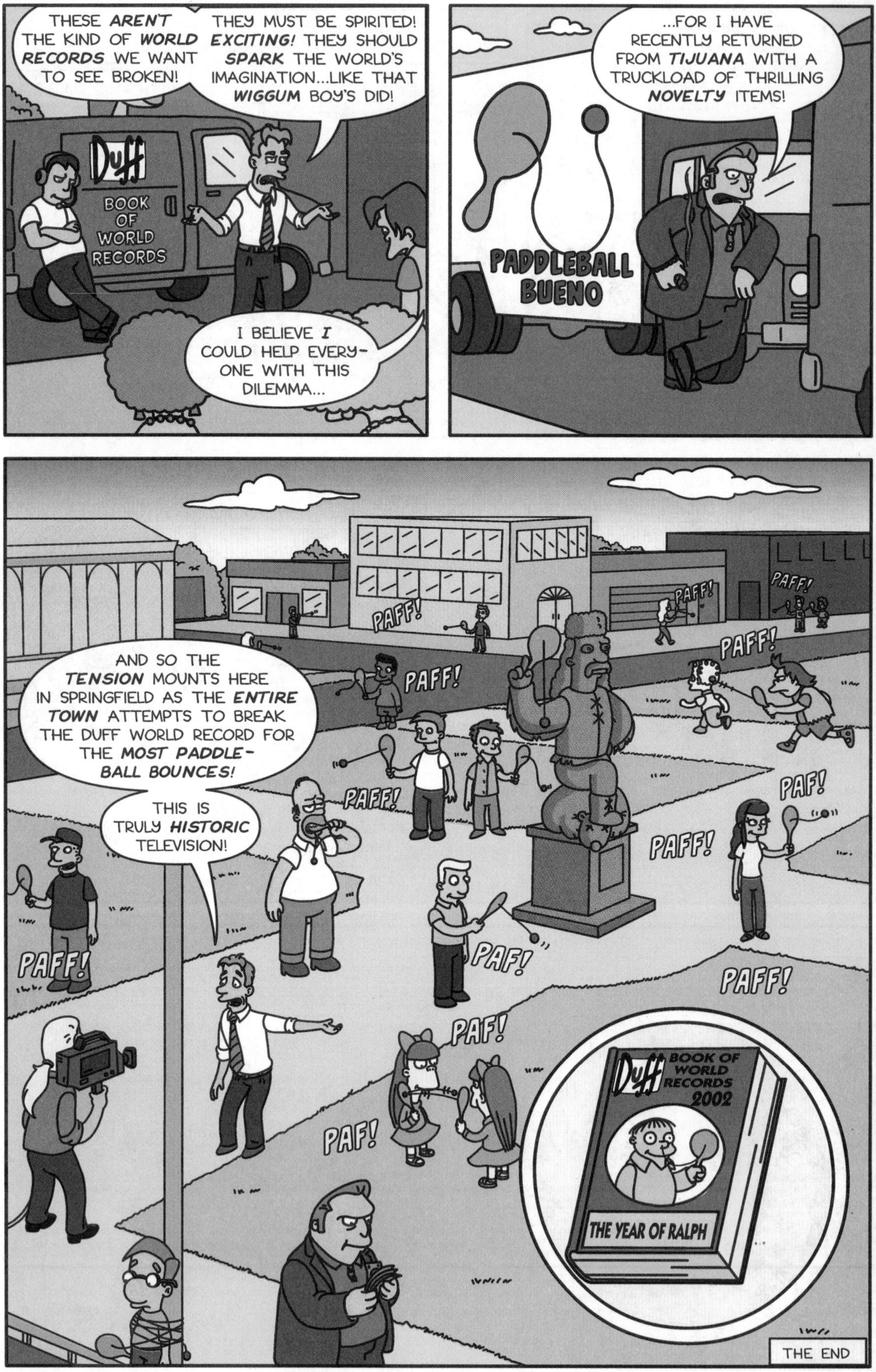
THESE *AREN'T* THE KIND OF *WORLD RECORDS* WE WANT TO SEE BROKEN!
THEY MUST BE SPIRITED! *EXCITING!* THEY SHOULD *SPARK* THE WORLD'S IMAGINATION...LIKE THAT *WIGGUM* BOY'S DID!
DUFF
BOOK OF WORLD RECORDS
I BELIEVE *I* COULD HELP EVERY-ONE WITH THIS DILEMMA...
...FOR I HAVE RECENTLY RETURNED FROM *TIJUANA* WITH A TRUCKLOAD OF THRILLING *NOVELTY* ITEMS!
PADDLEBALL BUENO
PAFF!
PAFF!
PAFF!
PAFF!
PAFF!
AND SO THE *TENSION* MOUNTS HERE IN SPRINGFIELD AS THE *ENTIRE TOWN* ATTEMPTS TO BREAK THE DUFF WORLD RECORD FOR THE *MOST PADDLE-BALL BOUNCES!*
THIS IS TRULY *HISTORIC* TELEVISION!
PAFF!
PAF!
PAFF!
PAFF!
PAF!
PAFF!
PAF!
PAF!
DUFF BOOK OF WORLD RECORDS 2002
THE YEAR OF RALPH
THE END

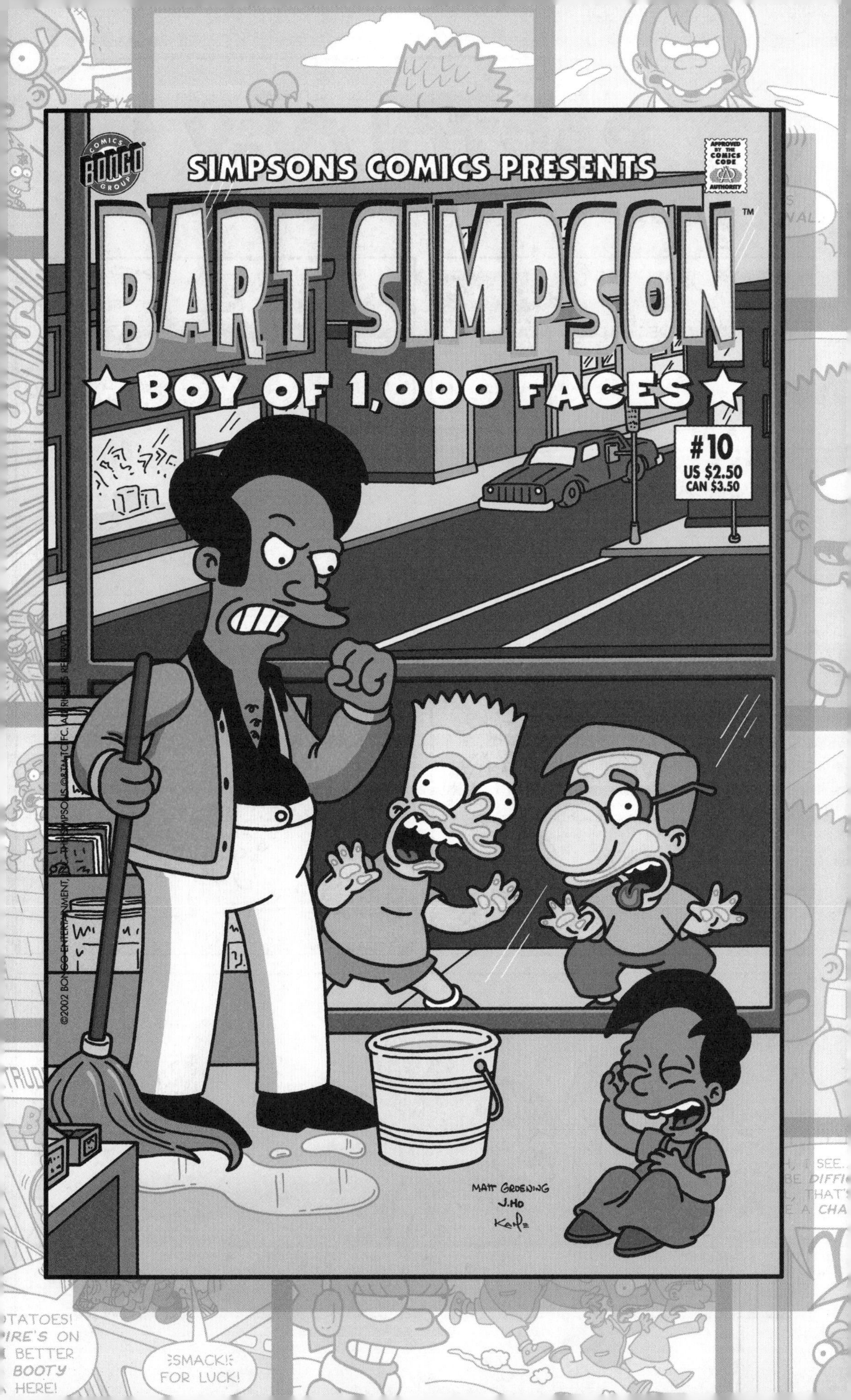
SIMPSONS COMICS PRESENTS
BART SIMPSON
BOY OF 1,000 FACES
#10
US $2.50
CAN $3.50
MATT GROENING
J.HO
SMACK!!
FOR LUCK!
BETTER
BOOTY
HERE!
I SEE.

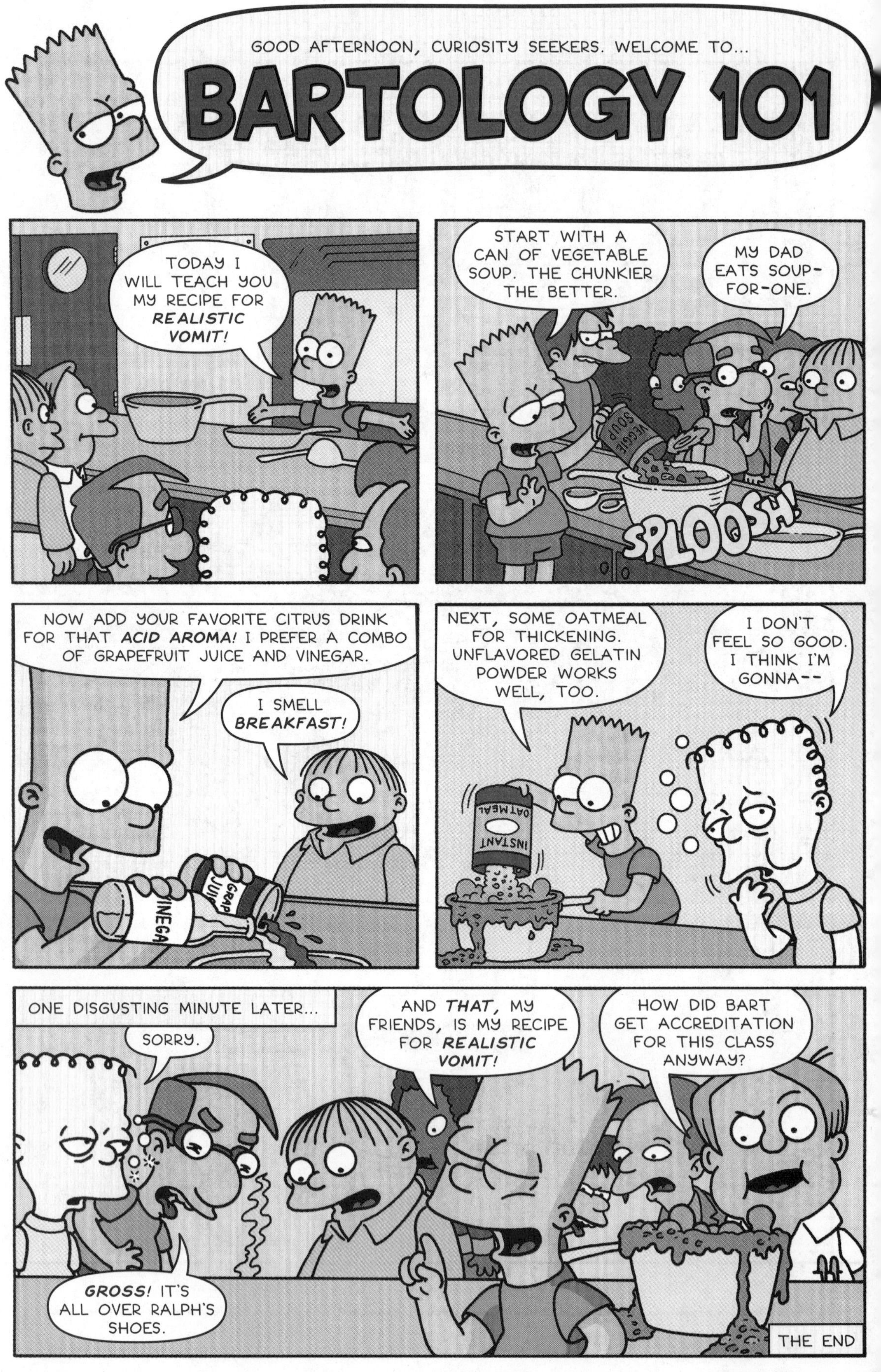
GOOD AFTERNOON, CURIOSITY SEEKERS. WELCOME TO...
BARTOLOGY 101
TODAY I WILL TEACH YOU MY RECIPE FOR REALISTIC VOMIT!
START WITH A CAN OF VEGETABLE SOUP. THE CHUNKIER THE BETTER.
VEGGIE SOUP
MY DAD EATS SOUP-FOR-ONE.
SPLOOSH!
NOW ADD YOUR FAVORITE CITRUS DRINK FOR THAT ACID AROMA! I PREFER A COMBO OF GRAPEFRUIT JUICE AND VINEGAR.
I SMELL BREAKFAST!
NEXT, SOME OATMEAL FOR THICKENING. UNFLAVORED GELATIN POWDER WORKS WELL, TOO.
I DON'T FEEL SO GOOD. I THINK I'M GONNA--
INSTANT OATMEAL
ONE DISGUSTING MINUTE LATER...
SORRY.
AND THAT, MY FRIENDS, IS MY RECIPE FOR REALISTIC VOMIT!
HOW DID BART GET ACCREDITATION FOR THIS CLASS ANYWAY?
GROSS! IT'S ALL OVER RALPH'S SHOES.
THE END

BART SIMPSON IN BART'S BEARD

I'M HERE TO TELL YOU ABOUT THE MIRACLE OF "OX-O-CLEAN." A NEW *CLEANING PRODUCT* THAT HARNESSES *THE POWER AND SMELL OF OXEN!*

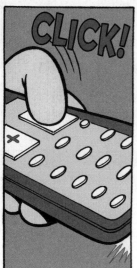

CLICK!

THE WIFETIME NETWORK IS NOW PROUD TO PRESENT MARKIE POST AS WILMA LOMAN IN "DEATH OF A NON-GENDER-SPECIFIC SALES ASSOCIATE."

Wifetime
Televison for Housewives

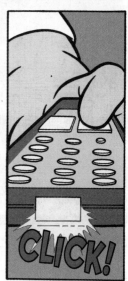

CLICK!

WANNA SEE WHAT KIND OF *TROUBLE* CLOWNS GET INTO WHEN THEY STOP *PLAYING NICE?* WELL, NOW YOU *CAN* WITH "CLOWNS GONE WILD!"

JAMES BATES
SCRIPT

OSCAR GONZALEZ LOYO
PENCILS

MIKE DECARLO
INKS

ART VILLANUEVA
COLORS

KAREN BATES
LETTERS

BILL MORRISON
EDITOR

MATT GROENING
CARTOONIST GONE WILD

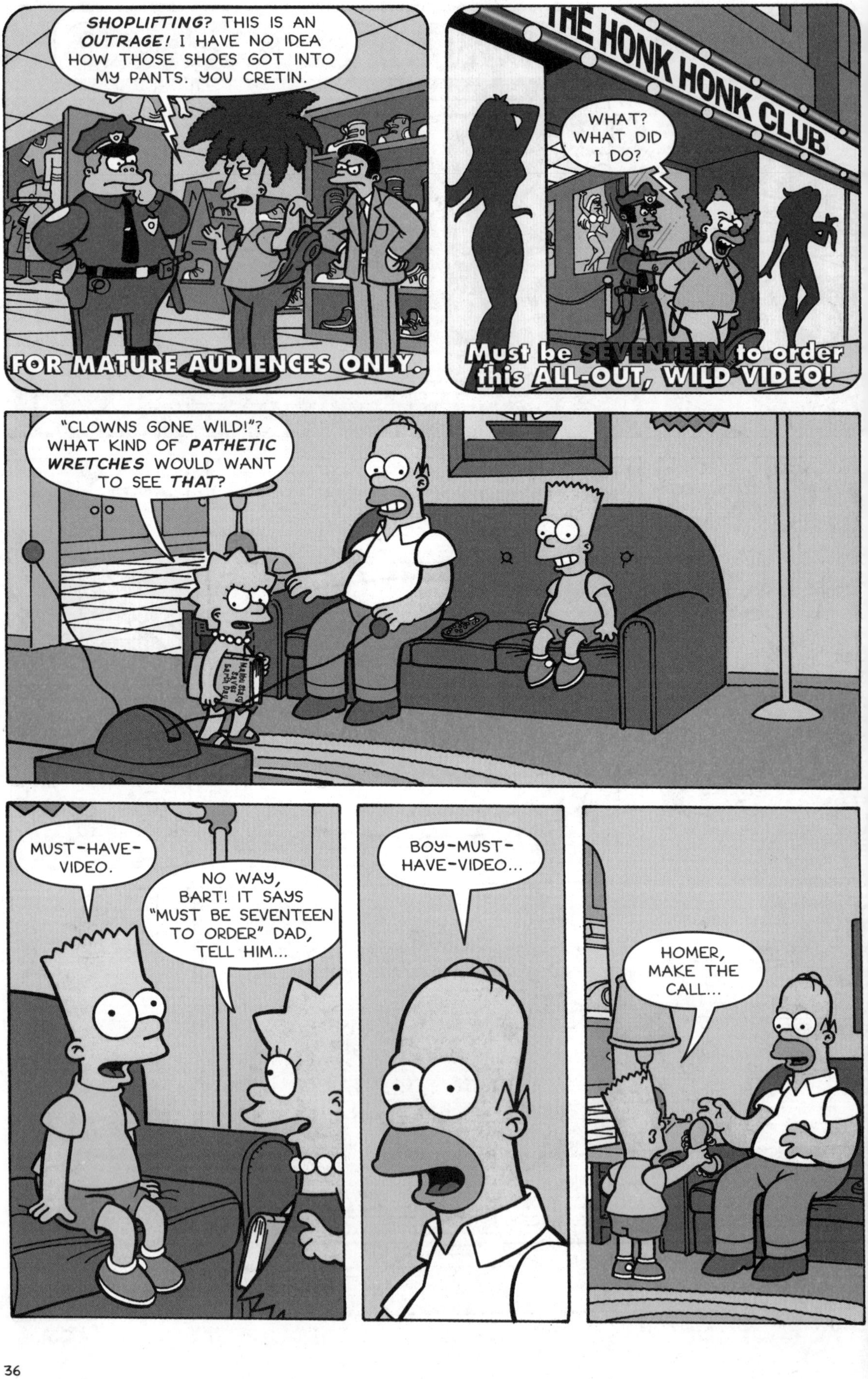
SHOPLIFTING? THIS IS AN OUTRAGE! I HAVE NO IDEA HOW THOSE SHOES GOT INTO MY PANTS. YOU CRETIN.
FOR MATURE AUDIENCES ONLY.
THE HONK HONK CLUB
WHAT? WHAT DID I DO?
Must be SEVENTEEN to order this ALL-OUT, WILD VIDEO!
"CLOWNS GONE WILD!"? WHAT KIND OF PATHETIC WRETCHES WOULD WANT TO SEE THAT?
MUST-HAVE-VIDEO.
NO WAY, BART! IT SAYS "MUST BE SEVENTEEN TO ORDER" DAD, TELL HIM...
BOY-MUST-HAVE-VIDEO...
HOMER, MAKE THE CALL...

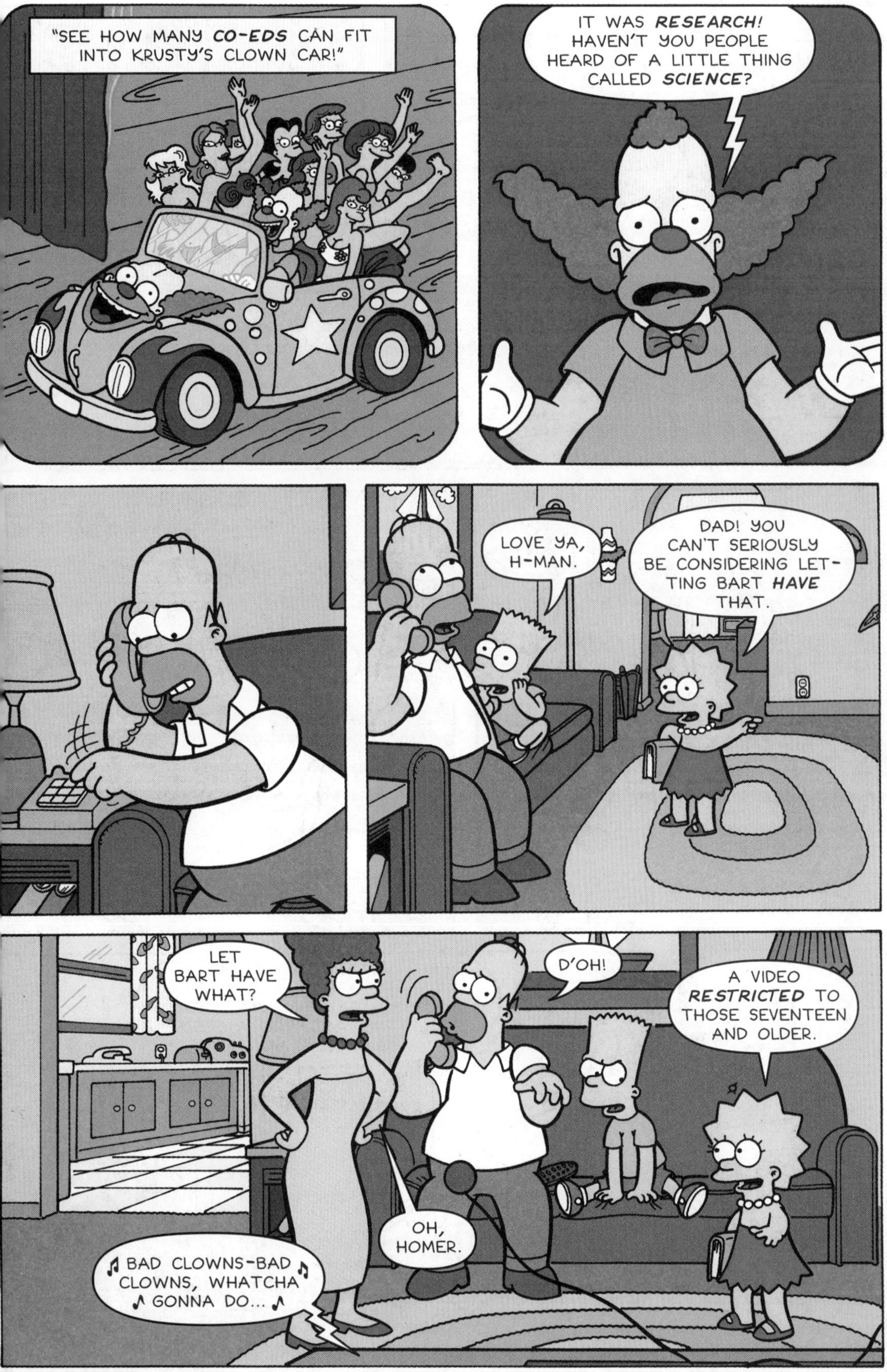
"SEE HOW MANY CO-EDS CAN FIT INTO KRUSTY'S CLOWN CAR!"
IT WAS RESEARCH! HAVEN'T YOU PEOPLE HEARD OF A LITTLE THING CALLED SCIENCE?
LOVE YA, H-MAN.
DAD! YOU CAN'T SERIOUSLY BE CONSIDERING LET-TING BART HAVE THAT.
LET BART HAVE WHAT?
D'OH!
A VIDEO RESTRICTED TO THOSE SEVENTEEN AND OLDER.
OH, HOMER.
♪ BAD CLOWNS-BAD ♪ CLOWNS, WHATCHA ♪ GONNA DO... ♪

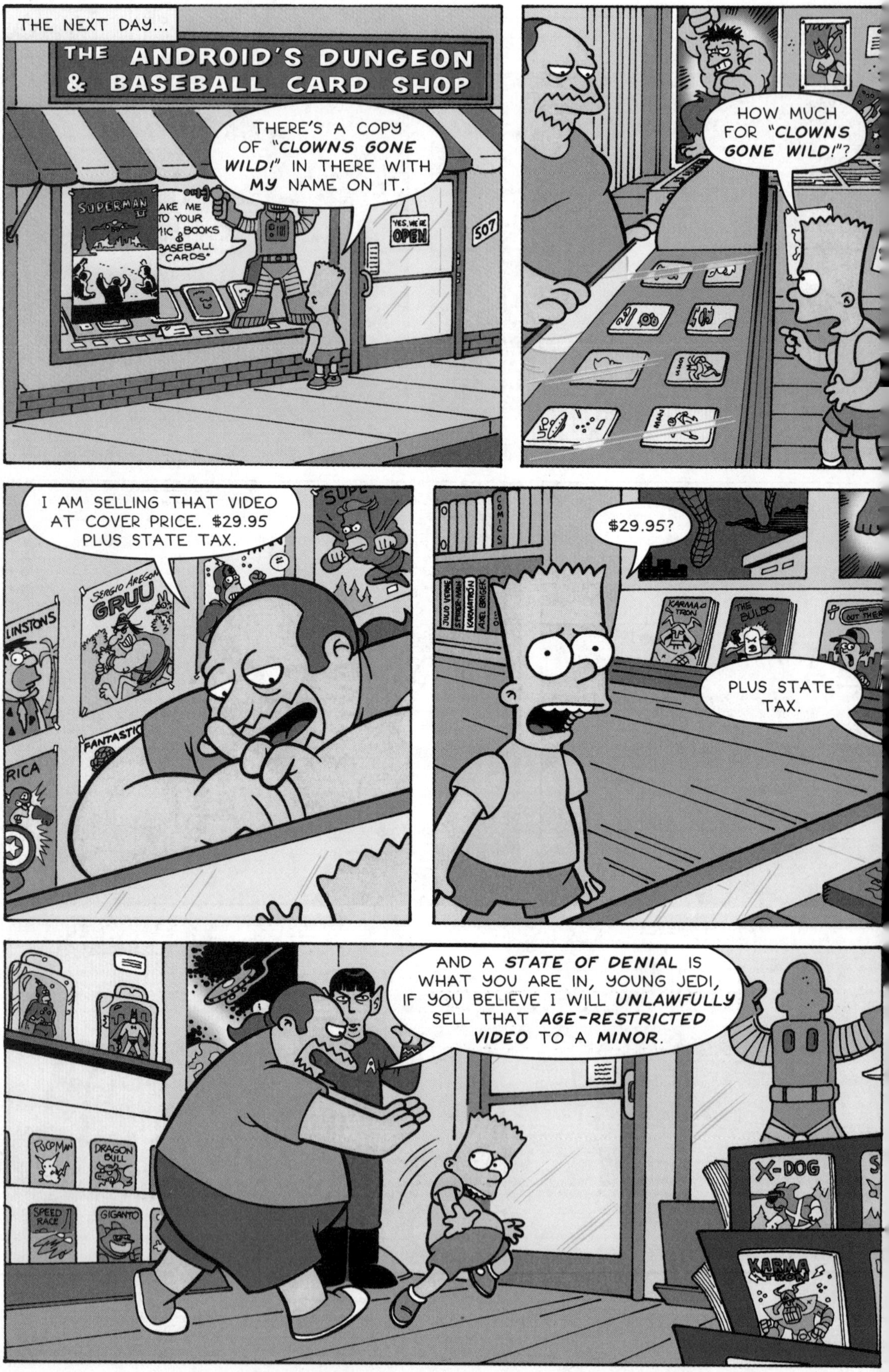
THE NEXT DAY...
THE ANDROID'S DUNGEON & BASEBALL CARD SHOP
THERE'S A COPY OF "CLOWNS GONE WILD!" IN THERE WITH MY NAME ON IT.
YES, WE'RE OPEN
507
HOW MUCH FOR "CLOWNS GONE WILD!"?
I AM SELLING THAT VIDEO AT COVER PRICE. $29.95 PLUS STATE TAX.
$29.95?
PLUS STATE TAX.
AND A STATE OF DENIAL IS WHAT YOU ARE IN, YOUNG JEDI, IF YOU BELIEVE I WILL UNLAWFULLY SELL THAT AGE-RESTRICTED VIDEO TO A MINOR.

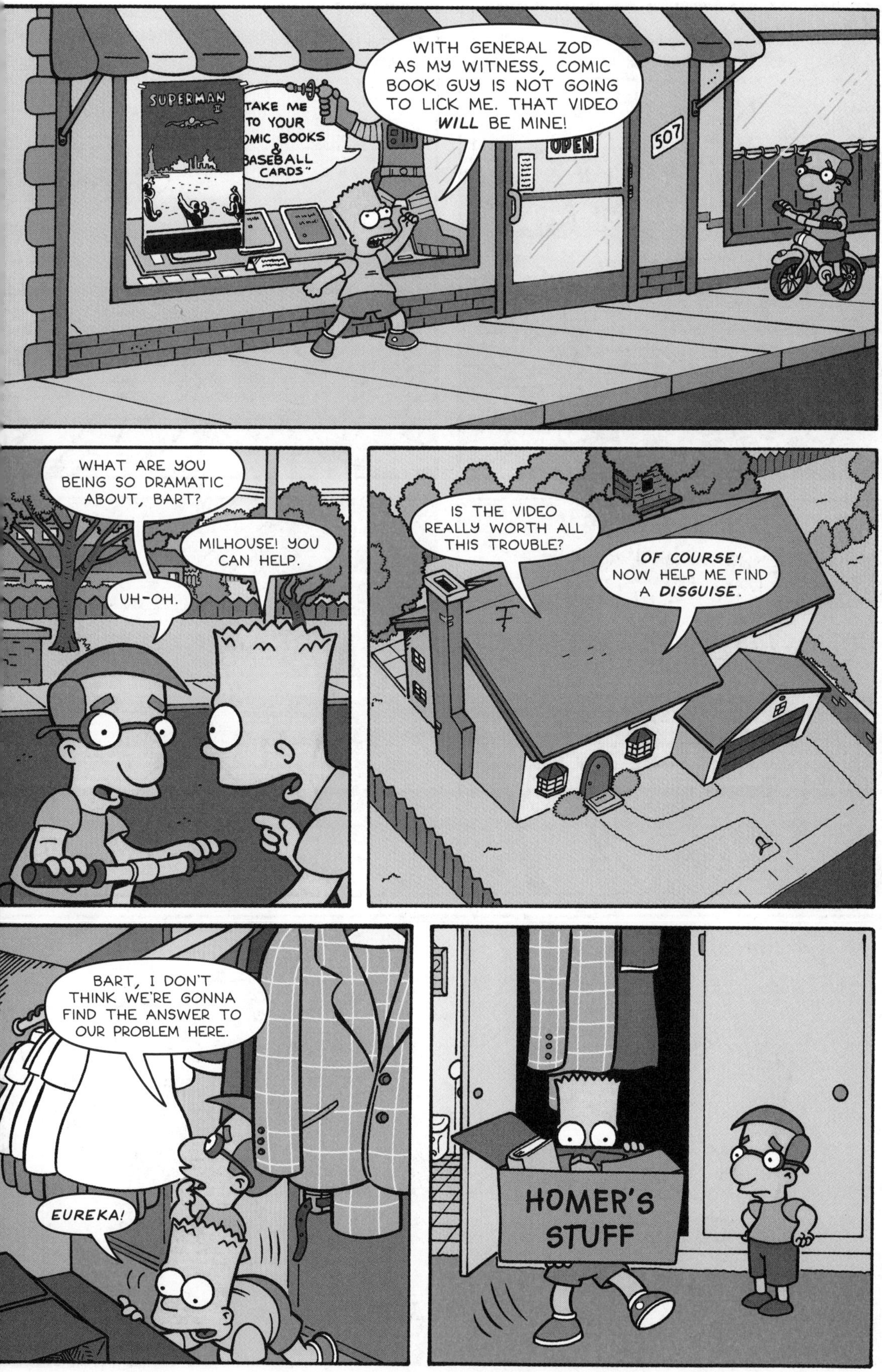
WITH GENERAL ZOD AS MY WITNESS, COMIC BOOK GUY IS NOT GOING TO LICK ME. THAT VIDEO **WILL** BE MINE!
SUPERMAN II
TAKE ME TO YOUR COMIC BOOKS & BASEBALL CARDS"
OPEN
507
WHAT ARE YOU BEING SO DRAMATIC ABOUT, BART?
MILHOUSE! YOU CAN HELP.
UH-OH.
IS THE VIDEO REALLY WORTH ALL THIS TROUBLE?
OF COURSE! NOW HELP ME FIND A **DISGUISE**.
BART, I DON'T THINK WE'RE GONNA FIND THE ANSWER TO OUR PROBLEM HERE.
EUREKA!
HOMER'S STUFF

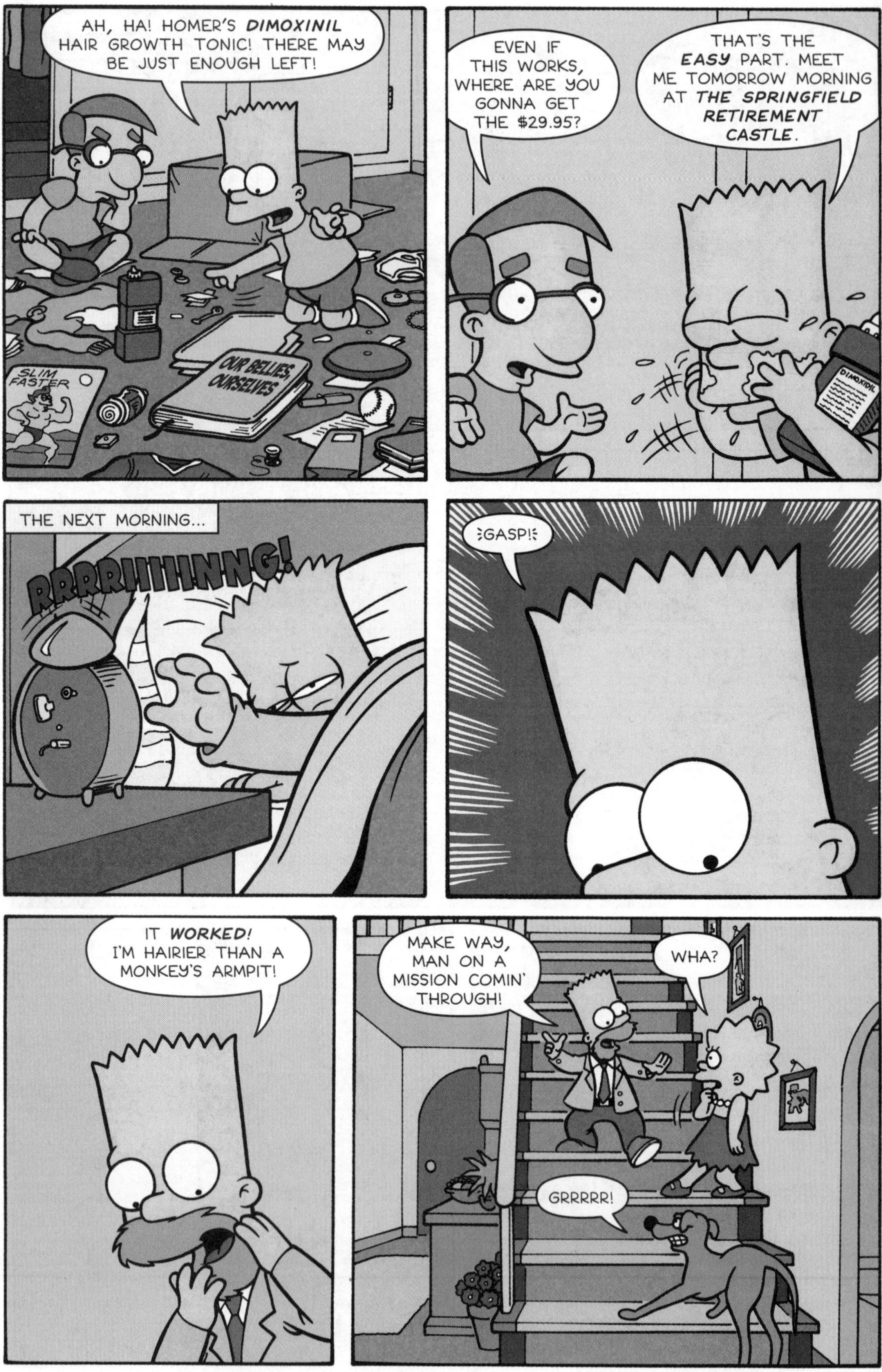
AH, HA! HOMER'S DIMOXINIL HAIR GROWTH TONIC! THERE MAY BE JUST ENOUGH LEFT!
SLIM FASTER
OUR BELLIES, OURSELVES
EVEN IF THIS WORKS, WHERE ARE YOU GONNA GET THE $29.95?
THAT'S THE EASY PART. MEET ME TOMORROW MORNING AT THE SPRINGFIELD RETIREMENT CASTLE.
DIMOXIDIL
THE NEXT MORNING...
RRRRIIIIINNG!
GASP!
IT WORKED! I'M HAIRIER THAN A MONKEY'S ARMPIT!
MAKE WAY, MAN ON A MISSION COMIN' THROUGH!
WHA?
GRRRRR!

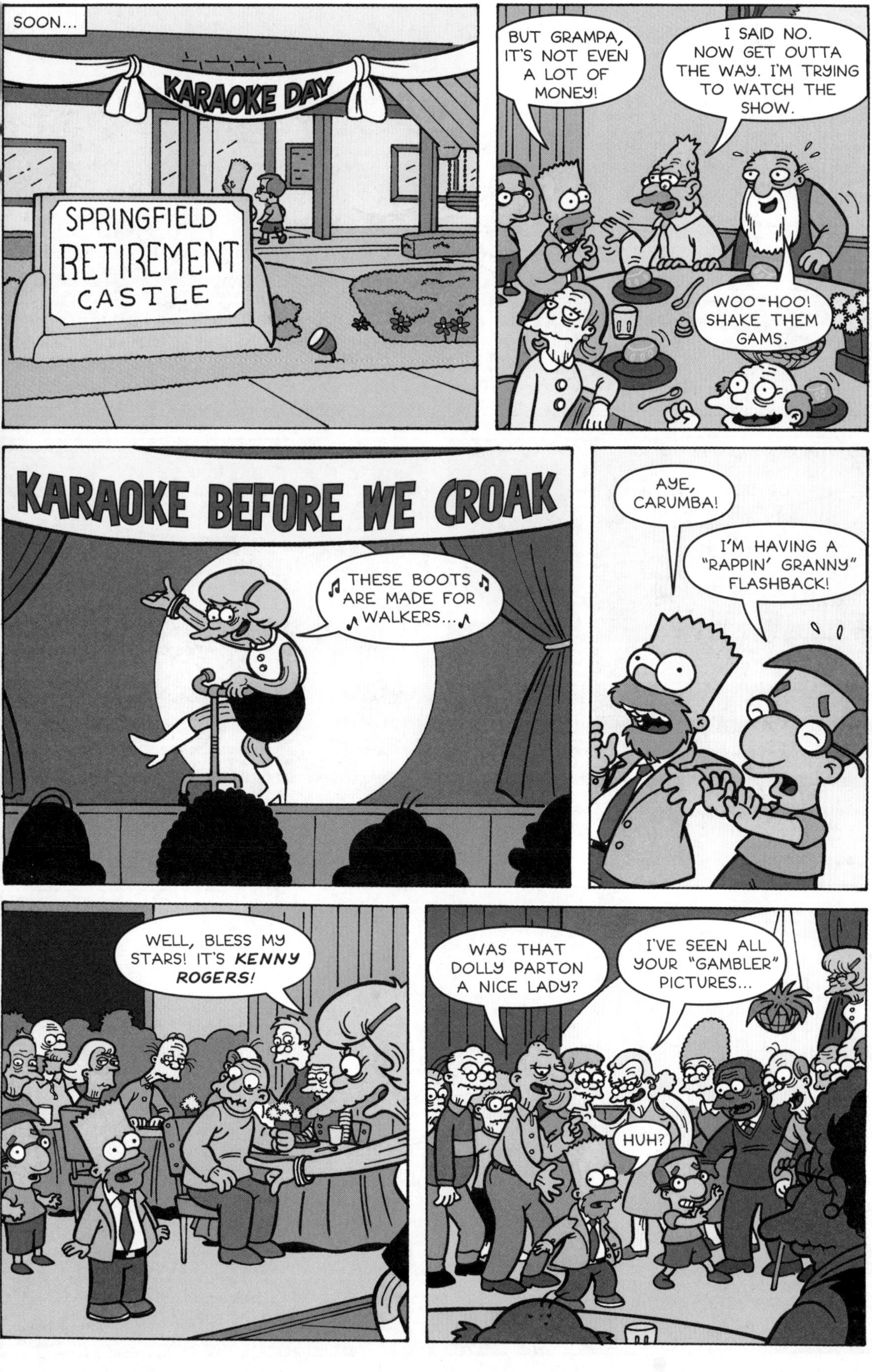
SOON...
KARAOKE DAY
SPRINGFIELD RETIREMENT CASTLE
BUT GRAMPA, IT'S NOT EVEN A LOT OF MONEY!
I SAID NO. NOW GET OUTTA THE WAY. I'M TRYING TO WATCH THE SHOW.
WOO-HOO! SHAKE THEM GAMS.
KARAOKE BEFORE WE CROAK
THESE BOOTS ARE MADE FOR WALKERS...
AYE, CARUMBA!
I'M HAVING A "RAPPIN' GRANNY" FLASHBACK!
WELL, BLESS MY STARS! IT'S KENNY ROGERS!
WAS THAT DOLLY PARTON A NICE LADY?
I'VE SEEN ALL YOUR "GAMBLER" PICTURES...
HUH?

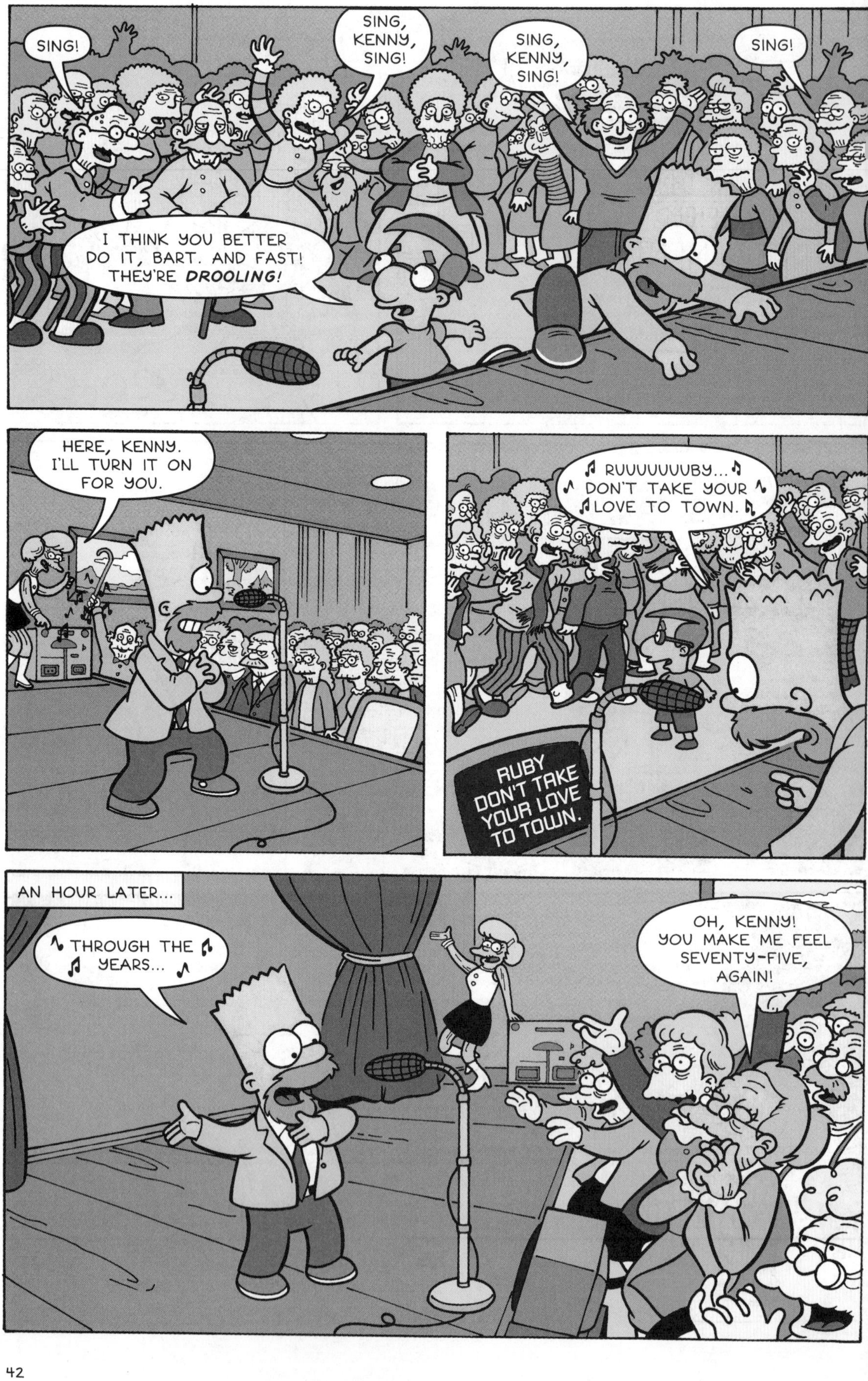
SING!
SING, KENNY, SING!
SING, KENNY, SING!
SING!
I THINK YOU BETTER DO IT, BART. AND FAST! THEY'RE *DROOLING!*
HERE, KENNY. I'LL TURN IT ON FOR YOU.
♫ RUUUUUUUBY... ♫ DON'T TAKE YOUR LOVE TO TOWN. ♫
RUBY DON'T TAKE YOUR LOVE TO TOWN.
AN HOUR LATER...
♫ THROUGH THE YEARS... ♫
OH, KENNY! YOU MAKE ME FEEL SEVENTY-FIVE, AGAIN!

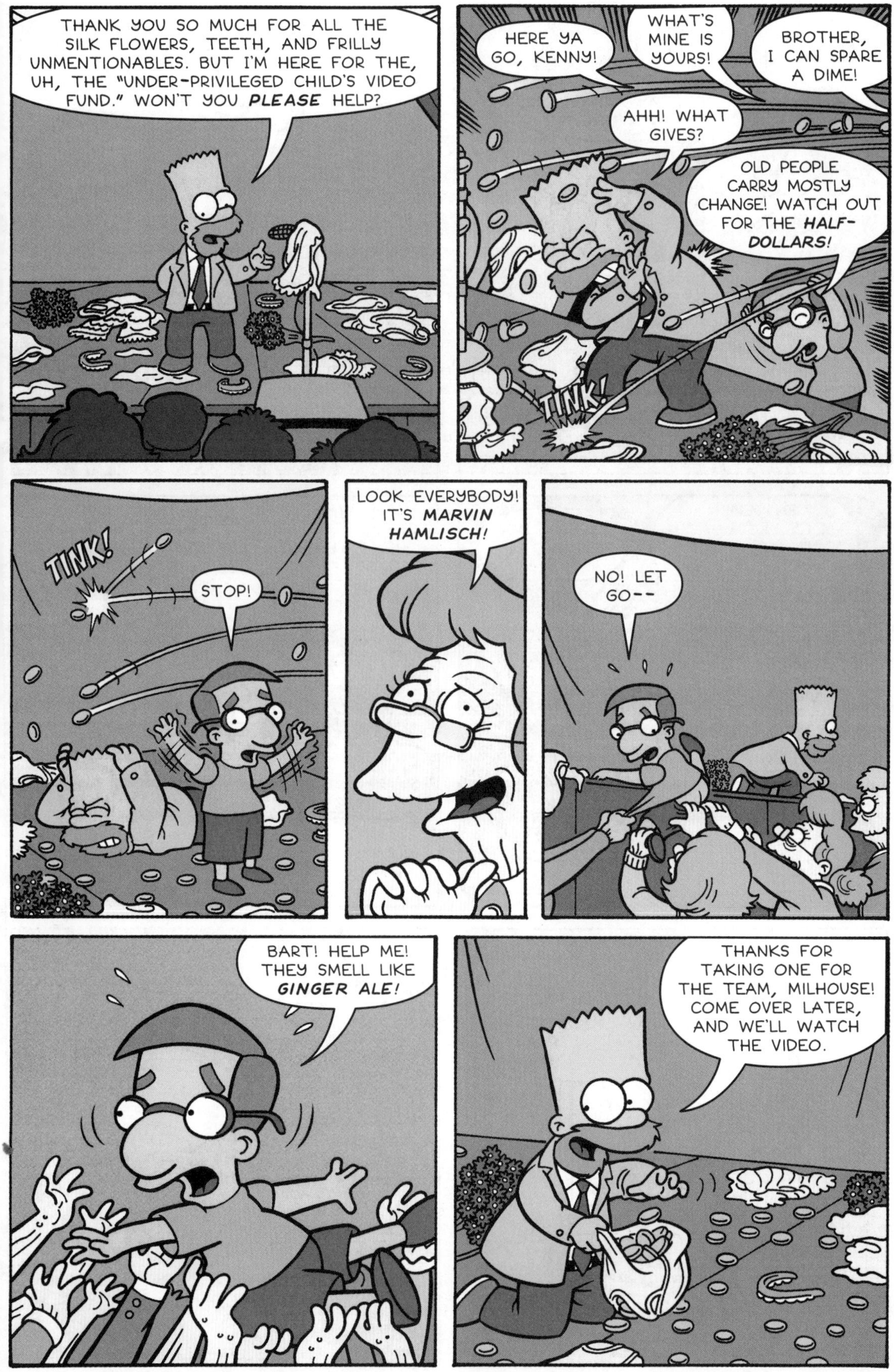
THANK YOU SO MUCH FOR ALL THE SILK FLOWERS, TEETH, AND FRILLY UNMENTIONABLES. BUT I'M HERE FOR THE, UH, THE "UNDER-PRIVILEGED CHILD'S VIDEO FUND." WON'T YOU **PLEASE** HELP?
HERE YA GO, KENNY!
WHAT'S MINE IS YOURS!
BROTHER, I CAN SPARE A DIME!
AHH! WHAT GIVES?
OLD PEOPLE CARRY MOSTLY CHANGE! WATCH OUT FOR THE **HALF-DOLLARS**!
TINK!
TINK!
STOP!
LOOK EVERYBODY! IT'S **MARVIN HAMLISCH**!
NO! LET GO--
BART! HELP ME! THEY SMELL LIKE **GINGER ALE**!
THANKS FOR TAKING ONE FOR THE TEAM, MILHOUSE! COME OVER LATER, AND WE'LL WATCH THE VIDEO.

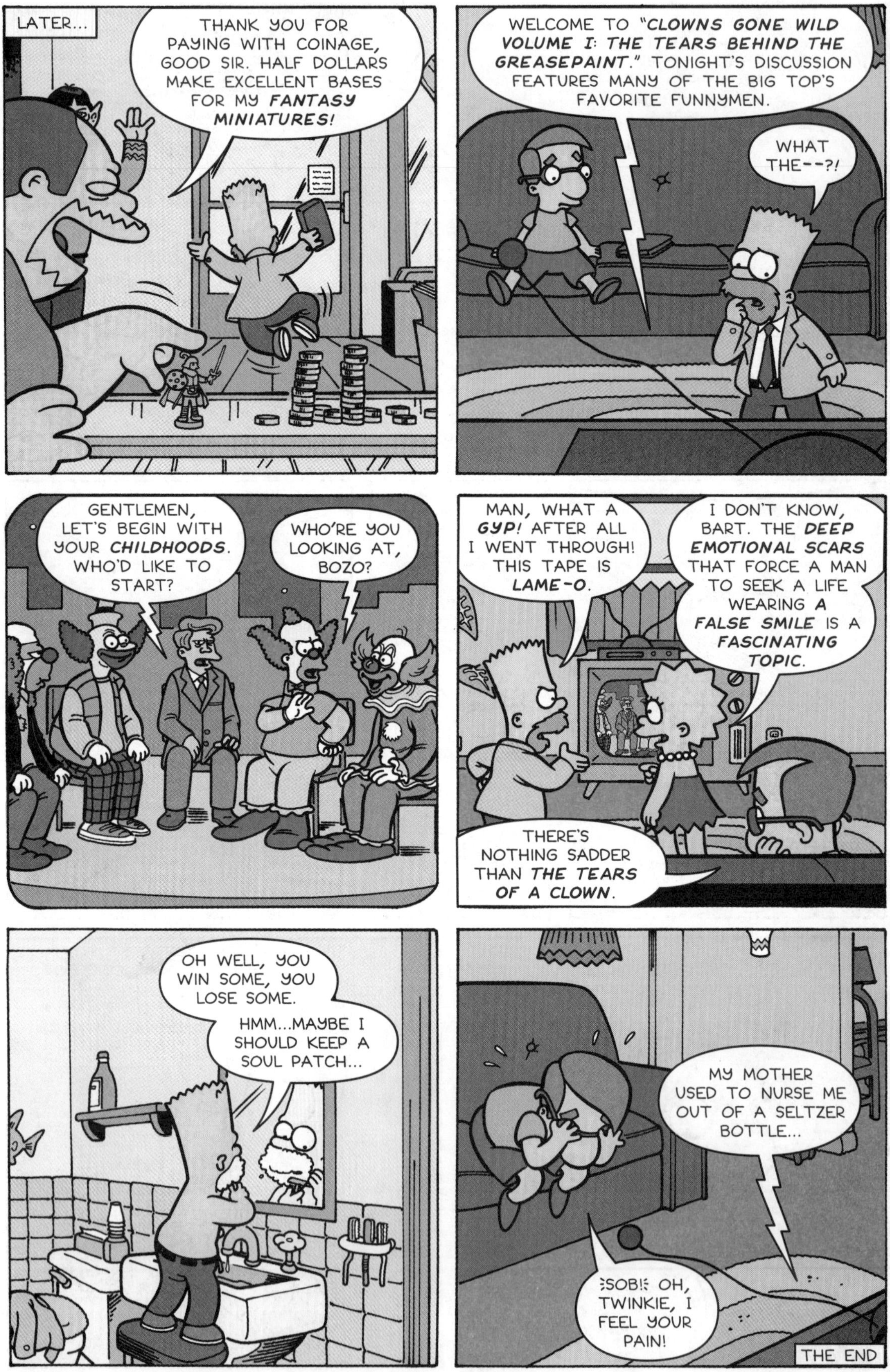
LATER...
THANK YOU FOR PAYING WITH COINAGE, GOOD SIR. HALF DOLLARS MAKE EXCELLENT BASES FOR MY FANTASY MINIATURES!
WELCOME TO "CLOWNS GONE WILD VOLUME I: THE TEARS BEHIND THE GREASEPAINT." TONIGHT'S DISCUSSION FEATURES MANY OF THE BIG TOP'S FAVORITE FUNNYMEN.
WHAT THE--?!
GENTLEMEN, LET'S BEGIN WITH YOUR CHILDHOODS. WHO'D LIKE TO START?
WHO'RE YOU LOOKING AT, BOZO?
MAN, WHAT A GYP! AFTER ALL I WENT THROUGH! THIS TAPE IS LAME-O.
I DON'T KNOW, BART. THE DEEP EMOTIONAL SCARS THAT FORCE A MAN TO SEEK A LIFE WEARING A FALSE SMILE IS A FASCINATING TOPIC.
THERE'S NOTHING SADDER THAN THE TEARS OF A CLOWN.
OH WELL, YOU WIN SOME, YOU LOSE SOME.
HMM...MAYBE I SHOULD KEEP A SOUL PATCH...
MY MOTHER USED TO NURSE ME OUT OF A SELTZER BOTTLE...
:SOB!: OH, TWINKIE, I FEEL YOUR PAIN!
THE END

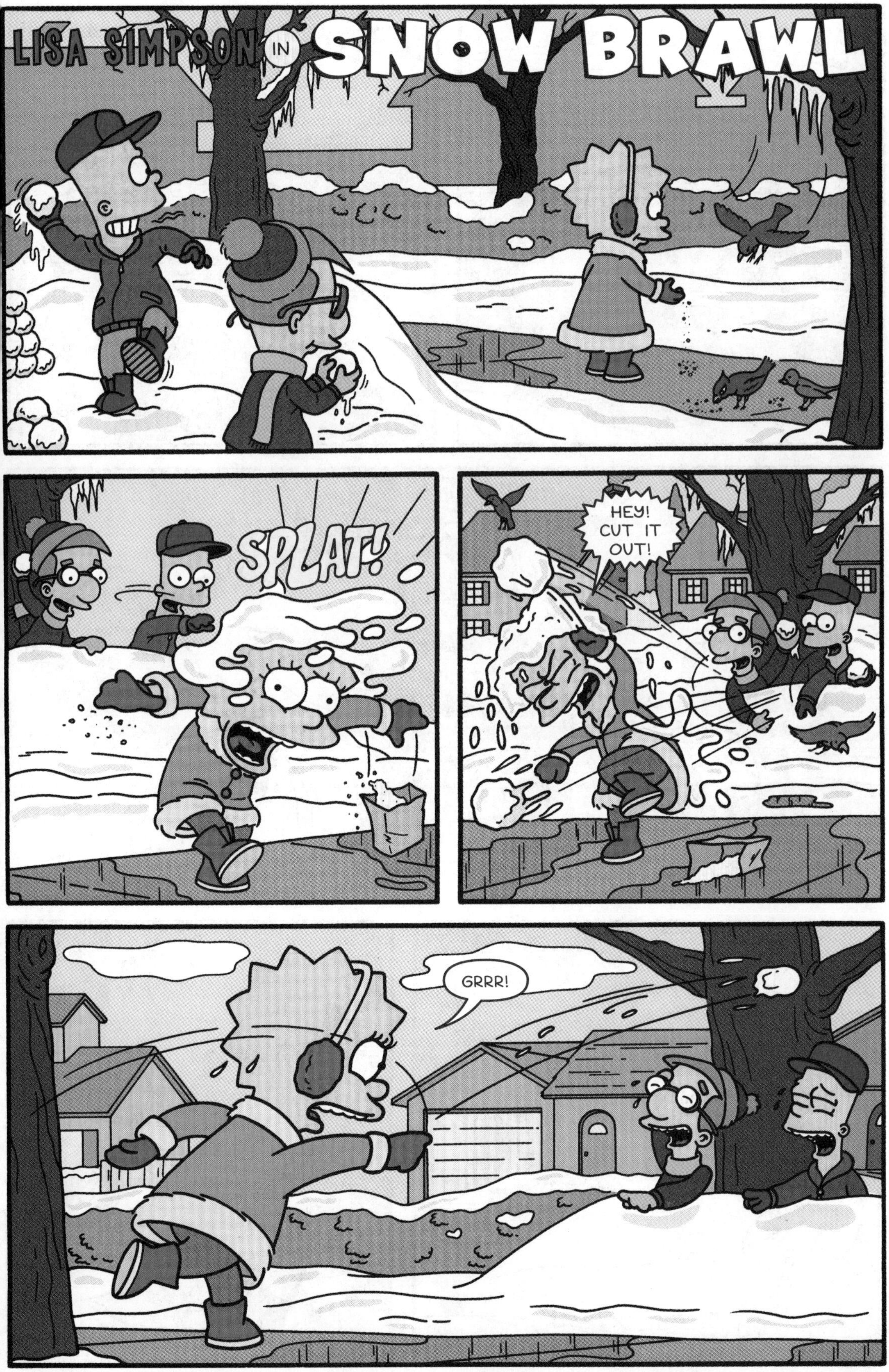
LISA SIMPSON IN SNOW BRAWL
SPLAT!
HEY! CUT IT OUT!
GRRR!

CHRIS YAMBAR SCRIPT · MIKE WORLEY PENCILS · MIKE ROTE INKS · KAREN BATES COLORS/LETTERS · BILL MORRISON EDITOR · MATT GROENING SLUSH-BALL KING

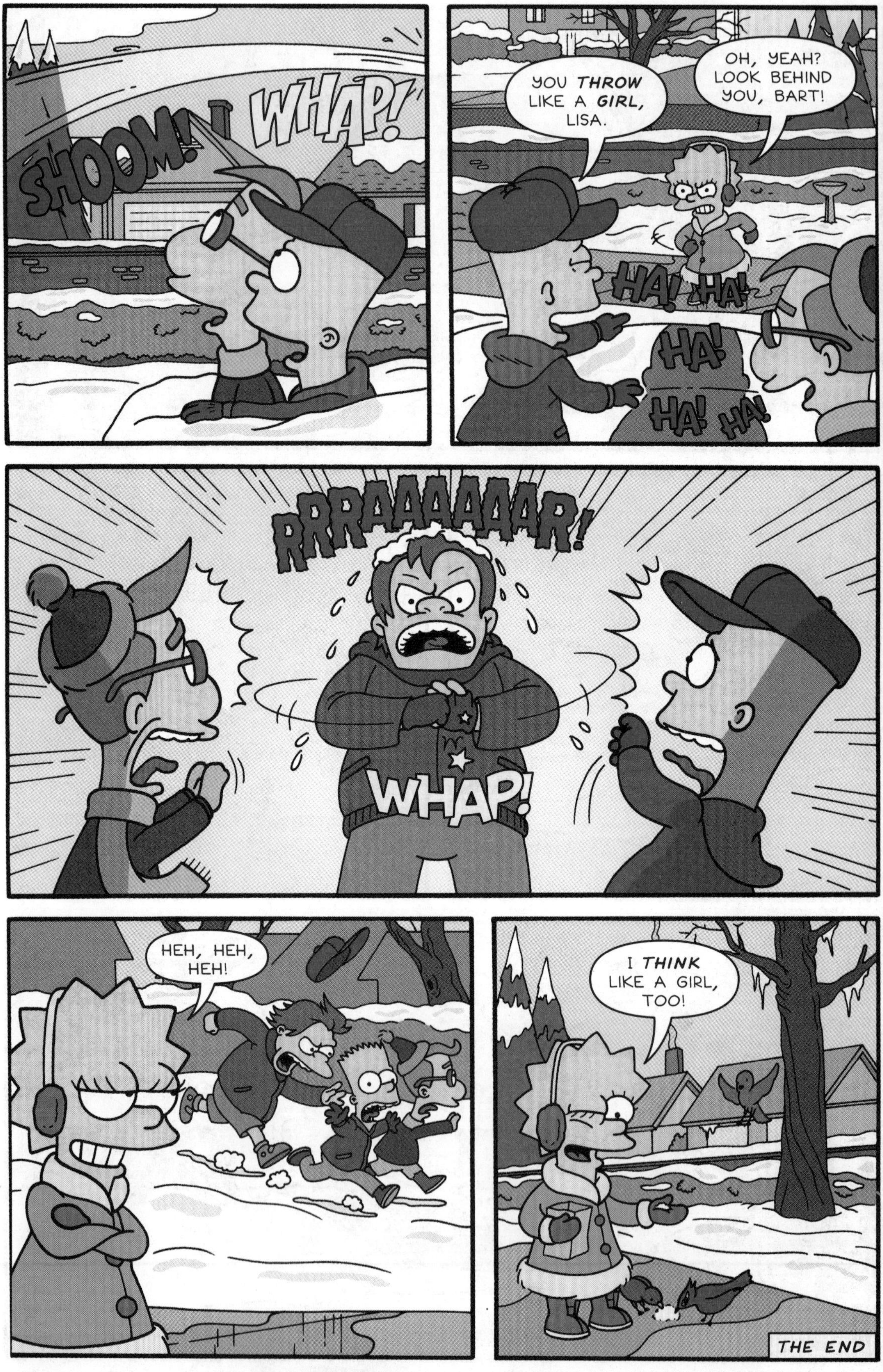
SHOOM!
WHAP!
YOU THROW LIKE A GIRL, LISA.
OH, YEAH? LOOK BEHIND YOU, BART!
HA! HA!
HA!
HA! HA!
RRRAAAAAAAR!
WHAP!
HEH, HEH, HEH!
I THINK LIKE A GIRL, TOO!
THE END

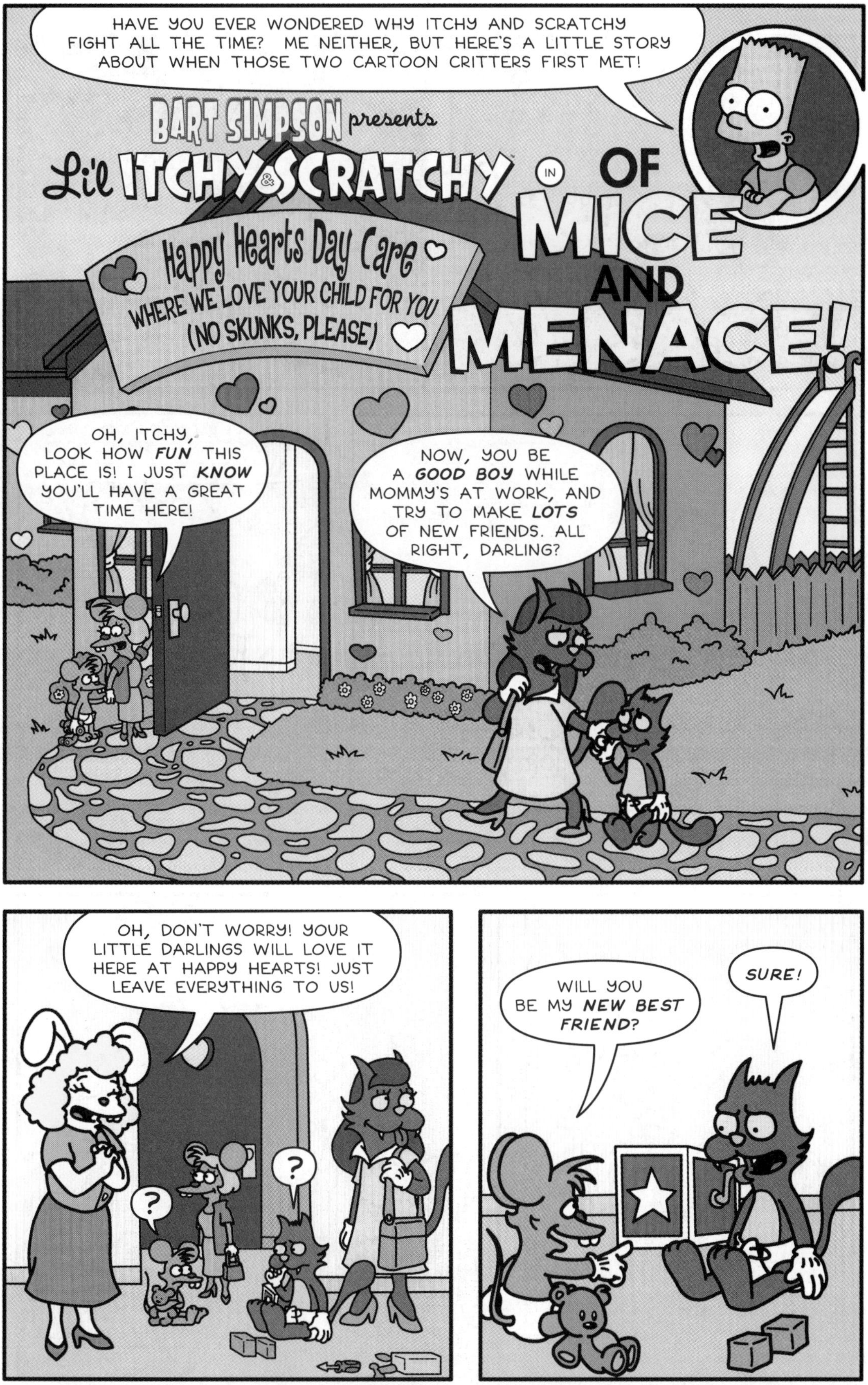
HAVE YOU EVER WONDERED WHY ITCHY AND SCRATCHY FIGHT ALL THE TIME? ME NEITHER, BUT HERE'S A LITTLE STORY ABOUT WHEN THOSE TWO CARTOON CRITTERS FIRST MET!
BART SIMPSON presents
Li'l ITCHY & SCRATCHY IN OF MICE AND MENACE!
Happy Hearts Day Care
WHERE WE LOVE YOUR CHILD FOR YOU
(NO SKUNKS, PLEASE)
OH, ITCHY, LOOK HOW *FUN* THIS PLACE IS! I JUST *KNOW* YOU'LL HAVE A GREAT TIME HERE!
NOW, YOU BE A *GOOD BOY* WHILE MOMMY'S AT WORK, AND TRY TO MAKE *LOTS* OF NEW FRIENDS. ALL RIGHT, DARLING?
OH, DON'T WORRY! YOUR LITTLE DARLINGS WILL LOVE IT HERE AT HAPPY HEARTS! JUST LEAVE EVERYTHING TO US!
?
?
WILL YOU BE MY *NEW BEST FRIEND*?
SURE!

GAIL SIMONE SCRIPT — *KIM LE* PENCILS — *JAME HUANG* INKS — *ART VILLANUEVA* COLORS — *KAREN BATES* LETTERS — *BILL MORRISON* EDITOR — *MATT GROENING* PRESCHOOL PRANKSTER

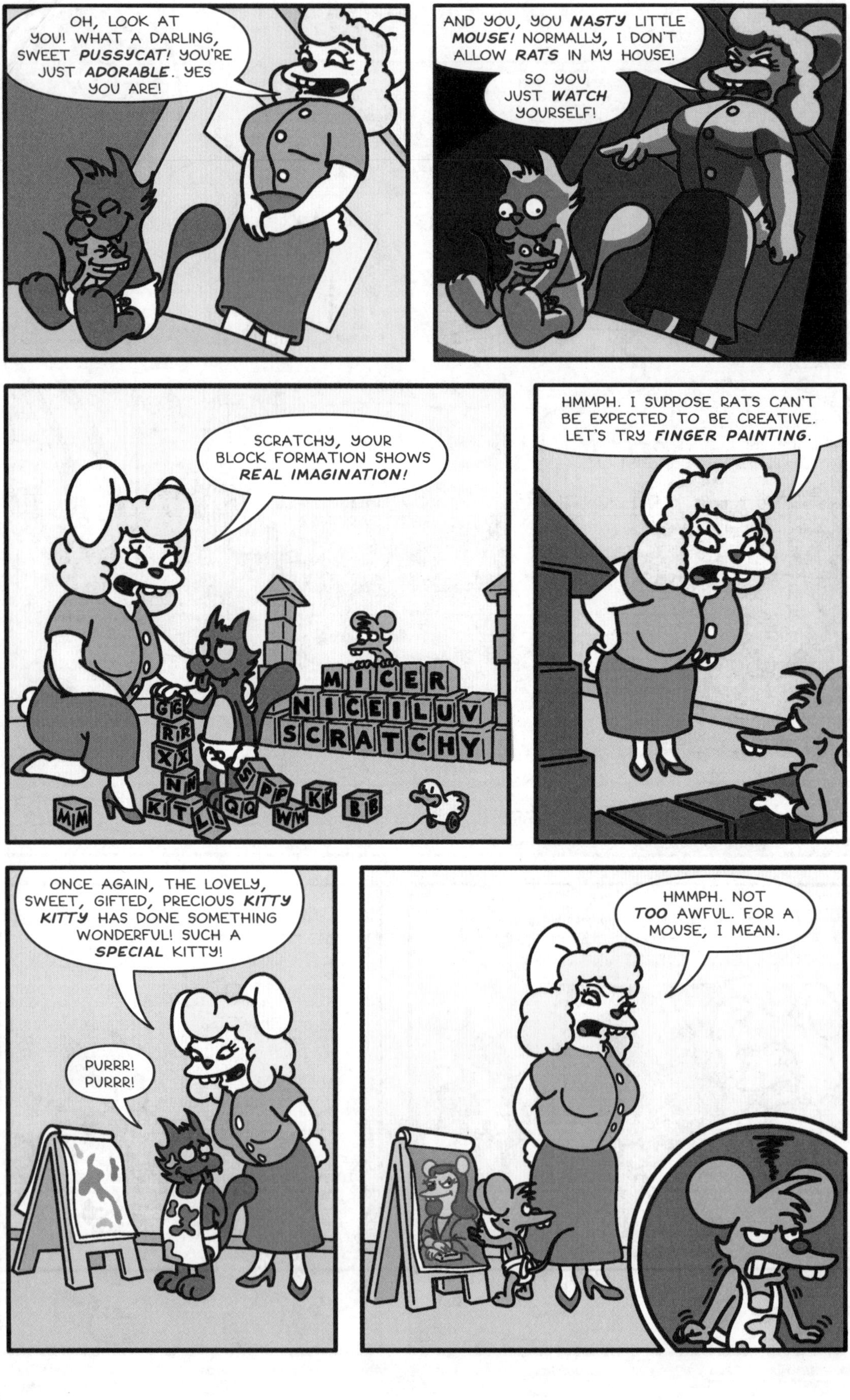
OH, LOOK AT YOU! WHAT A DARLING, SWEET PUSSYCAT! YOU'RE JUST ADORABLE. YES YOU ARE!
AND YOU, YOU NASTY LITTLE MOUSE! NORMALLY, I DON'T ALLOW RATS IN MY HOUSE!
SO YOU JUST WATCH YOURSELF!
SCRATCHY, YOUR BLOCK FORMATION SHOWS REAL IMAGINATION!
MICER
NICEILUV
SCRATCHY
HMMPH. I SUPPOSE RATS CAN'T BE EXPECTED TO BE CREATIVE. LET'S TRY FINGER PAINTING.
ONCE AGAIN, THE LOVELY, SWEET, GIFTED, PRECIOUS KITTY KITTY HAS DONE SOMETHING WONDERFUL! SUCH A SPECIAL KITTY!
PURRR! PURRR!
HMMPH. NOT TOO AWFUL. FOR A MOUSE, I MEAN.

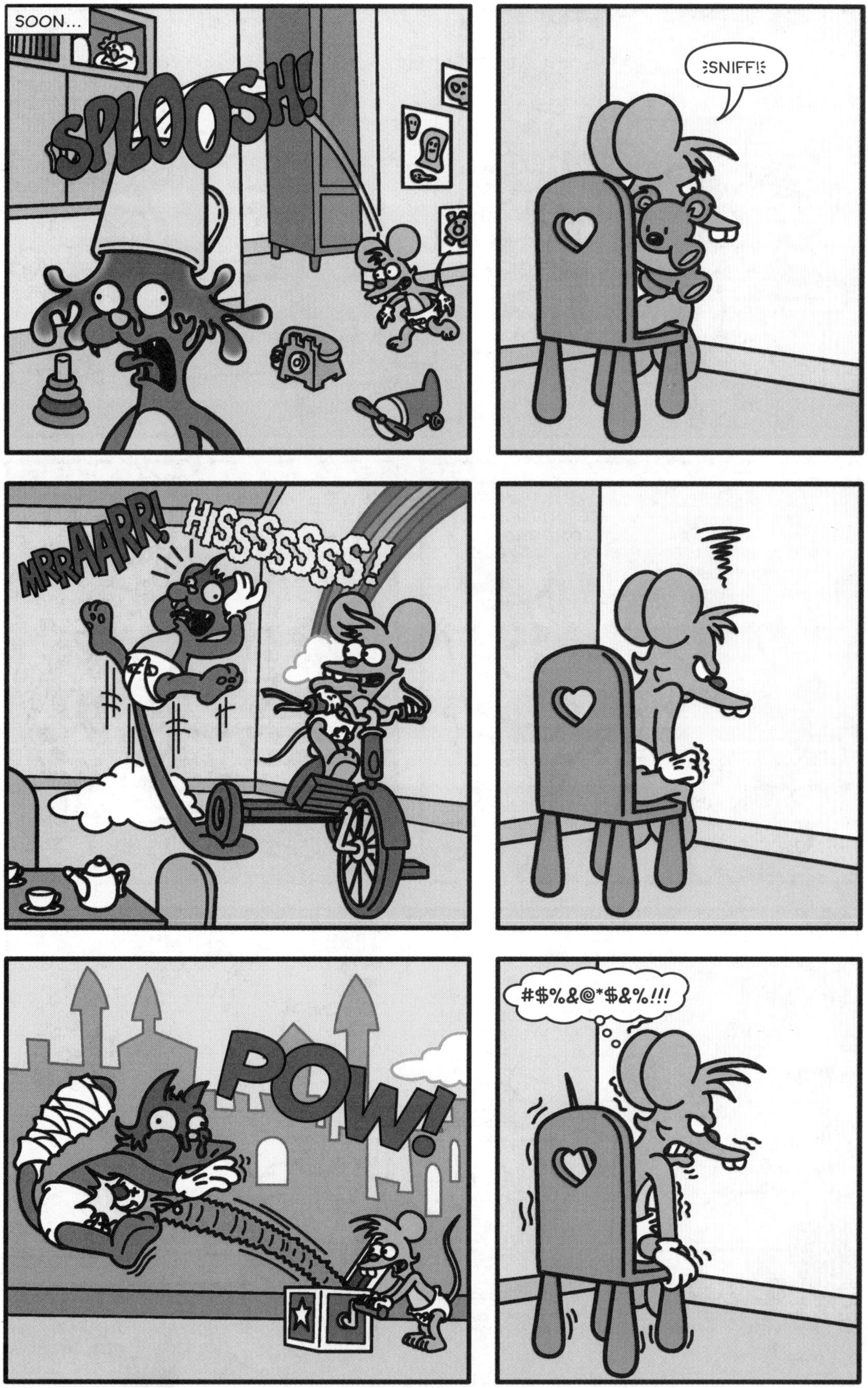
SOON...
SPLOOSH!
SNIFF!
MRRAARR!
HISSSSSSS!
POW!
#$%&@*$&%!!!

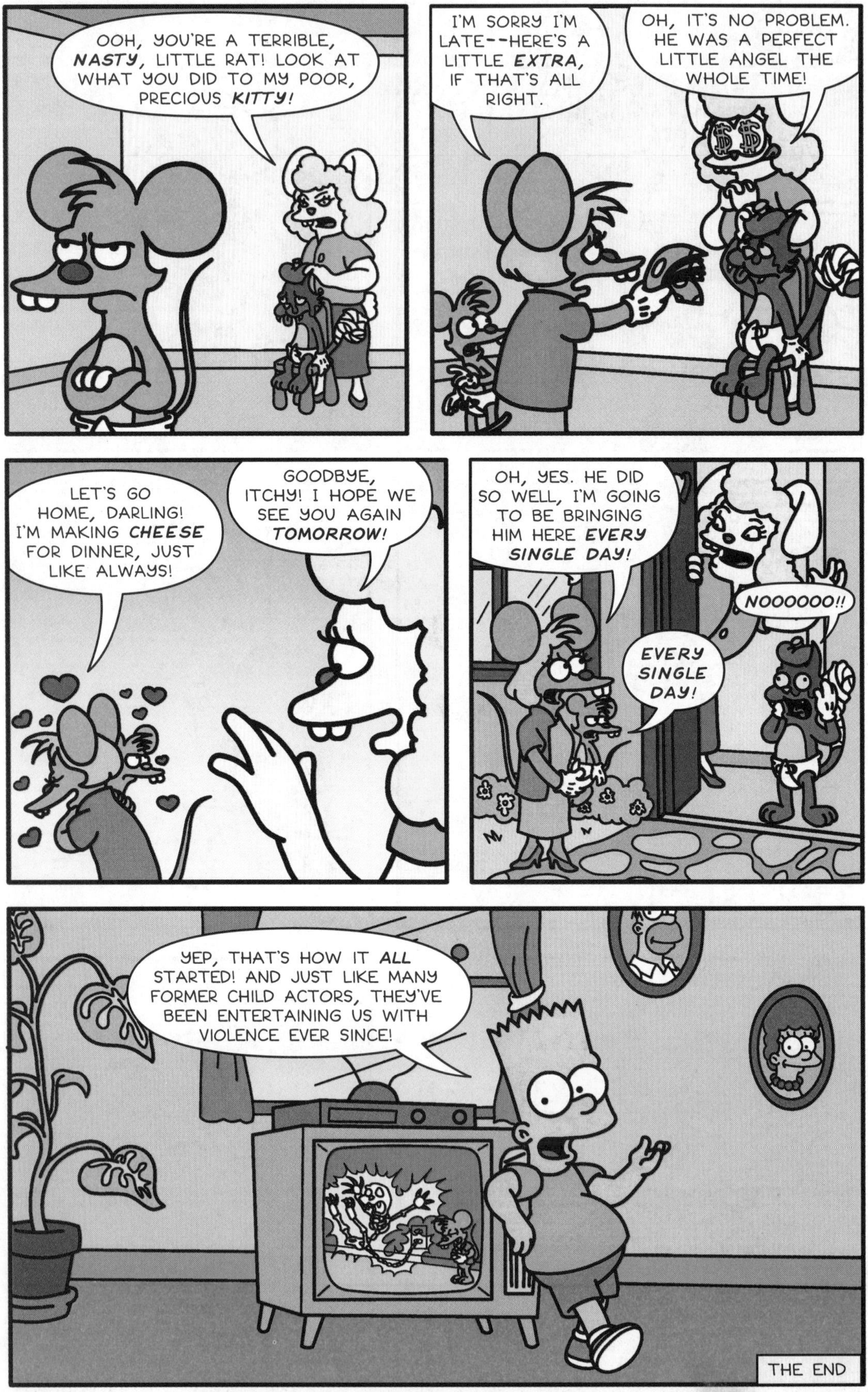
OOH, YOU'RE A TERRIBLE, NASTY, LITTLE RAT! LOOK AT WHAT YOU DID TO MY POOR, PRECIOUS KITTY!
I'M SORRY I'M LATE--HERE'S A LITTLE EXTRA, IF THAT'S ALL RIGHT.
OH, IT'S NO PROBLEM. HE WAS A PERFECT LITTLE ANGEL THE WHOLE TIME!
LET'S GO HOME, DARLING! I'M MAKING CHEESE FOR DINNER, JUST LIKE ALWAYS!
GOODBYE, ITCHY! I HOPE WE SEE YOU AGAIN TOMORROW!
OH, YES. HE DID SO WELL, I'M GOING TO BE BRINGING HIM HERE EVERY SINGLE DAY!
NOOOOOO!!
EVERY SINGLE DAY!
YEP, THAT'S HOW IT ALL STARTED! AND JUST LIKE MANY FORMER CHILD ACTORS, THEY'VE BEEN ENTERTAINING US WITH VIOLENCE EVER SINCE!
THE END

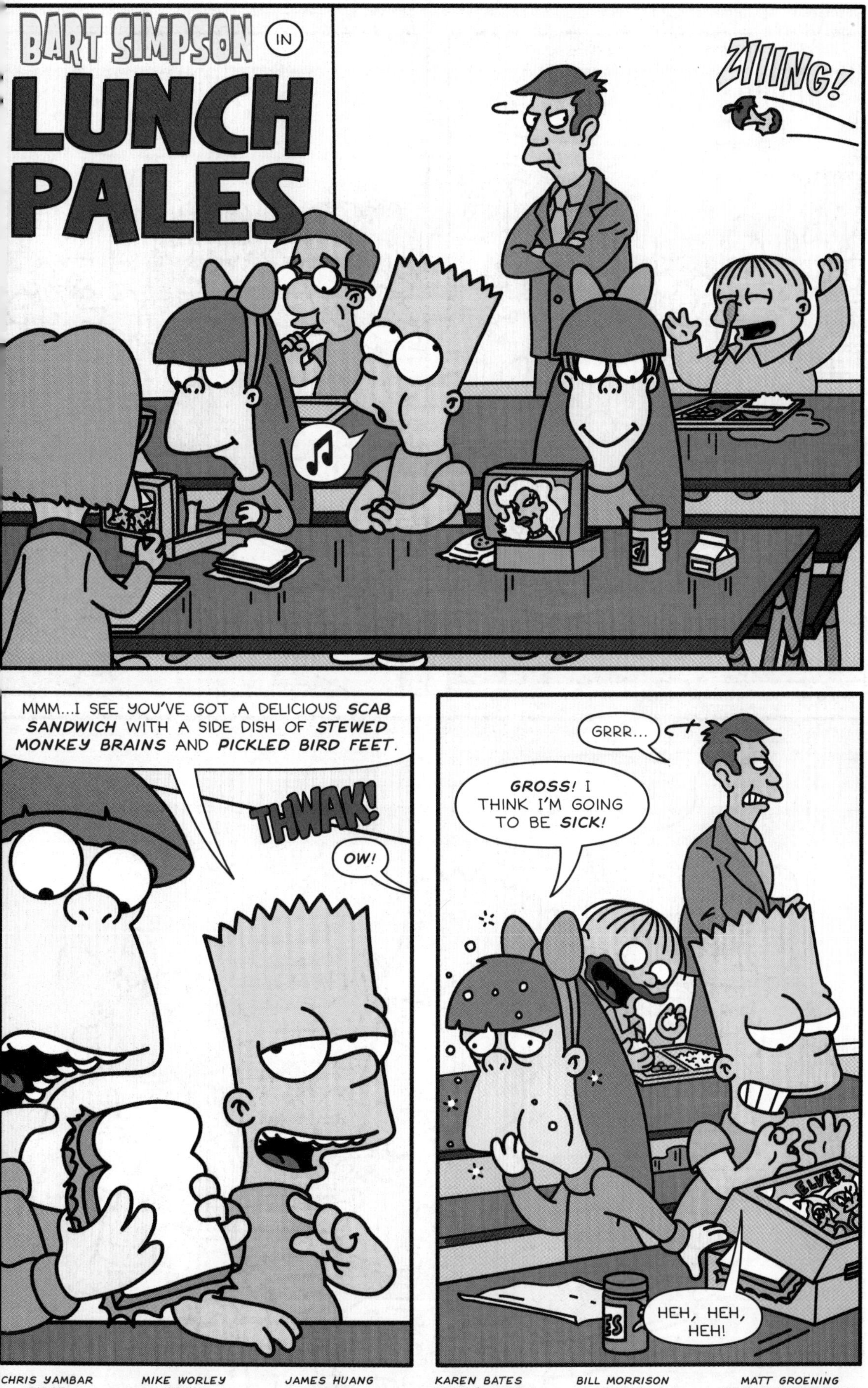
BART SIMPSON IN
LUNCH PALES
ZIIING!
MMM...I SEE YOU'VE GOT A DELICIOUS SCAB SANDWICH WITH A SIDE DISH OF STEWED MONKEY BRAINS AND PICKLED BIRD FEET.
THWAK!
OW!
GRRR...
GROSS! I THINK I'M GOING TO BE SICK!
HEH, HEH, HEH!

CHRIS YAMBAR SCRIPT · MIKE WORLEY PENCILS · JAMES HUANG INKS · KAREN BATES COLORS/LETTERS · BILL MORRISON EDITOR · MATT GROENING LUNCH MENU SUPERVISOR

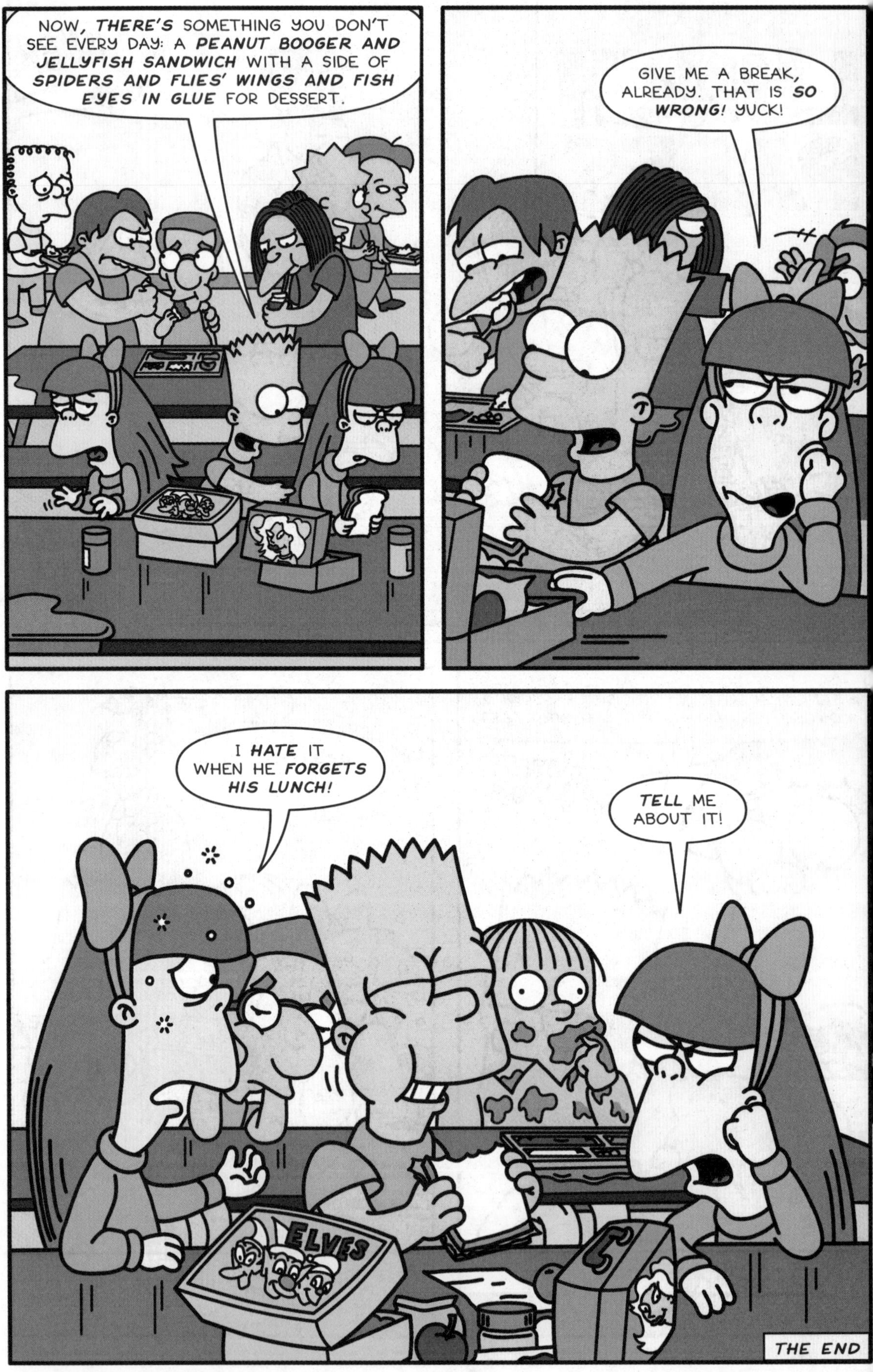
NOW, *THERE'S* SOMETHING YOU DON'T SEE EVERY DAY: A *PEANUT BOOGER AND JELLYFISH SANDWICH* WITH A SIDE OF *SPIDERS AND FLIES' WINGS AND FISH EYES IN GLUE* FOR DESSERT.
GIVE ME A BREAK, ALREADY. THAT IS *SO WRONG!* YUCK!
I *HATE* IT WHEN HE *FORGETS HIS LUNCH!*
TELL ME ABOUT IT!
ELVES
THE END

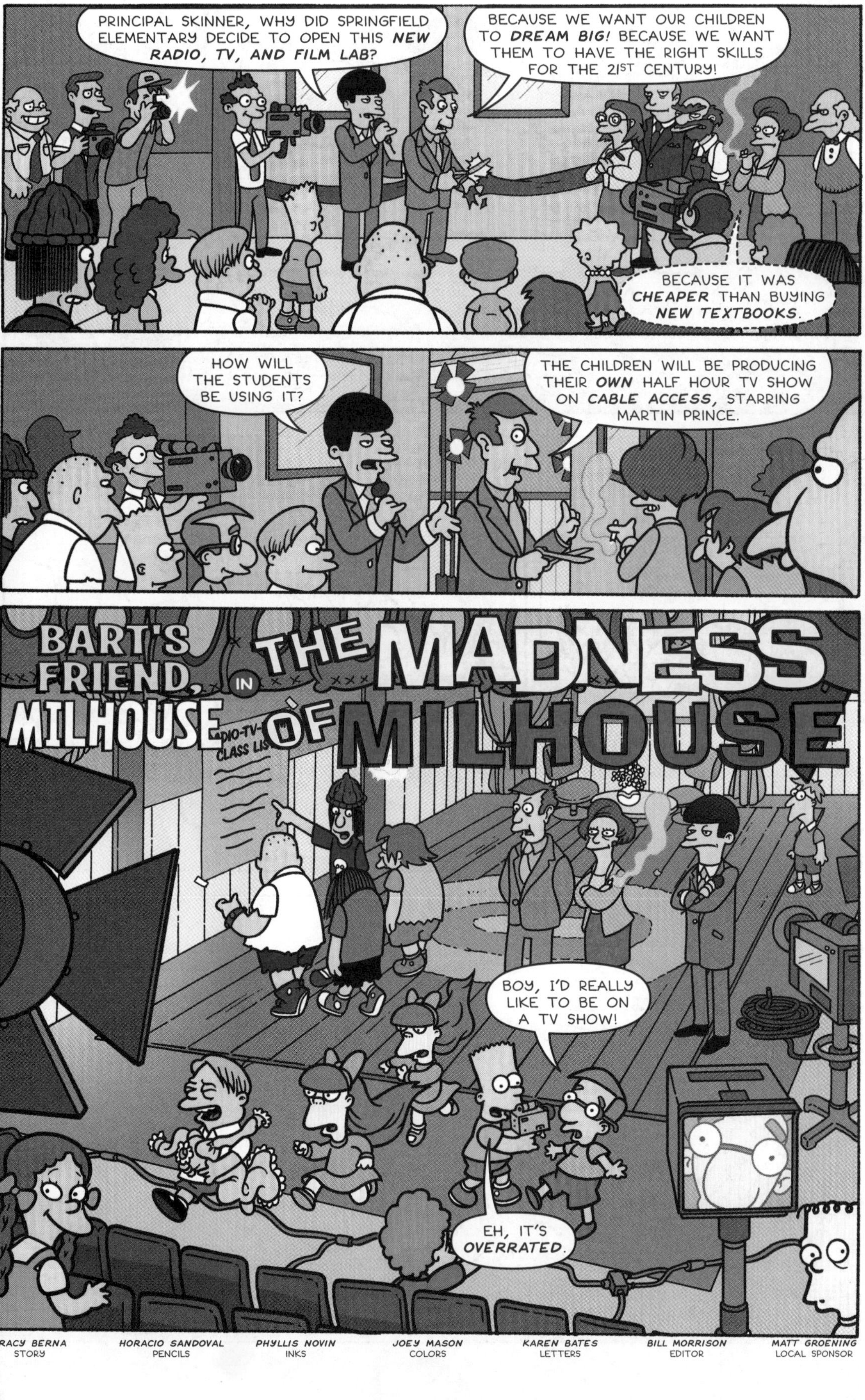
PRINCIPAL SKINNER, WHY DID SPRINGFIELD ELEMENTARY DECIDE TO OPEN THIS NEW RADIO, TV, AND FILM LAB?
BECAUSE WE WANT OUR CHILDREN TO DREAM BIG! BECAUSE WE WANT THEM TO HAVE THE RIGHT SKILLS FOR THE 21ST CENTURY!
BECAUSE IT WAS CHEAPER THAN BUYING NEW TEXTBOOKS.
HOW WILL THE STUDENTS BE USING IT?
THE CHILDREN WILL BE PRODUCING THEIR OWN HALF HOUR TV SHOW ON CABLE ACCESS, STARRING MARTIN PRINCE.
BART'S FRIEND, MILHOUSE IN THE MADNESS OF MILHOUSE
BOY, I'D REALLY LIKE TO BE ON A TV SHOW!
EH, IT'S OVERRATED.

TRACY BERNA STORY · HORACIO SANDOVAL PENCILS · PHYLLIS NOVIN INKS · JOEY MASON COLORS · KAREN BATES LETTERS · BILL MORRISON EDITOR · MATT GROENING LOCAL SPONSOR

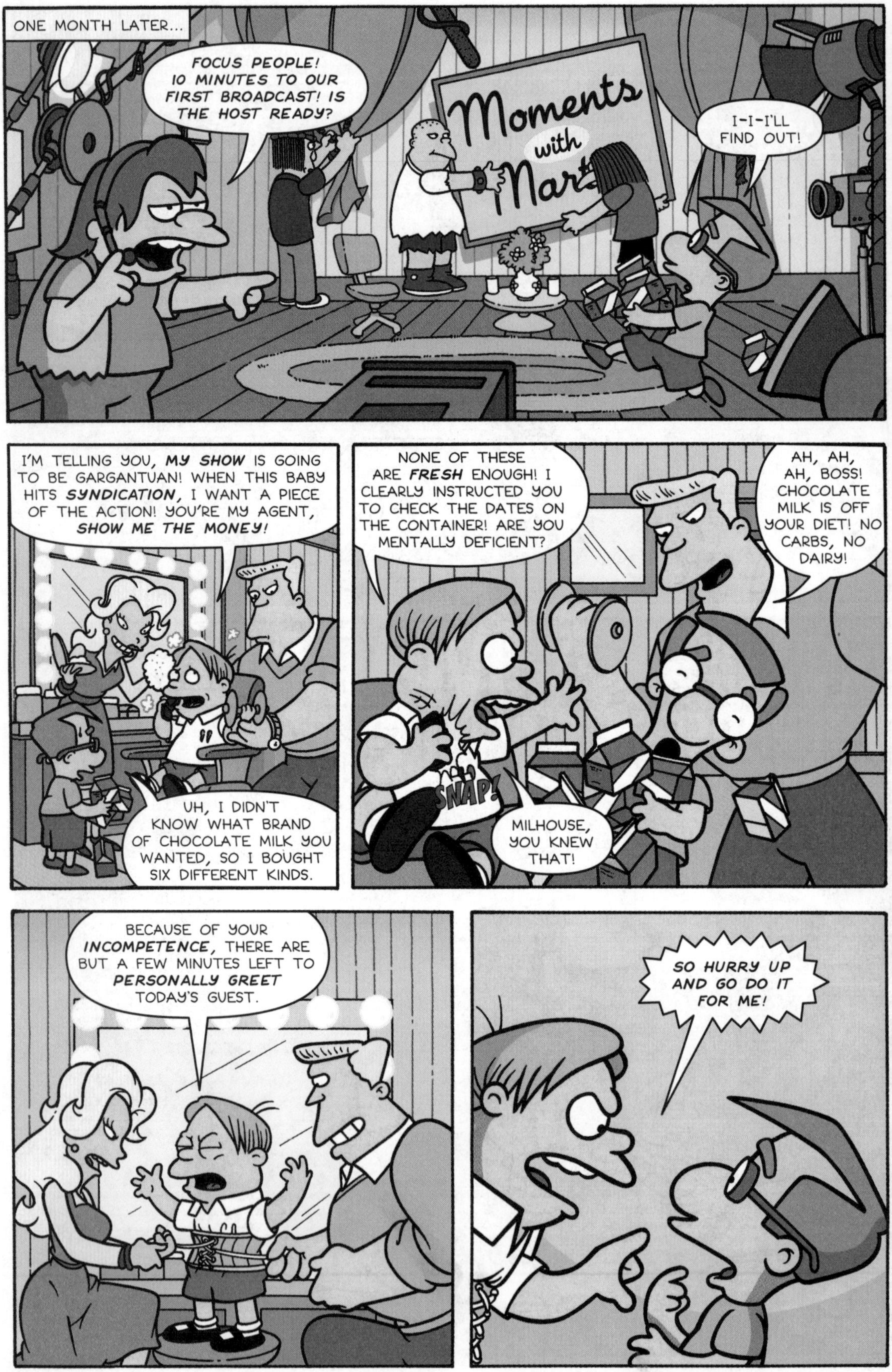
ONE MONTH LATER...
FOCUS PEOPLE! 10 MINUTES TO OUR FIRST BROADCAST! IS THE HOST READY?
Moments
with
I-I-I'LL FIND OUT!
I'M TELLING YOU, MY SHOW IS GOING TO BE GARGANTUAN! WHEN THIS BABY HITS SYNDICATION, I WANT A PIECE OF THE ACTION! YOU'RE MY AGENT, SHOW ME THE MONEY!
UH, I DIDN'T KNOW WHAT BRAND OF CHOCOLATE MILK YOU WANTED, SO I BOUGHT SIX DIFFERENT KINDS.
NONE OF THESE ARE FRESH ENOUGH! I CLEARLY INSTRUCTED YOU TO CHECK THE DATES ON THE CONTAINER! ARE YOU MENTALLY DEFICIENT?
AH, AH, AH, BOSS! CHOCOLATE MILK IS OFF YOUR DIET! NO CARBS, NO DAIRY!
SNAP!
MILHOUSE, YOU KNEW THAT!
BECAUSE OF YOUR INCOMPETENCE, THERE ARE BUT A FEW MINUTES LEFT TO PERSONALLY GREET TODAY'S GUEST.
SO HURRY UP AND GO DO IT FOR ME!

LOOK, DUDES, IT'S MILHOUSE THE *WONDER GOFER!*

FASTER THAN A FLYING MILK CARTON! STRONGER THAN MARTIN'S GIRDLE!

ABLE TO LEAP WHENEVER HIS BOSS SAYS SO!

{PANT, PANT!} YOU'RE WANTED ON THE SET, MR. {PANT!} BROCKMAN.

GOOD! I JUST FINISHED THE LAST LAYER OF *SPACKLING!*

UM, MARTIN WOULD LIKE TO WELCOME YOU PERSONALLY TO THE SHOW, SIR.

OH, MY PLEASURE! I'M GLAD TO BE LENDING MY ILLUSION OF *RESPECTABILITY* TO YOU KIDS.

OKAY, THREE SECONDS 'TIL OUR FIRST SHOW EVER! THREE, TWO...

Moments with Martin

...ONE ...*YOU'RE* ON!

UNNNHHH...

SAY SOMETHING, KID!

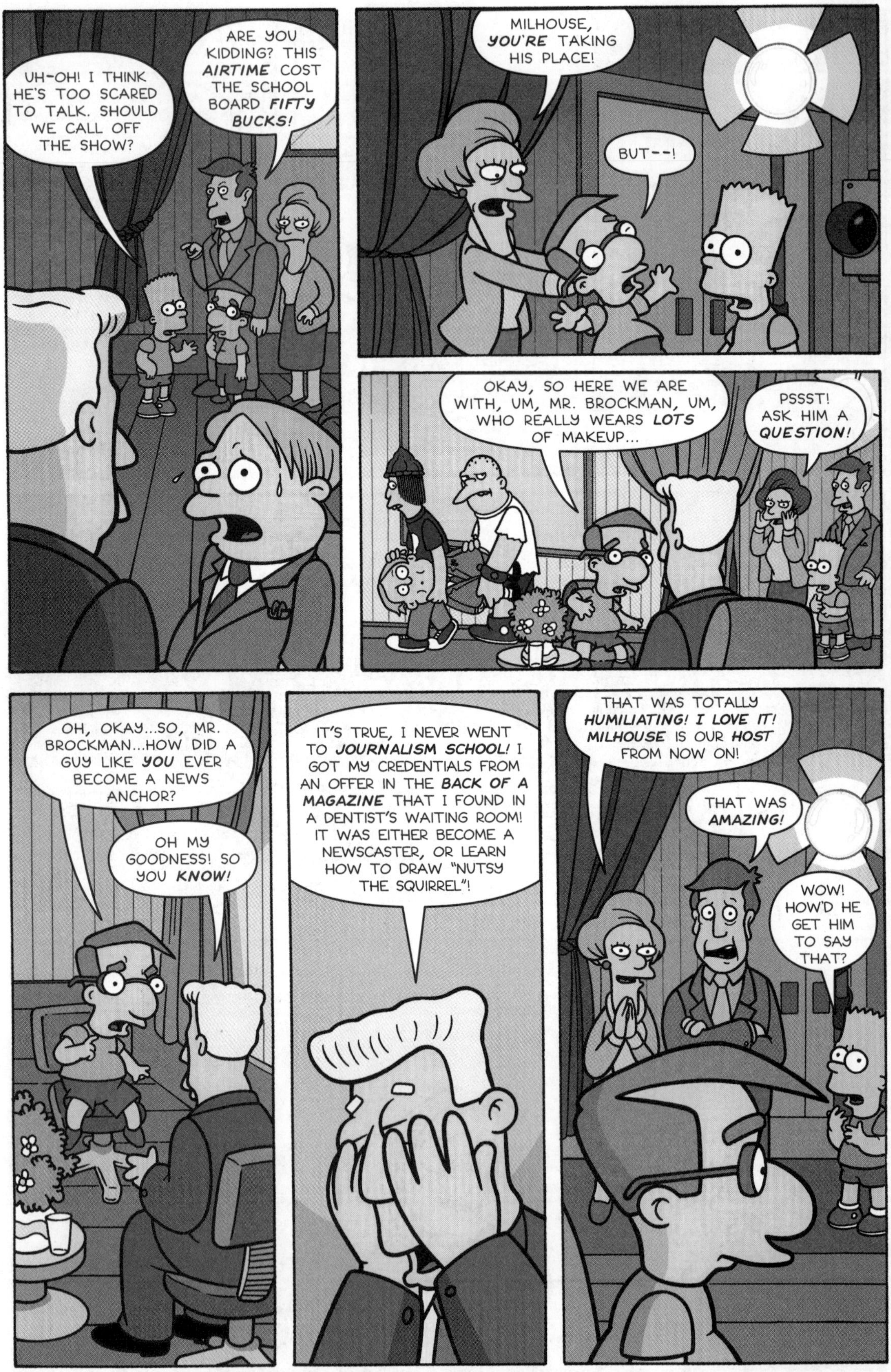
UH-OH! I THINK HE'S TOO SCARED TO TALK. SHOULD WE CALL OFF THE SHOW?
ARE YOU KIDDING? THIS AIRTIME COST THE SCHOOL BOARD FIFTY BUCKS!
MILHOUSE, YOU'RE TAKING HIS PLACE!
BUT--!
OKAY, SO HERE WE ARE WITH, UM, MR. BROCKMAN, UM, WHO REALLY WEARS LOTS OF MAKEUP...
PSSST! ASK HIM A QUESTION!
OH, OKAY...SO, MR. BROCKMAN...HOW DID A GUY LIKE YOU EVER BECOME A NEWS ANCHOR?
OH MY GOODNESS! SO YOU KNOW!
IT'S TRUE, I NEVER WENT TO JOURNALISM SCHOOL! I GOT MY CREDENTIALS FROM AN OFFER IN THE BACK OF A MAGAZINE THAT I FOUND IN A DENTIST'S WAITING ROOM! IT WAS EITHER BECOME A NEWSCASTER, OR LEARN HOW TO DRAW "NUTSY THE SQUIRREL"!
THAT WAS TOTALLY HUMILIATING! I LOVE IT! MILHOUSE IS OUR HOST FROM NOW ON!
THAT WAS AMAZING!
WOW! HOW'D HE GET HIM TO SAY THAT?

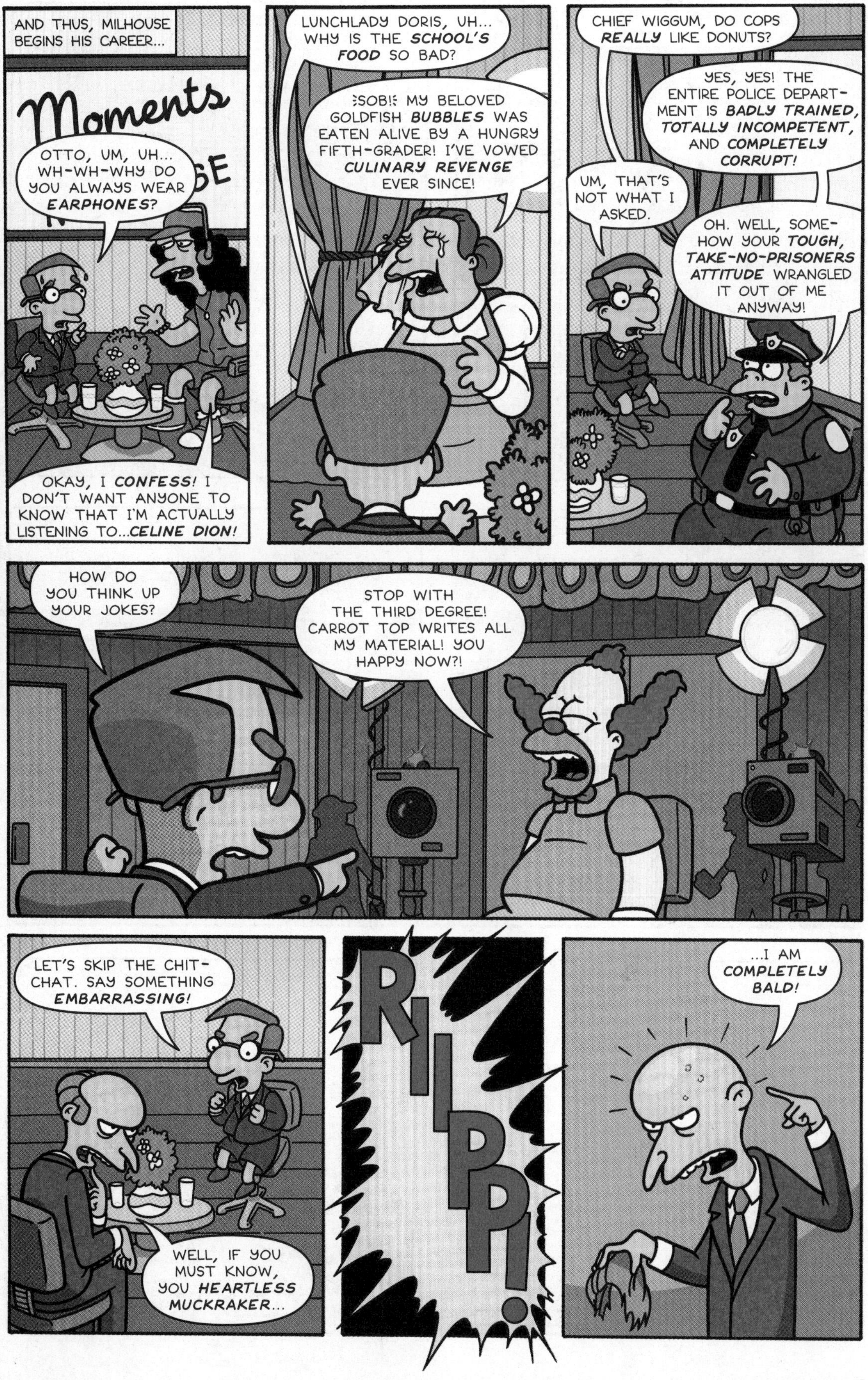
AND THUS, MILHOUSE BEGINS HIS CAREER...
Moments
OTTO, UM, UH... WH-WH-WHY DO YOU ALWAYS WEAR EARPHONES?
OKAY, I CONFESS! I DON'T WANT ANYONE TO KNOW THAT I'M ACTUALLY LISTENING TO...CELINE DION!
LUNCHLADY DORIS, UH... WHY IS THE SCHOOL'S FOOD SO BAD?
SOB! MY BELOVED GOLDFISH BUBBLES WAS EATEN ALIVE BY A HUNGRY FIFTH-GRADER! I'VE VOWED CULINARY REVENGE EVER SINCE!
CHIEF WIGGUM, DO COPS REALLY LIKE DONUTS?
YES, YES! THE ENTIRE POLICE DEPARTMENT IS BADLY TRAINED, TOTALLY INCOMPETENT, AND COMPLETELY CORRUPT!
UM, THAT'S NOT WHAT I ASKED.
OH. WELL, SOMEHOW YOUR TOUGH, TAKE-NO-PRISONERS ATTITUDE WRANGLED IT OUT OF ME ANYWAY!
HOW DO YOU THINK UP YOUR JOKES?
STOP WITH THE THIRD DEGREE! CARROT TOP WRITES ALL MY MATERIAL! YOU HAPPY NOW?!
LET'S SKIP THE CHIT-CHAT. SAY SOMETHING EMBARRASSING!
WELL, IF YOU MUST KNOW, YOU HEARTLESS MUCKRAKER...
RIIPP!
...I AM COMPLETELY BALD!

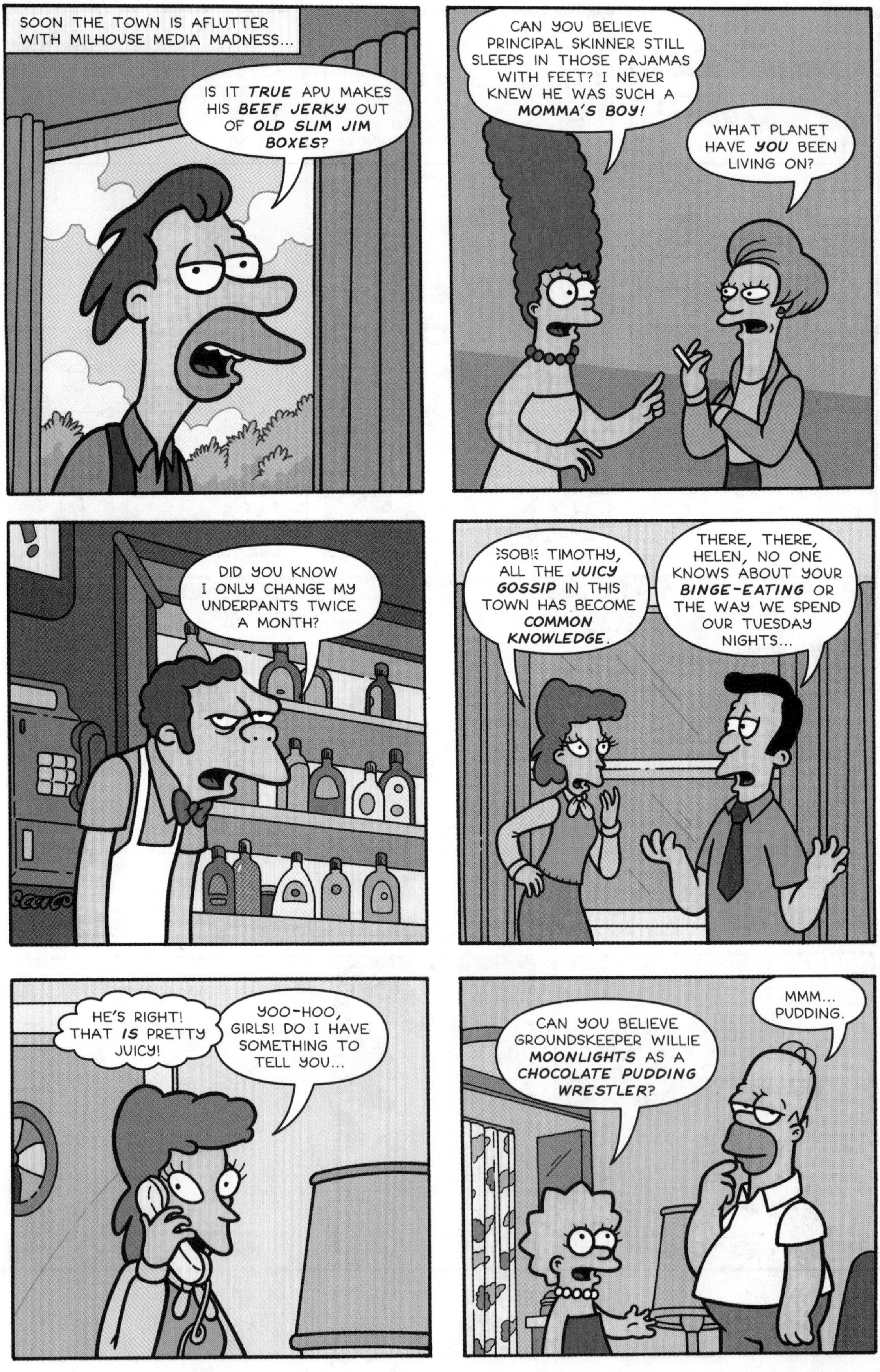
SOON THE TOWN IS AFLUTTER WITH MILHOUSE MEDIA MADNESS...
IS IT TRUE APU MAKES HIS BEEF JERKY OUT OF OLD SLIM JIM BOXES?
CAN YOU BELIEVE PRINCIPAL SKINNER STILL SLEEPS IN THOSE PAJAMAS WITH FEET? I NEVER KNEW HE WAS SUCH A MOMMA'S BOY!
WHAT PLANET HAVE YOU BEEN LIVING ON?
DID YOU KNOW I ONLY CHANGE MY UNDERPANTS TWICE A MONTH?
SOB! TIMOTHY, ALL THE JUICY GOSSIP IN THIS TOWN HAS BECOME COMMON KNOWLEDGE.
THERE, THERE, HELEN, NO ONE KNOWS ABOUT YOUR BINGE-EATING OR THE WAY WE SPEND OUR TUESDAY NIGHTS...
HE'S RIGHT! THAT IS PRETTY JUICY!
YOO-HOO, GIRLS! DO I HAVE SOMETHING TO TELL YOU...
CAN YOU BELIEVE GROUNDSKEEPER WILLIE MOONLIGHTS AS A CHOCOLATE PUDDING WRESTLER?
MMM... PUDDING.

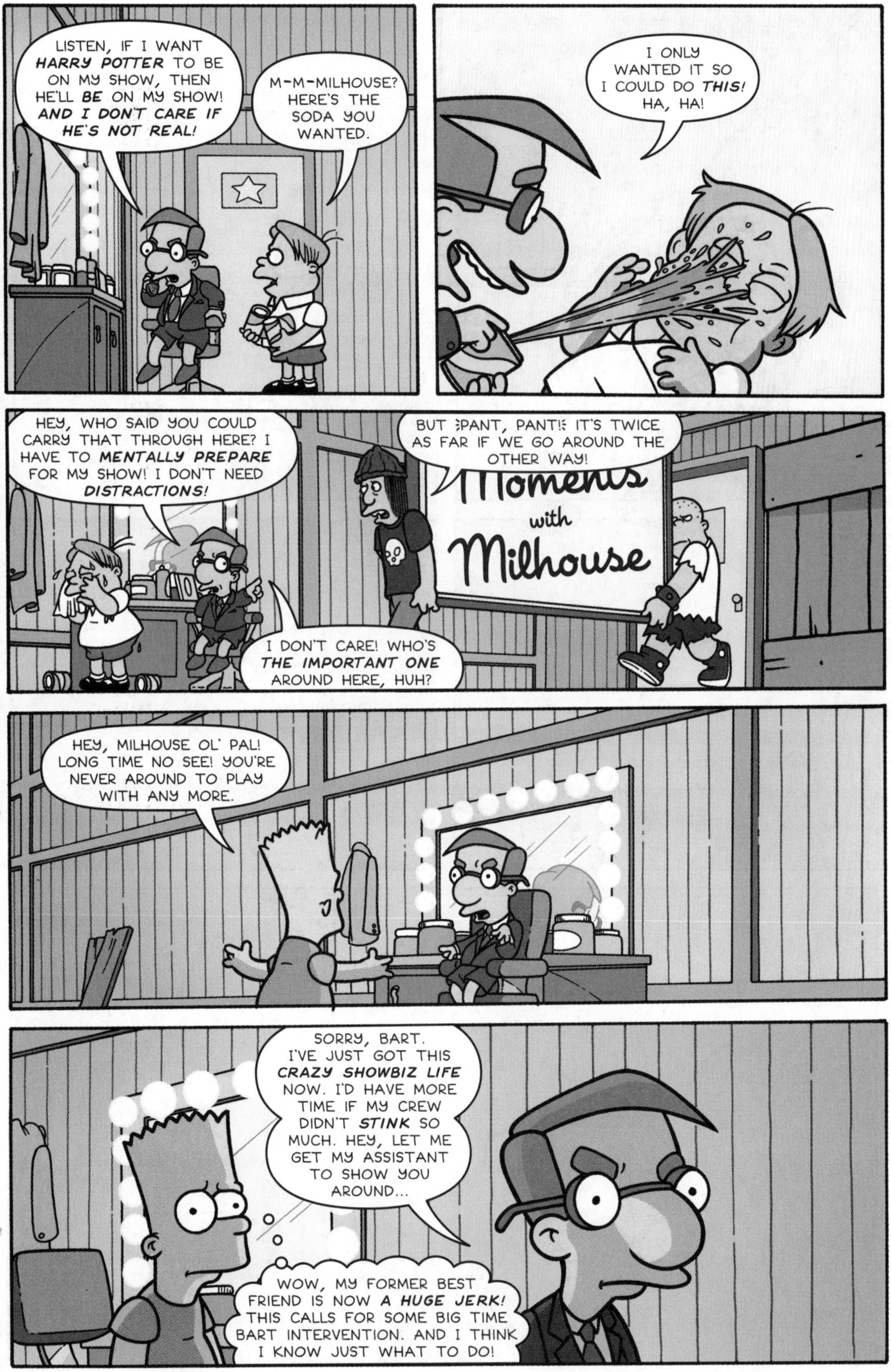
LISTEN, IF I WANT HARRY POTTER TO BE ON MY SHOW, THEN HE'LL BE ON MY SHOW! AND I DON'T CARE IF HE'S NOT REAL!
M-M-MILHOUSE? HERE'S THE SODA YOU WANTED.
I ONLY WANTED IT SO I COULD DO THIS! HA, HA!
HEY, WHO SAID YOU COULD CARRY THAT THROUGH HERE? I HAVE TO MENTALLY PREPARE FOR MY SHOW! I DON'T NEED DISTRACTIONS!
BUT *PANT, PANT!* IT'S TWICE AS FAR IF WE GO AROUND THE OTHER WAY!
Moments with Milhouse
I DON'T CARE! WHO'S THE IMPORTANT ONE AROUND HERE, HUH?
HEY, MILHOUSE OL' PAL! LONG TIME NO SEE! YOU'RE NEVER AROUND TO PLAY WITH ANY MORE.
SORRY, BART. I'VE JUST GOT THIS CRAZY SHOWBIZ LIFE NOW. I'D HAVE MORE TIME IF MY CREW DIDN'T STINK SO MUCH. HEY, LET ME GET MY ASSISTANT TO SHOW YOU AROUND...
WOW, MY FORMER BEST FRIEND IS NOW A HUGE JERK! THIS CALLS FOR SOME BIG TIME BART INTERVENTION. AND I THINK I KNOW JUST WHAT TO DO!

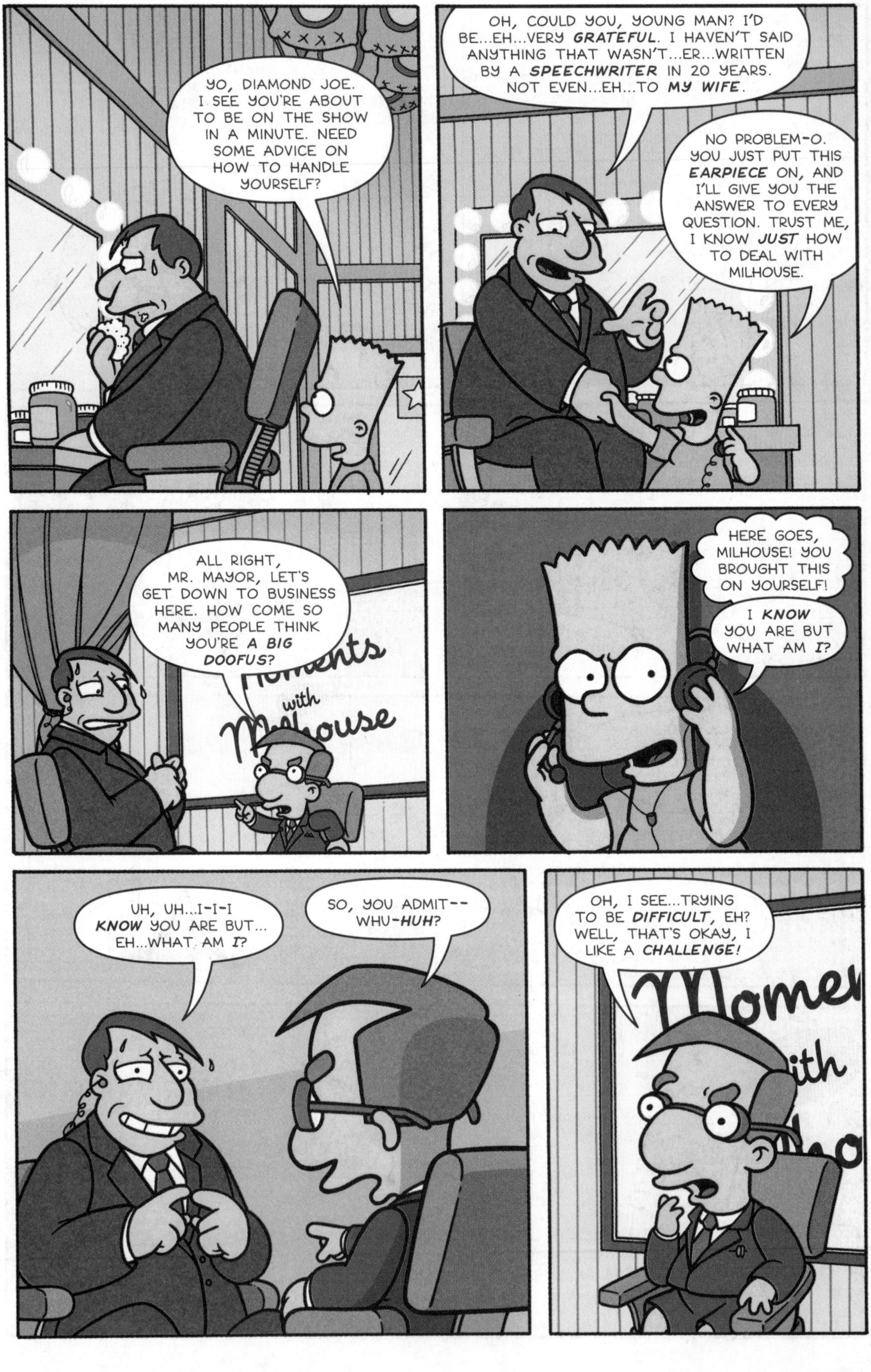
YO, DIAMOND JOE. I SEE YOU'RE ABOUT TO BE ON THE SHOW IN A MINUTE. NEED SOME ADVICE ON HOW TO HANDLE YOURSELF?
OH, COULD YOU, YOUNG MAN? I'D BE...EH...VERY **GRATEFUL**. I HAVEN'T SAID ANYTHING THAT WASN'T...ER...WRITTEN BY A **SPEECHWRITER** IN 20 YEARS. NOT EVEN...EH...TO **MY WIFE**.
NO PROBLEM-O. YOU JUST PUT THIS **EARPIECE** ON, AND I'LL GIVE YOU THE ANSWER TO EVERY QUESTION. TRUST ME, I KNOW **JUST** HOW TO DEAL WITH MILHOUSE.
ALL RIGHT, MR. MAYOR, LET'S GET DOWN TO BUSINESS HERE. HOW COME SO MANY PEOPLE THINK YOU'RE **A BIG DOOFUS**?
HERE GOES, MILHOUSE! YOU BROUGHT THIS ON YOURSELF!
I **KNOW** YOU ARE BUT WHAT AM **I**?
UH, UH...I-I-I **KNOW** YOU ARE BUT... EH...WHAT AM **I**?
SO, YOU ADMIT-- WHU-**HUH**?
OH, I SEE...TRYING TO BE **DIFFICULT**, EH? WELL, THAT'S OKAY, I LIKE A **CHALLENGE**!

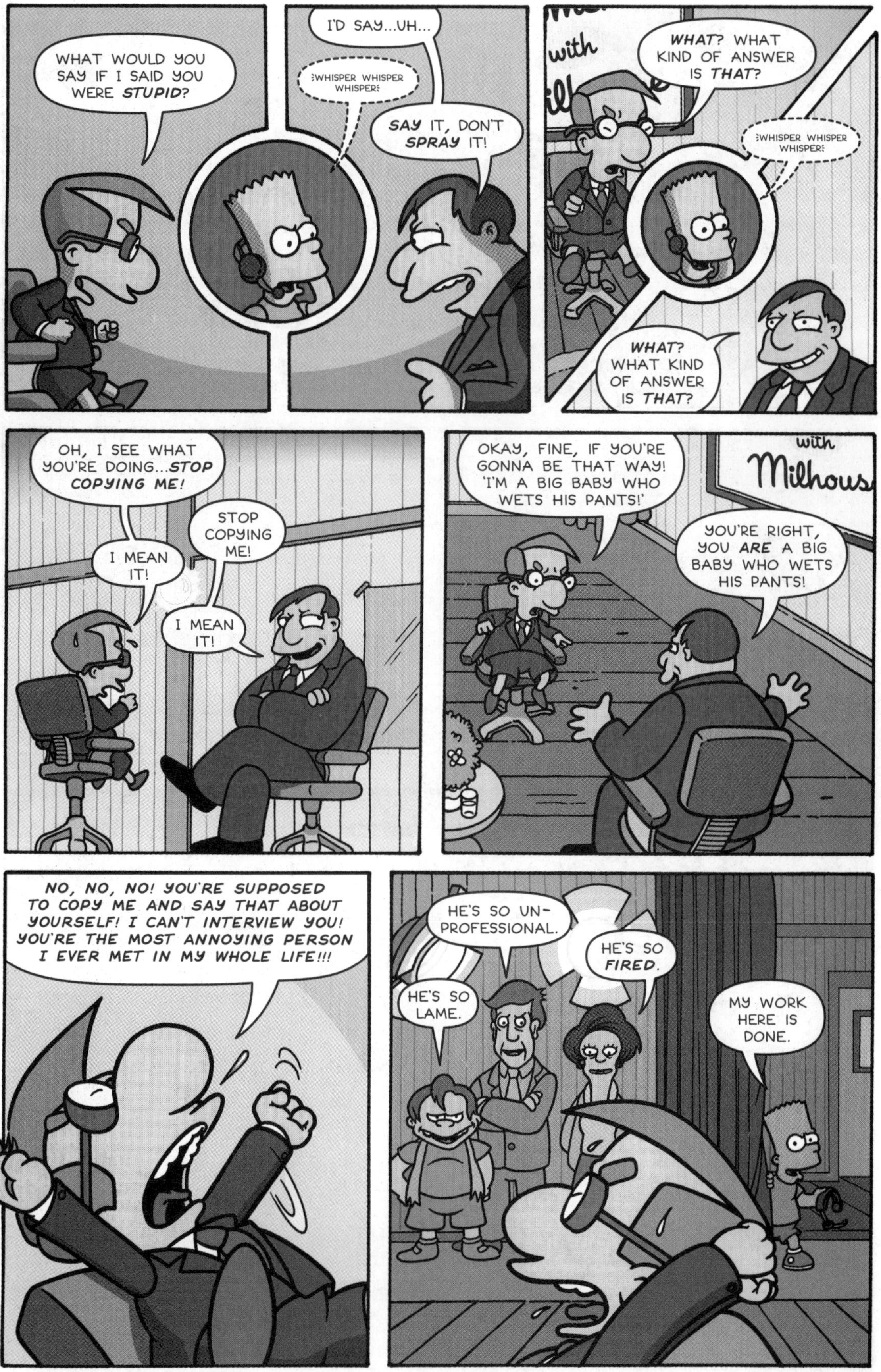
WHAT WOULD YOU SAY IF I SAID YOU WERE STUPID?
I'D SAY...UH...
WHISPER WHISPER WHISPER
SAY IT, DON'T SPRAY IT!
with
WHAT? WHAT KIND OF ANSWER IS THAT?
WHISPER WHISPER WHISPER
WHAT? WHAT KIND OF ANSWER IS THAT?
OH, I SEE WHAT YOU'RE DOING...STOP COPYING ME!
STOP COPYING ME!
I MEAN IT!
I MEAN IT!
with
Milhous
OKAY, FINE, IF YOU'RE GONNA BE THAT WAY! 'I'M A BIG BABY WHO WETS HIS PANTS!'
YOU'RE RIGHT, YOU ARE A BIG BABY WHO WETS HIS PANTS!
NO, NO, NO! YOU'RE SUPPOSED TO COPY ME AND SAY THAT ABOUT YOURSELF! I CAN'T INTERVIEW YOU! YOU'RE THE MOST ANNOYING PERSON I EVER MET IN MY WHOLE LIFE!!!
HE'S SO UN-PROFESSIONAL.
HE'S SO FIRED.
HE'S SO LAME.
MY WORK HERE IS DONE.

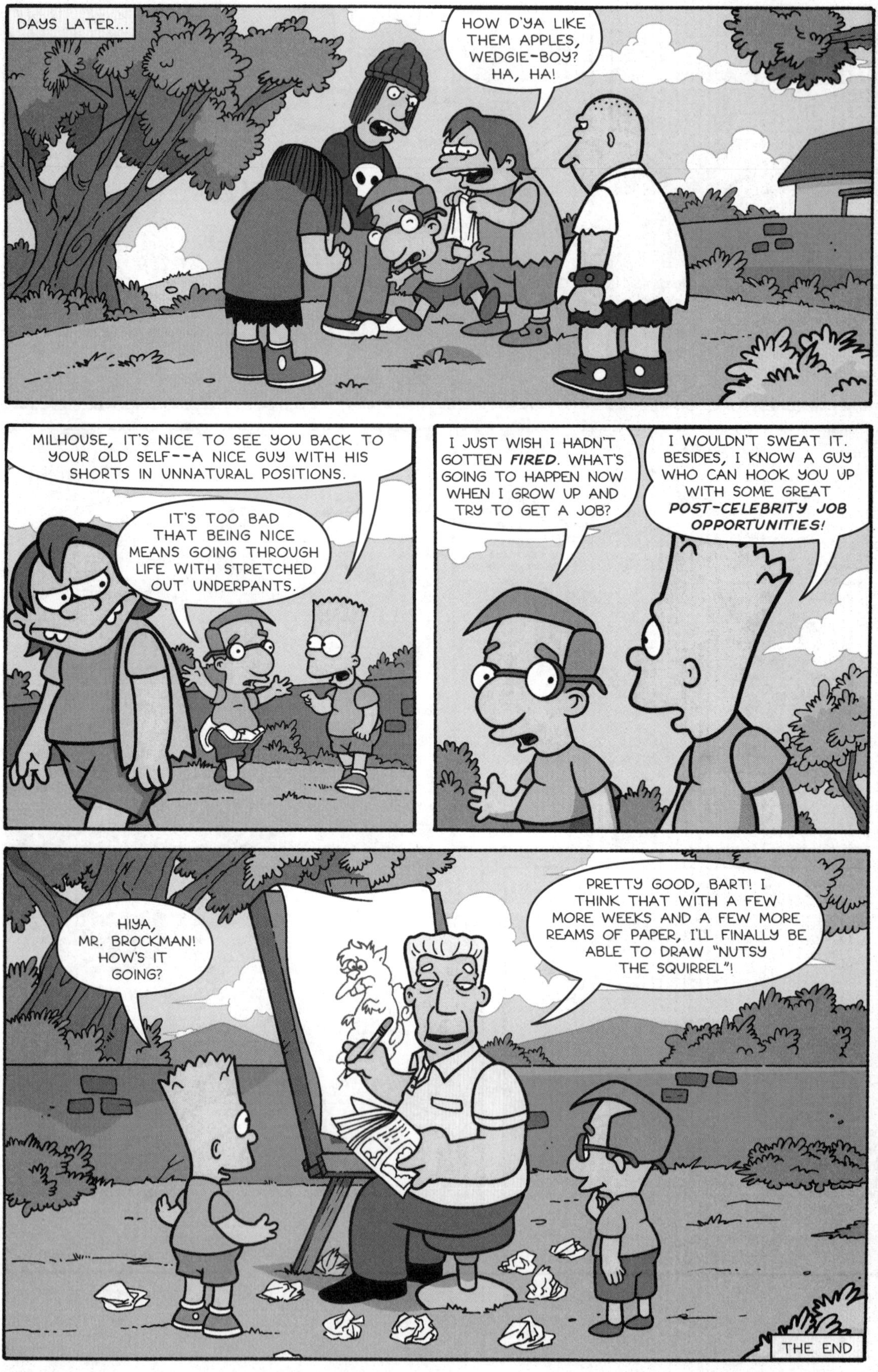
DAYS LATER...
HOW D'YA LIKE THEM APPLES, WEDGIE-BOY? HA, HA!
MILHOUSE, IT'S NICE TO SEE YOU BACK TO YOUR OLD SELF--A NICE GUY WITH HIS SHORTS IN UNNATURAL POSITIONS.
IT'S TOO BAD THAT BEING NICE MEANS GOING THROUGH LIFE WITH STRETCHED OUT UNDERPANTS.
I JUST WISH I HADN'T GOTTEN FIRED. WHAT'S GOING TO HAPPEN NOW WHEN I GROW UP AND TRY TO GET A JOB?
I WOULDN'T SWEAT IT. BESIDES, I KNOW A GUY WHO CAN HOOK YOU UP WITH SOME GREAT POST-CELEBRITY JOB OPPORTUNITIES!
HIYA, MR. BROCKMAN! HOW'S IT GOING?
PRETTY GOOD, BART! I THINK THAT WITH A FEW MORE WEEKS AND A FEW MORE REAMS OF PAPER, I'LL FINALLY BE ABLE TO DRAW "NUTSY THE SQUIRREL"!
THE END

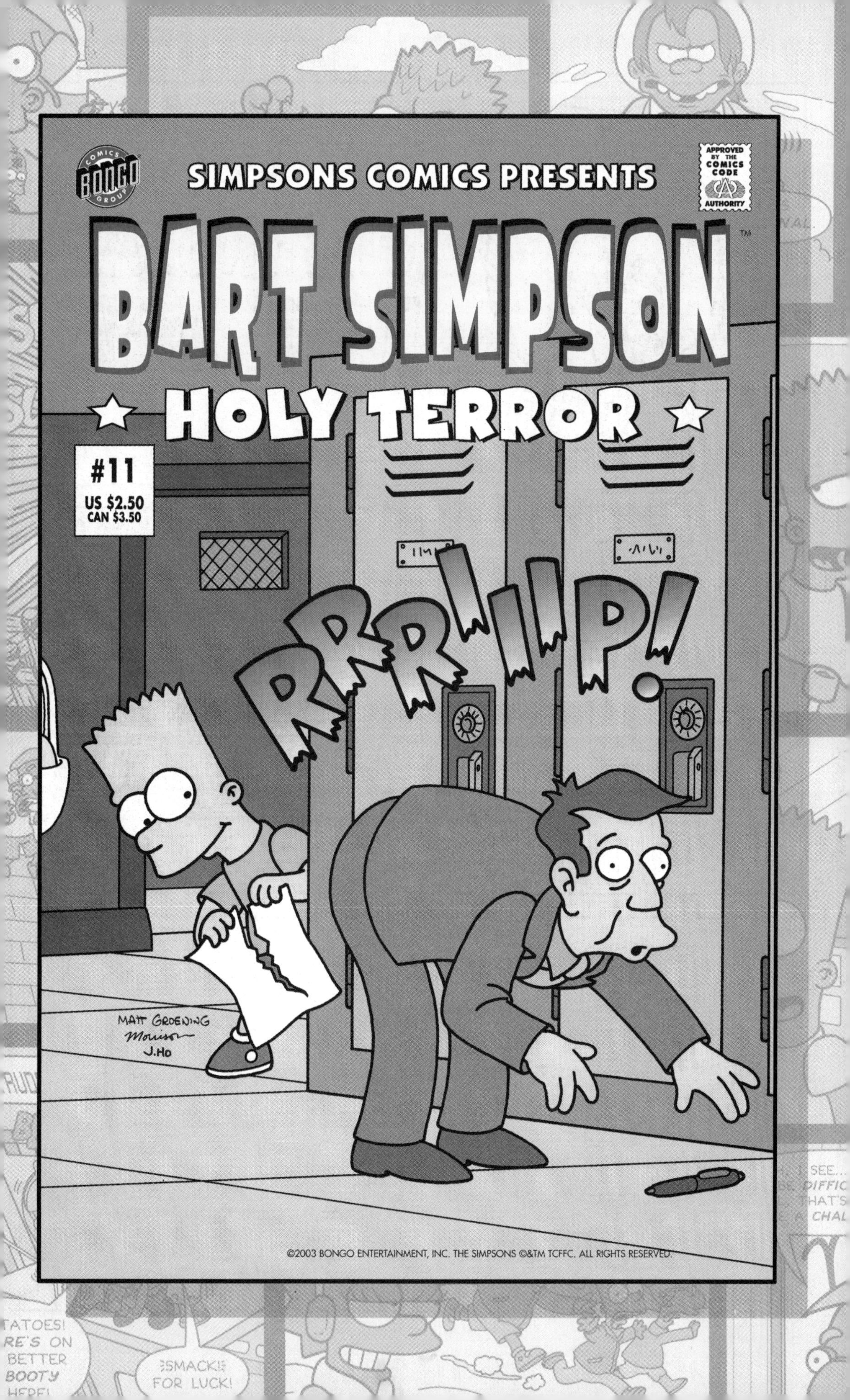

BONGO COMICS GROUP
SIMPSONS COMICS PRESENTS
APPROVED BY THE COMICS CODE AUTHORITY
BART SIMPSON™
HOLY TERROR
#11
US $2.50
CAN $3.50
RRIIIP!
MATT GROENING
J.HO
©2003 BONGO ENTERTAINMENT, INC. THE SIMPSONS ©&TM TCFFC. ALL RIGHTS RESERVED.
SMACK! FOR LUCK!

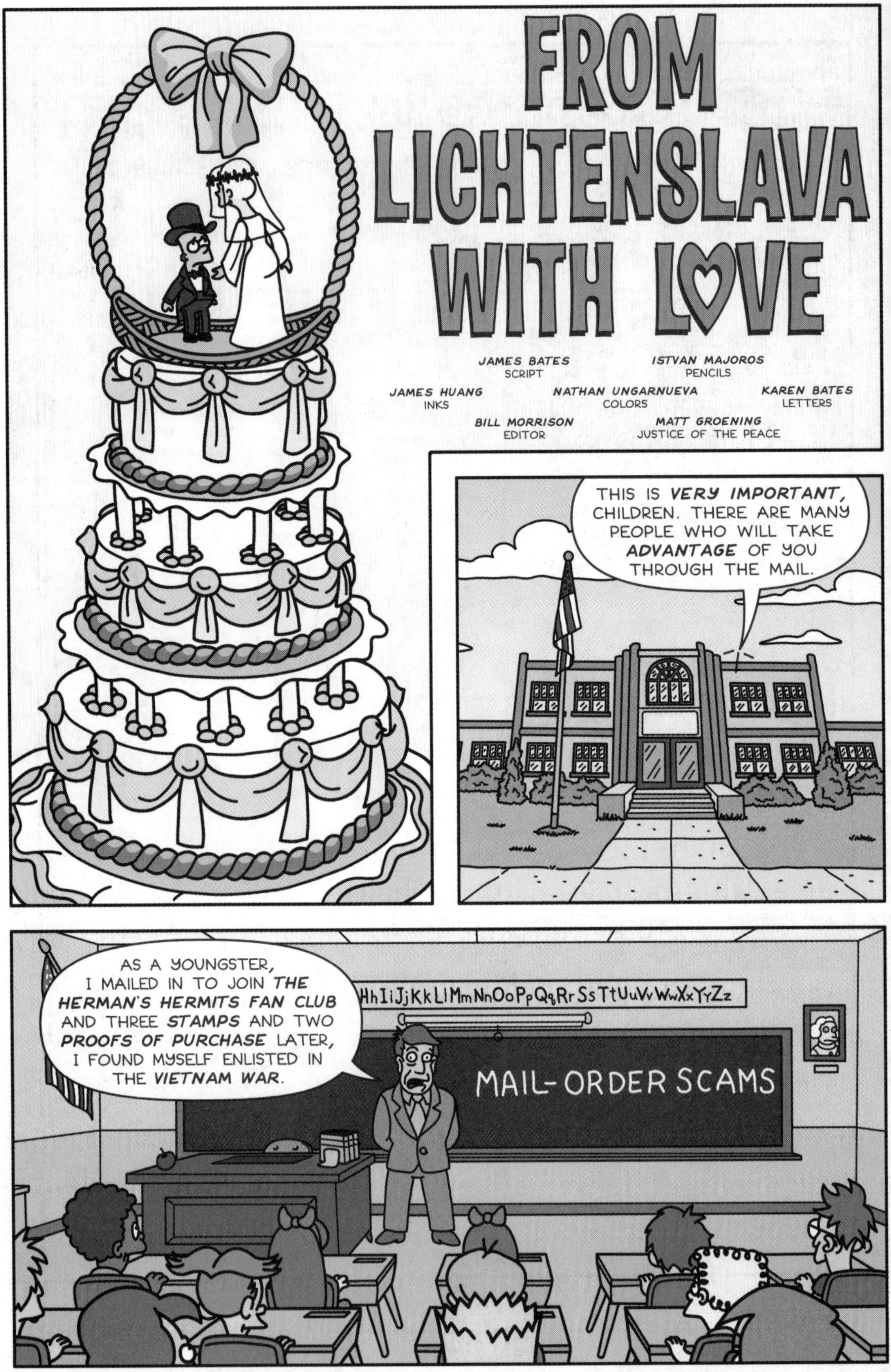
FROM LICHTENSLAVA WITH LOVE
JAMES BATES SCRIPT
ISTVAN MAJOROS PENCILS
JAMES HUANG INKS
NATHAN UNGARNUEVA COLORS
KAREN BATES LETTERS
BILL MORRISON EDITOR
MATT GROENING JUSTICE OF THE PEACE
THIS IS VERY IMPORTANT, CHILDREN. THERE ARE MANY PEOPLE WHO WILL TAKE ADVANTAGE OF YOU THROUGH THE MAIL.
AS A YOUNGSTER, I MAILED IN TO JOIN THE HERMAN'S HERMITS FAN CLUB AND THREE STAMPS AND TWO PROOFS OF PURCHASE LATER, I FOUND MYSELF ENLISTED IN THE VIETNAM WAR.
Hh Ii Jj Kk Ll Mm Nn Oo Pp Qq Rr Ss Tt Uu Vv Ww Xx Yy Zz
MAIL-ORDER SCAMS

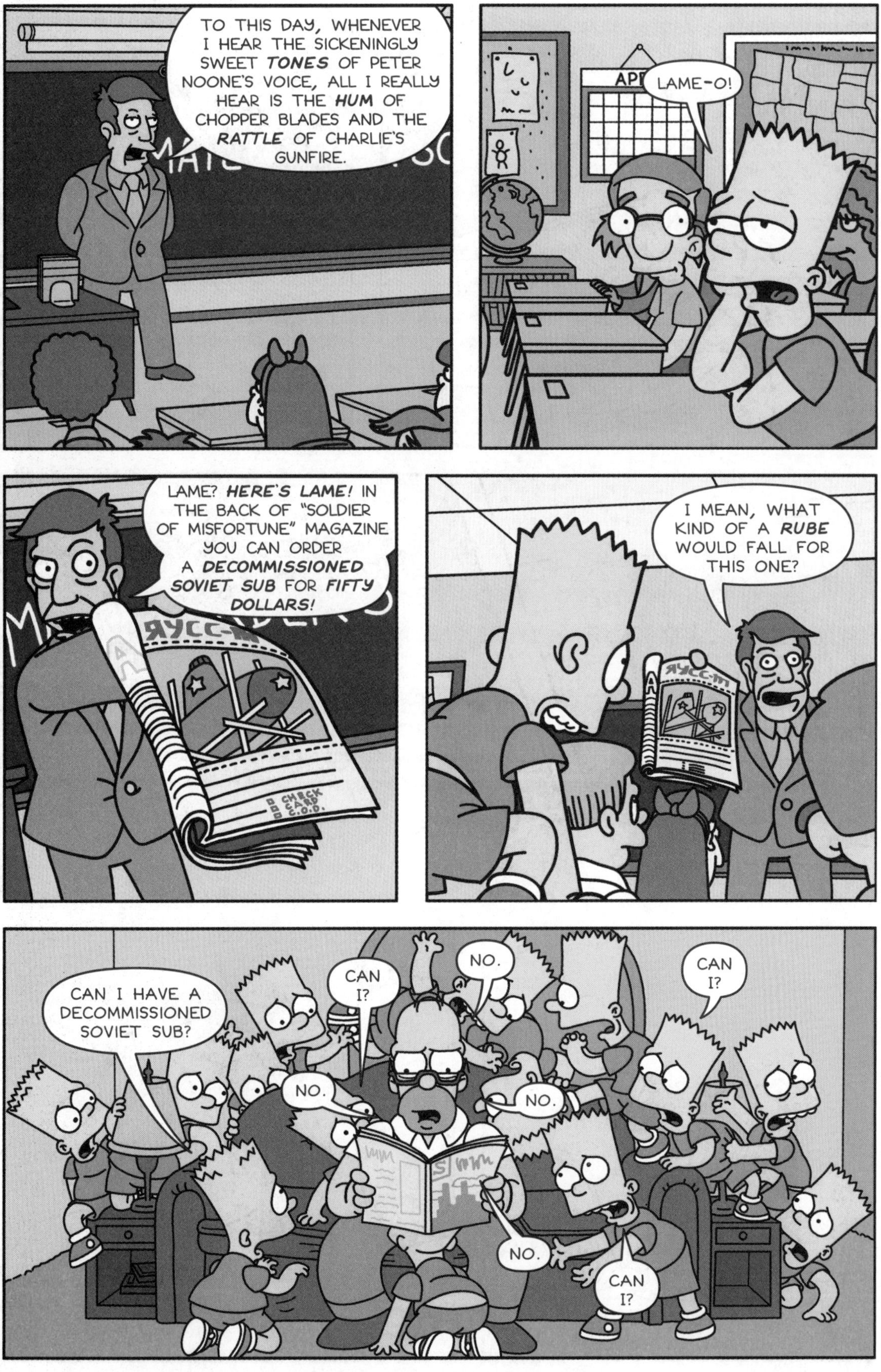
TO THIS DAY, WHENEVER I HEAR THE SICKENINGLY SWEET TONES OF PETER NOONE'S VOICE, ALL I REALLY HEAR IS THE HUM OF CHOPPER BLADES AND THE RATTLE OF CHARLIE'S GUNFIRE.
LAME-O!
LAME? HERE'S LAME! IN THE BACK OF "SOLDIER OF MISFORTUNE" MAGAZINE YOU CAN ORDER A DECOMMISSIONED SOVIET SUB FOR FIFTY DOLLARS!
CHECK
CARD
C.O.D.
I MEAN, WHAT KIND OF A RUBE WOULD FALL FOR THIS ONE?
CAN I HAVE A DECOMMISSIONED SOVIET SUB?
CAN I?
NO.
CAN I?
NO.
NO.
NO.
CAN I?

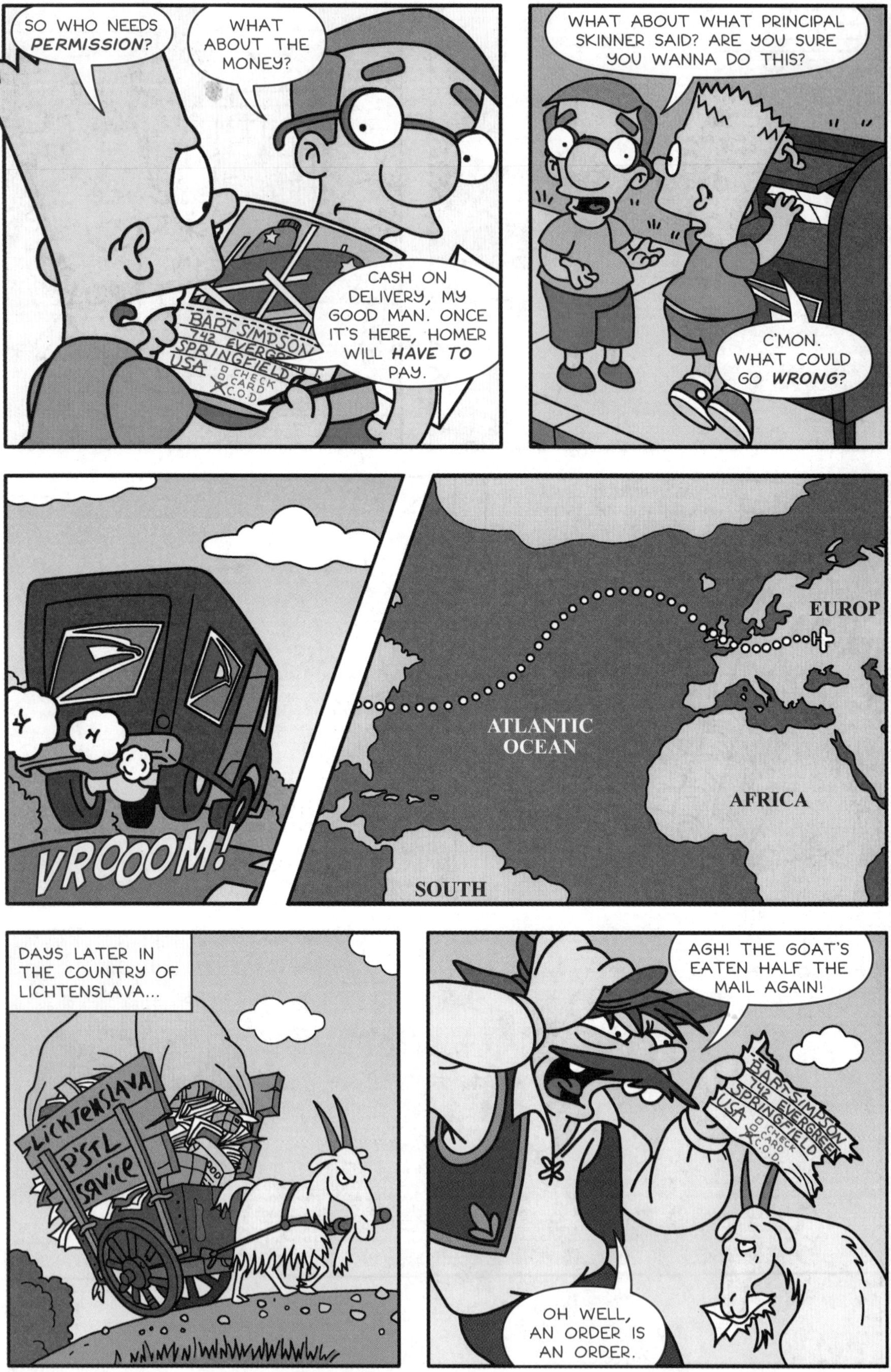

SO WHO NEEDS *PERMISSION*?
WHAT ABOUT THE MONEY?
BART SIMPSON 742 EVERGREEN SPRINGFIELD USA
CHECK CARD C.O.D
CASH ON DELIVERY, MY GOOD MAN. ONCE IT'S HERE, HOMER WILL *HAVE TO* PAY.
WHAT ABOUT WHAT PRINCIPAL SKINNER SAID? ARE YOU SURE YOU WANNA DO THIS?
C'MON. WHAT COULD GO *WRONG*?
VROOOM!
EUROP
ATLANTIC OCEAN
AFRICA
SOUTH
DAYS LATER IN THE COUNTRY OF LICHTENSLAVA...
LICHTENSLAVA P'STL SƎRVICE
AGH! THE GOAT'S EATEN HALF THE MAIL AGAIN!
BART SIMPSON 742 EVERGREEN SPRINGFIELD USA
CHECK CARD C.O.D
OH WELL, AN ORDER IS AN ORDER.

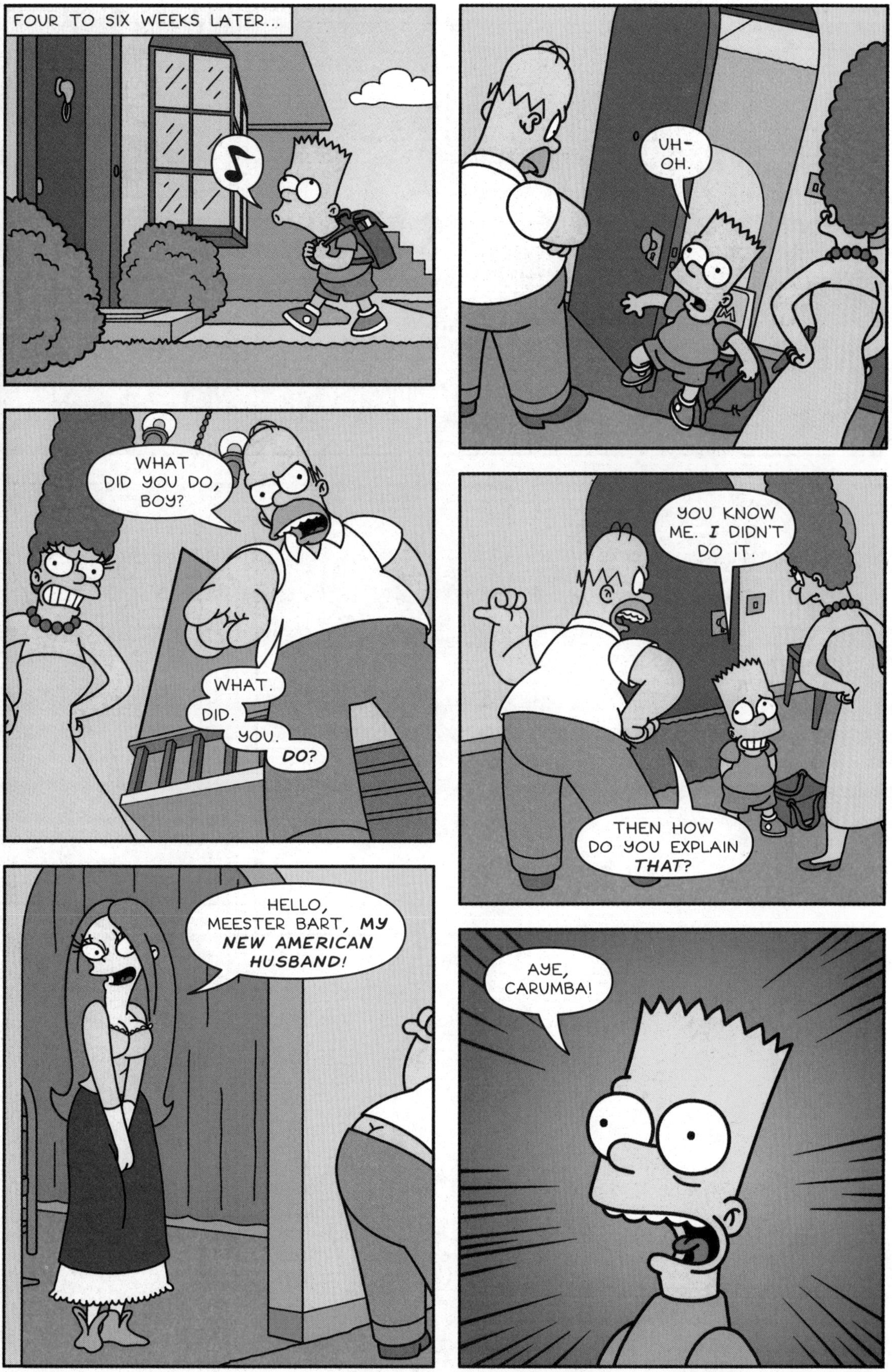
FOUR TO SIX WEEKS LATER...
UH-OH.
WHAT DID YOU DO, BOY?
WHAT. DID. YOU. *DO?*
YOU KNOW ME. *I* DIDN'T DO IT.
THEN HOW DO YOU EXPLAIN *THAT?*
HELLO, MEESTER BART, ***MY NEW AMERICAN HUSBAND!***
AYE, CARUMBA!

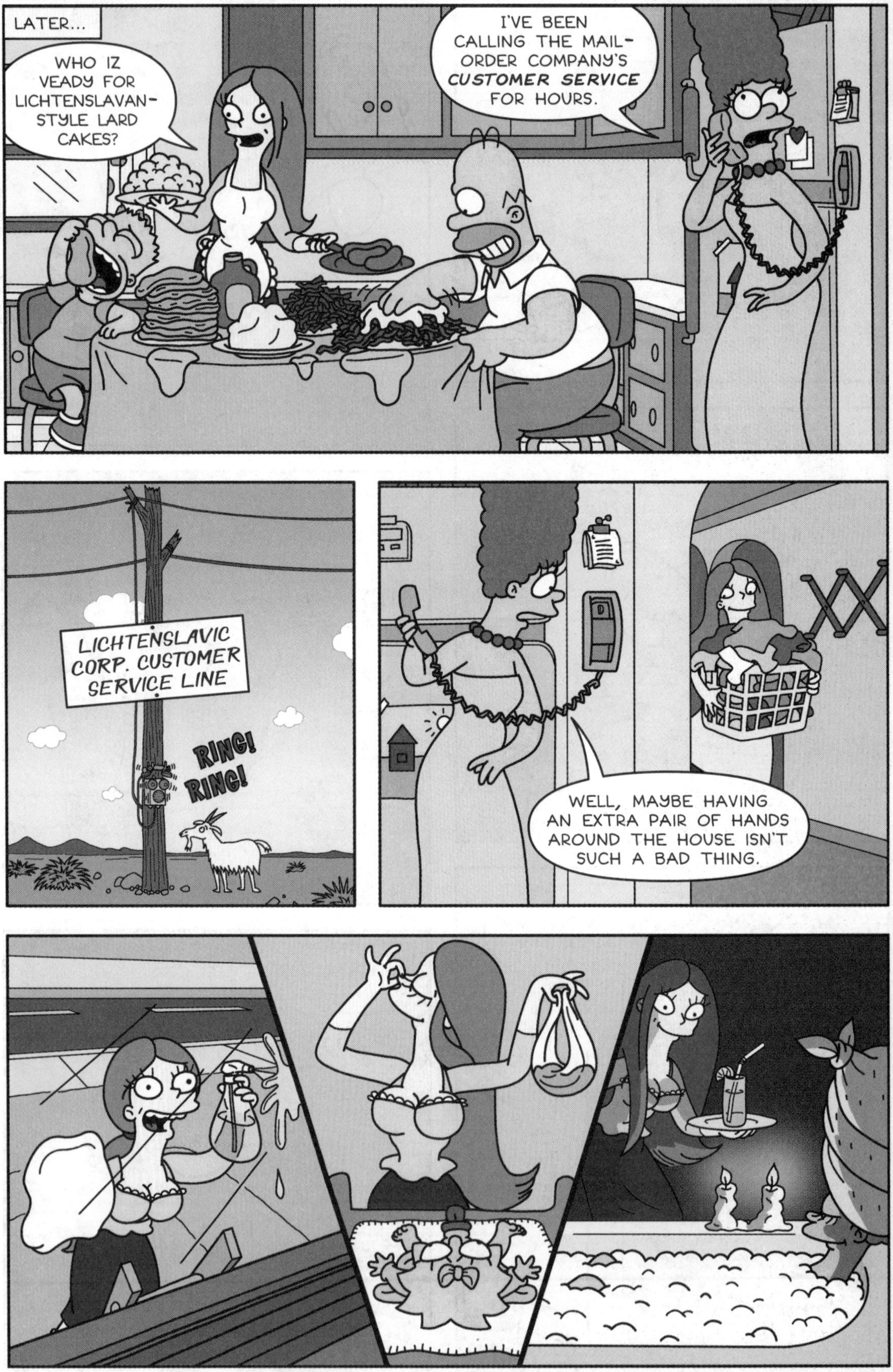
LATER...
WHO IZ VEADY FOR LICHTENSLAVAN-STYLE LARD CAKES?
I'VE BEEN CALLING THE MAIL-ORDER COMPANY'S CUSTOMER SERVICE FOR HOURS.
LICHTENSLAVIC CORP. CUSTOMER SERVICE LINE
RING! RING!
WELL, MAYBE HAVING AN EXTRA PAIR OF HANDS AROUND THE HOUSE ISN'T SUCH A BAD THING.

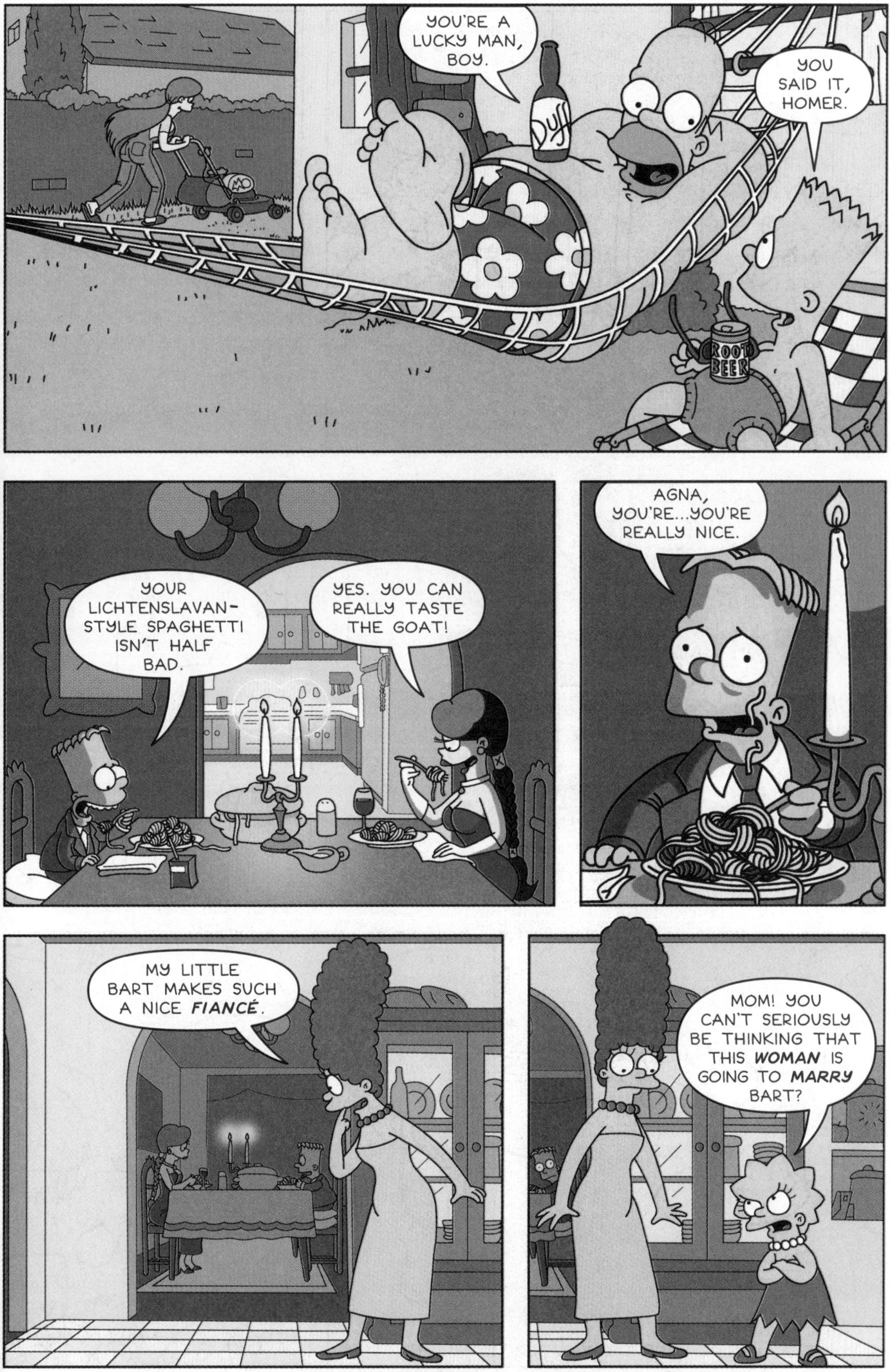

YOU'RE A LUCKY MAN, BOY.
YOU SAID IT, HOMER.
Duff
ROOT BEER
YOUR LICHTENSLAVAN-STYLE SPAGHETTI ISN'T HALF BAD.
YES. YOU CAN REALLY TASTE THE GOAT!
AGNA, YOU'RE...YOU'RE REALLY NICE.
MY LITTLE BART MAKES SUCH A NICE ***FIANCÉ***.
MOM! YOU CAN'T SERIOUSLY BE THINKING THAT THIS ***WOMAN*** IS GOING TO ***MARRY*** BART?

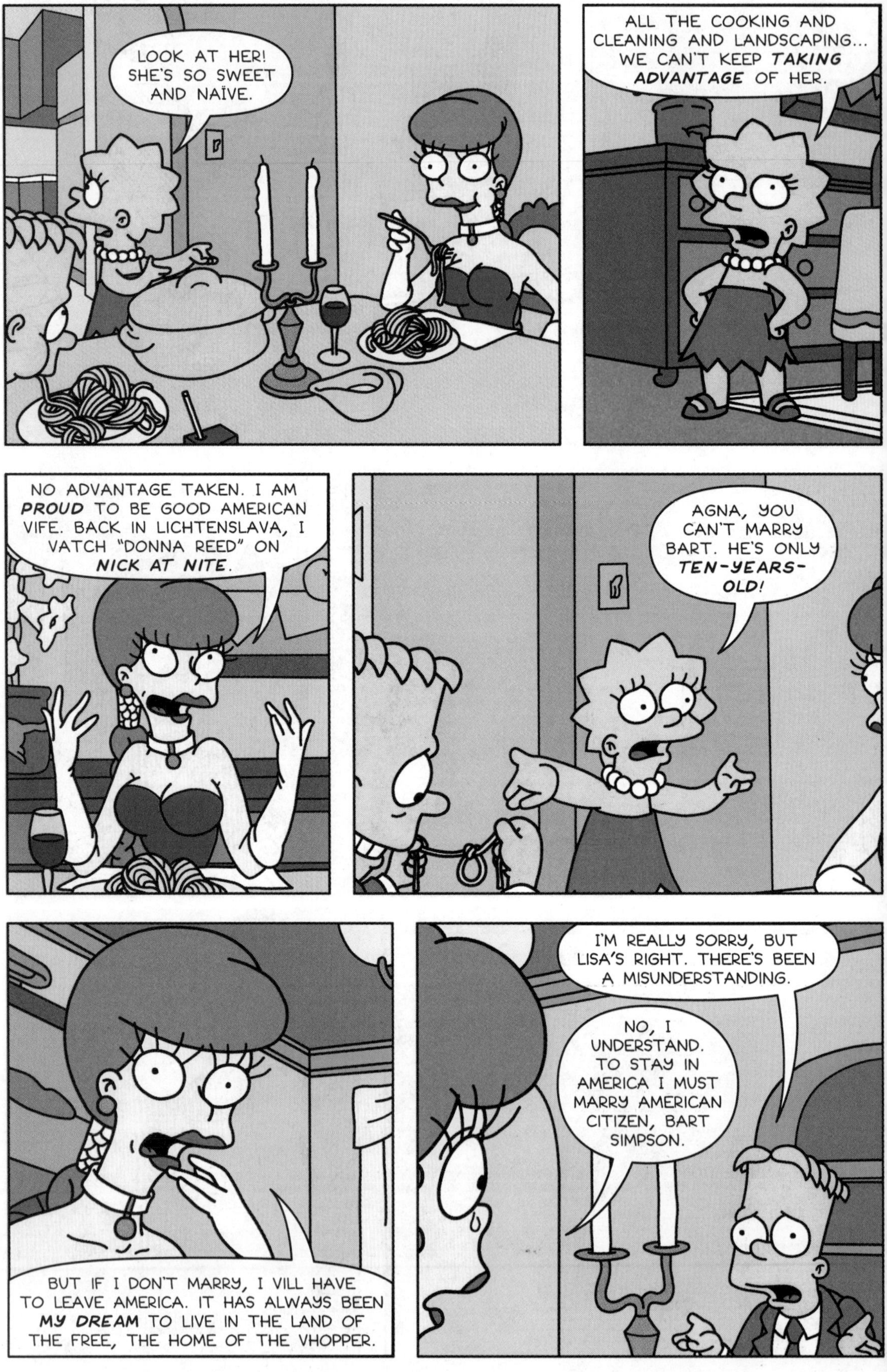
LOOK AT HER! SHE'S SO SWEET AND NAÏVE.
ALL THE COOKING AND CLEANING AND LANDSCAPING... WE CAN'T KEEP TAKING ADVANTAGE OF HER.
NO ADVANTAGE TAKEN. I AM PROUD TO BE GOOD AMERICAN VIFE. BACK IN LICHTENSLAVA, I VATCH "DONNA REED" ON NICK AT NITE.
AGNA, YOU CAN'T MARRY BART. HE'S ONLY TEN-YEARS-OLD!
BUT IF I DON'T MARRY, I VILL HAVE TO LEAVE AMERICA. IT HAS ALWAYS BEEN MY DREAM TO LIVE IN THE LAND OF THE FREE, THE HOME OF THE VHOPPER.
I'M REALLY SORRY, BUT LISA'S RIGHT. THERE'S BEEN A MISUNDERSTANDING.
NO, I UNDERSTAND. TO STAY IN AMERICA I MUST MARRY AMERICAN CITIZEN, BART SIMPSON.

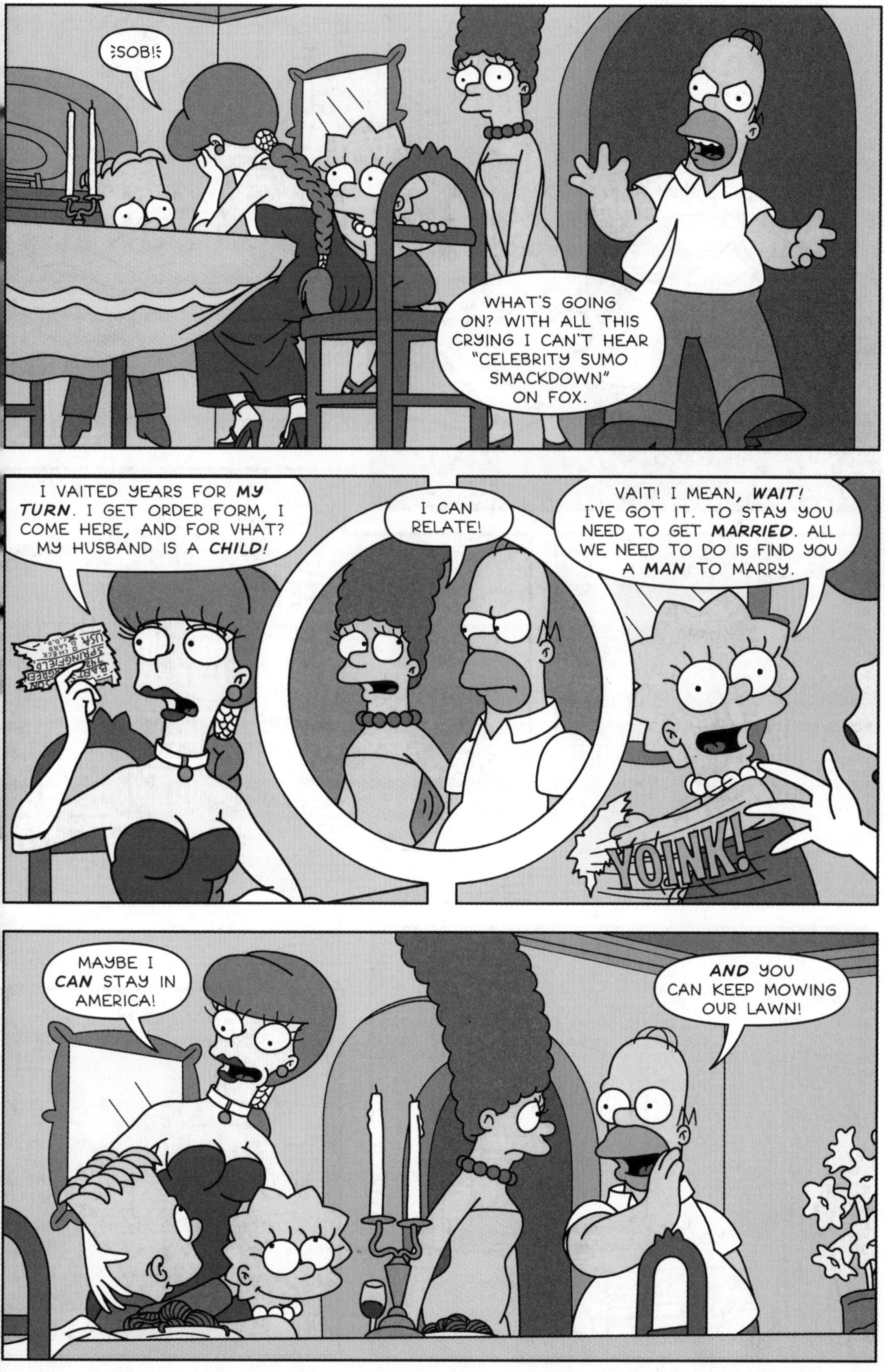
SOB!
WHAT'S GOING ON? WITH ALL THIS CRYING I CAN'T HEAR "CELEBRITY SUMO SMACKDOWN" ON FOX.
I VAITED YEARS FOR MY TURN. I GET ORDER FORM, I COME HERE, AND FOR VHAT? MY HUSBAND IS A CHILD!
I CAN RELATE!
VAIT! I MEAN, WAIT! I'VE GOT IT. TO STAY YOU NEED TO GET MARRIED. ALL WE NEED TO DO IS FIND YOU A MAN TO MARRY.
YOINK!
MAYBE I CAN STAY IN AMERICA!
AND YOU CAN KEEP MOWING OUR LAWN!

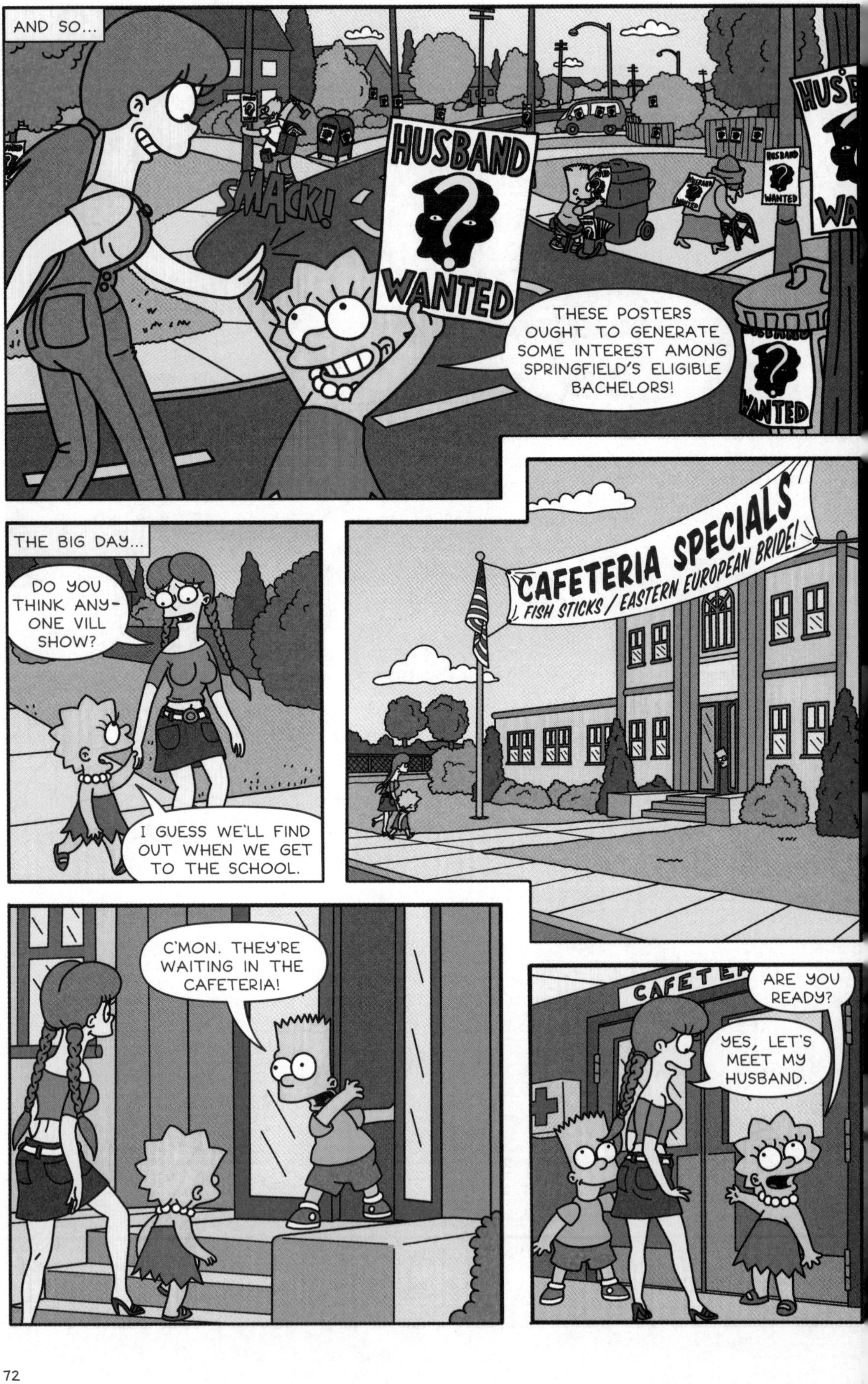
AND SO...
HUSBAND ? WANTED
SMACK!
THESE POSTERS OUGHT TO GENERATE SOME INTEREST AMONG SPRINGFIELD'S ELIGIBLE BACHELORS!
THE BIG DAY...
DO YOU THINK ANY-ONE VILL SHOW?
I GUESS WE'LL FIND OUT WHEN WE GET TO THE SCHOOL.
CAFETERIA SPECIALS
FISH STICKS / EASTERN EUROPEAN BRIDE!
C'MON. THEY'RE WAITING IN THE CAFETERIA!
ARE YOU READY?
YES, LET'S MEET MY HUSBAND.

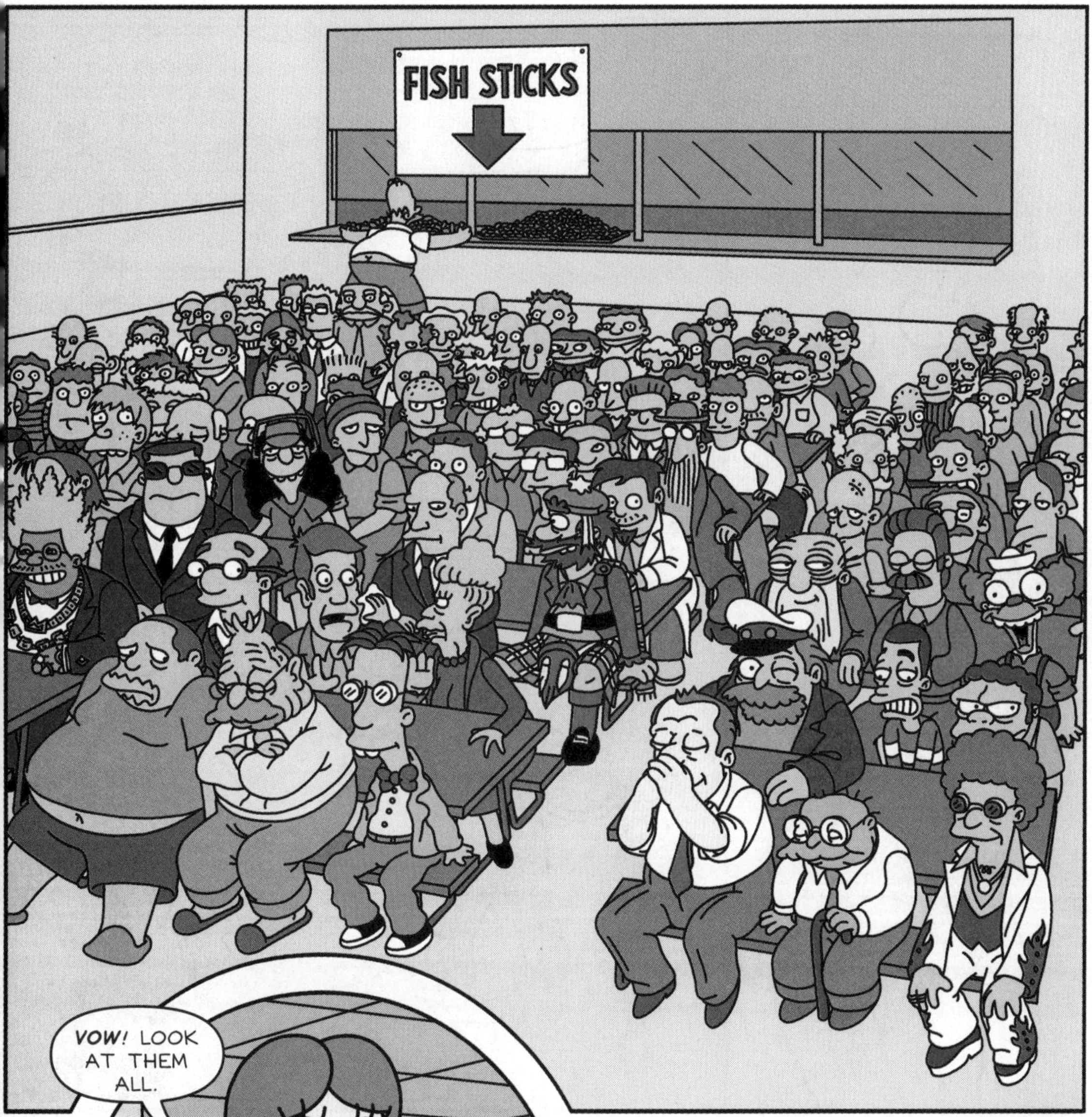
FISH STICKS

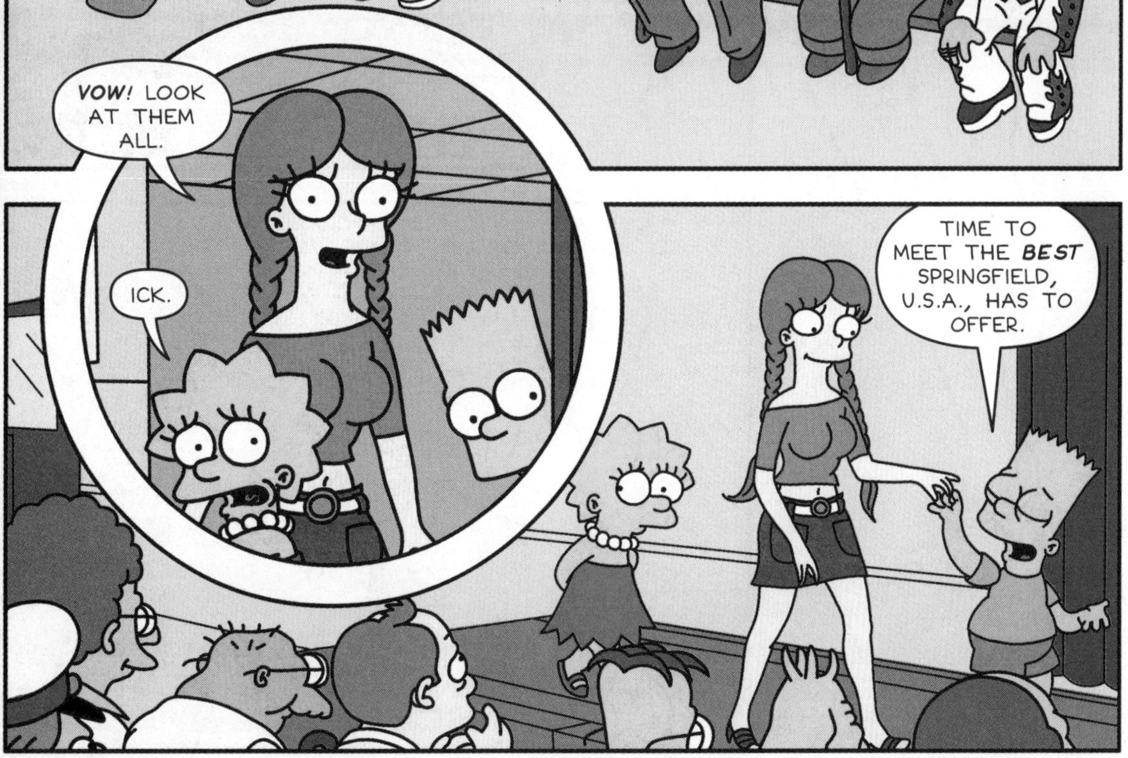
VOW! LOOK AT THEM ALL.
ICK.
TIME TO MEET THE BEST SPRINGFIELD, U.S.A., HAS TO OFFER.

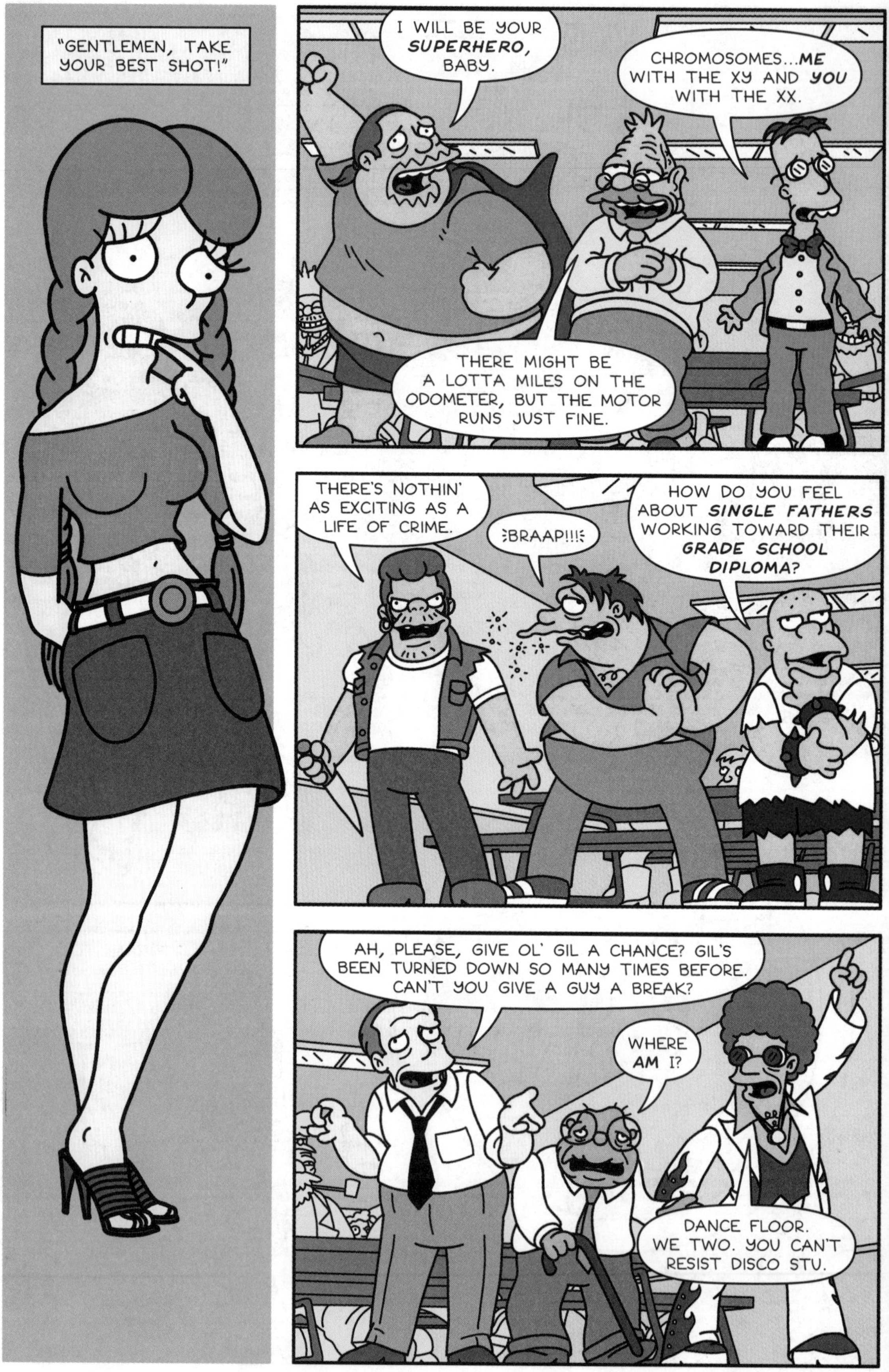
"GENTLEMEN, TAKE YOUR BEST SHOT!"
I WILL BE YOUR **SUPERHERO,** BABY.
CHROMOSOMES...**ME** WITH THE XY AND **YOU** WITH THE XX.
THERE MIGHT BE A LOTTA MILES ON THE ODOMETER, BUT THE MOTOR RUNS JUST FINE.
THERE'S NOTHIN' AS EXCITING AS A LIFE OF CRIME.
BRAAP!!!
HOW DO YOU FEEL ABOUT **SINGLE FATHERS** WORKING TOWARD THEIR **GRADE SCHOOL DIPLOMA?**
AH, PLEASE, GIVE OL' GIL A CHANCE? GIL'S BEEN TURNED DOWN SO MANY TIMES BEFORE. CAN'T YOU GIVE A GUY A BREAK?
WHERE **AM** I?
DANCE FLOOR. WE TWO. YOU CAN'T RESIST DISCO STU.

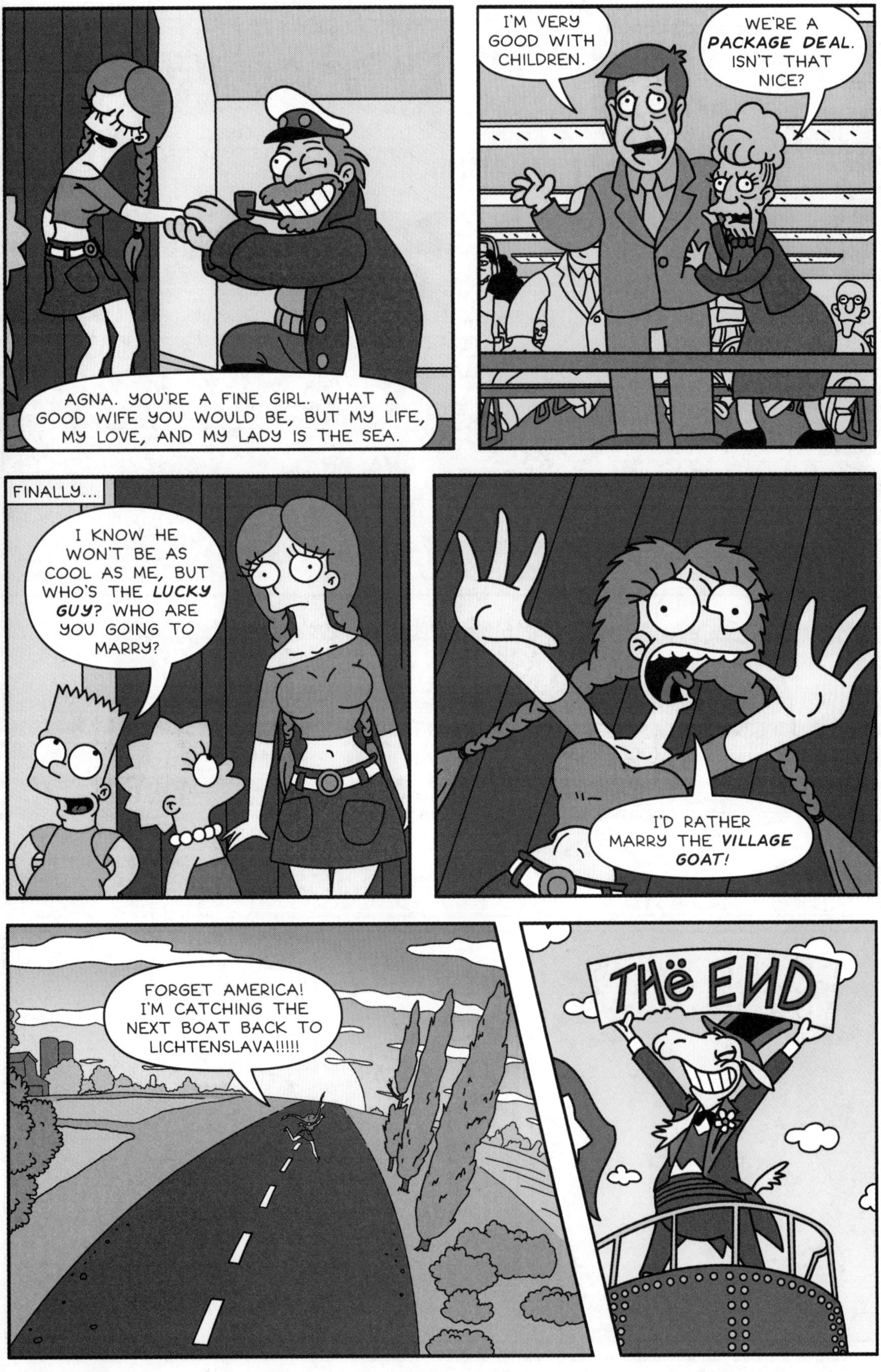
AGNA. YOU'RE A FINE GIRL. WHAT A GOOD WIFE YOU WOULD BE, BUT MY LIFE, MY LOVE, AND MY LADY IS THE SEA.
I'M VERY GOOD WITH CHILDREN.
WE'RE A **PACKAGE DEAL**. ISN'T THAT NICE?
FINALLY...
I KNOW HE WON'T BE AS COOL AS ME, BUT WHO'S THE **LUCKY GUY**? WHO ARE YOU GOING TO MARRY?
I'D RATHER MARRY THE **VILLAGE GOAT**!
FORGET AMERICA! I'M CATCHING THE NEXT BOAT BACK TO LICHTENSLAVA!!!!!
THË END

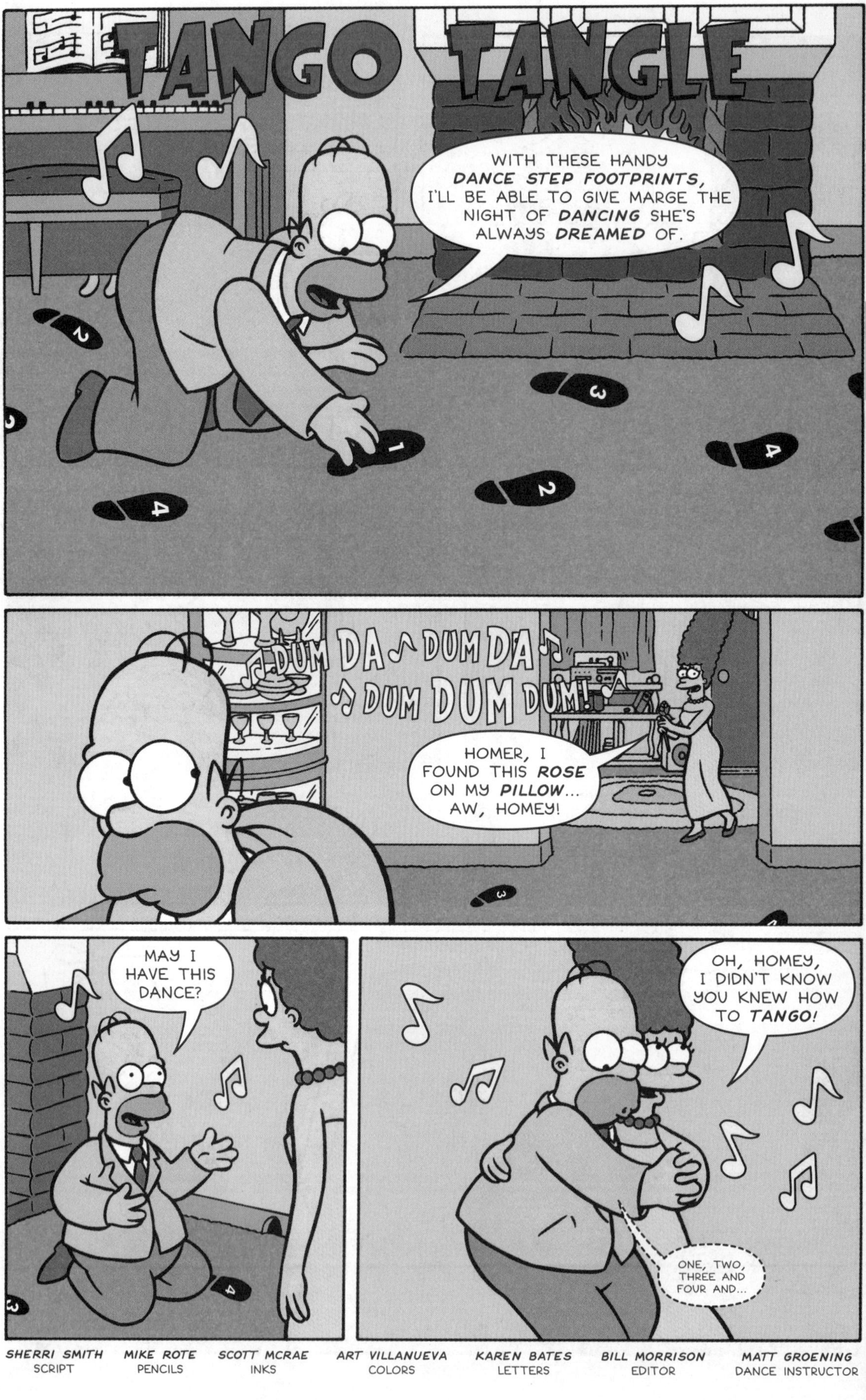
TANGO TANGLE
WITH THESE HANDY **DANCE STEP FOOTPRINTS,** I'LL BE ABLE TO GIVE MARGE THE NIGHT OF **DANCING** SHE'S ALWAYS **DREAMED** OF.
DUM DA DUM DA DUM DUM DUM!
HOMER, I FOUND THIS **ROSE** ON MY **PILLOW**... AW, HOMEY!
MAY I HAVE THIS DANCE?
OH, HOMEY, I DIDN'T KNOW YOU KNEW HOW TO **TANGO!**
ONE, TWO, THREE AND FOUR AND...

SHERRI SMITH SCRIPT — ***MIKE ROTE*** PENCILS — ***SCOTT MCRAE*** INKS — ***ART VILLANUEVA*** COLORS — ***KAREN BATES*** LETTERS — ***BILL MORRISON*** EDITOR — ***MATT GROENING*** DANCE INSTRUCTOR

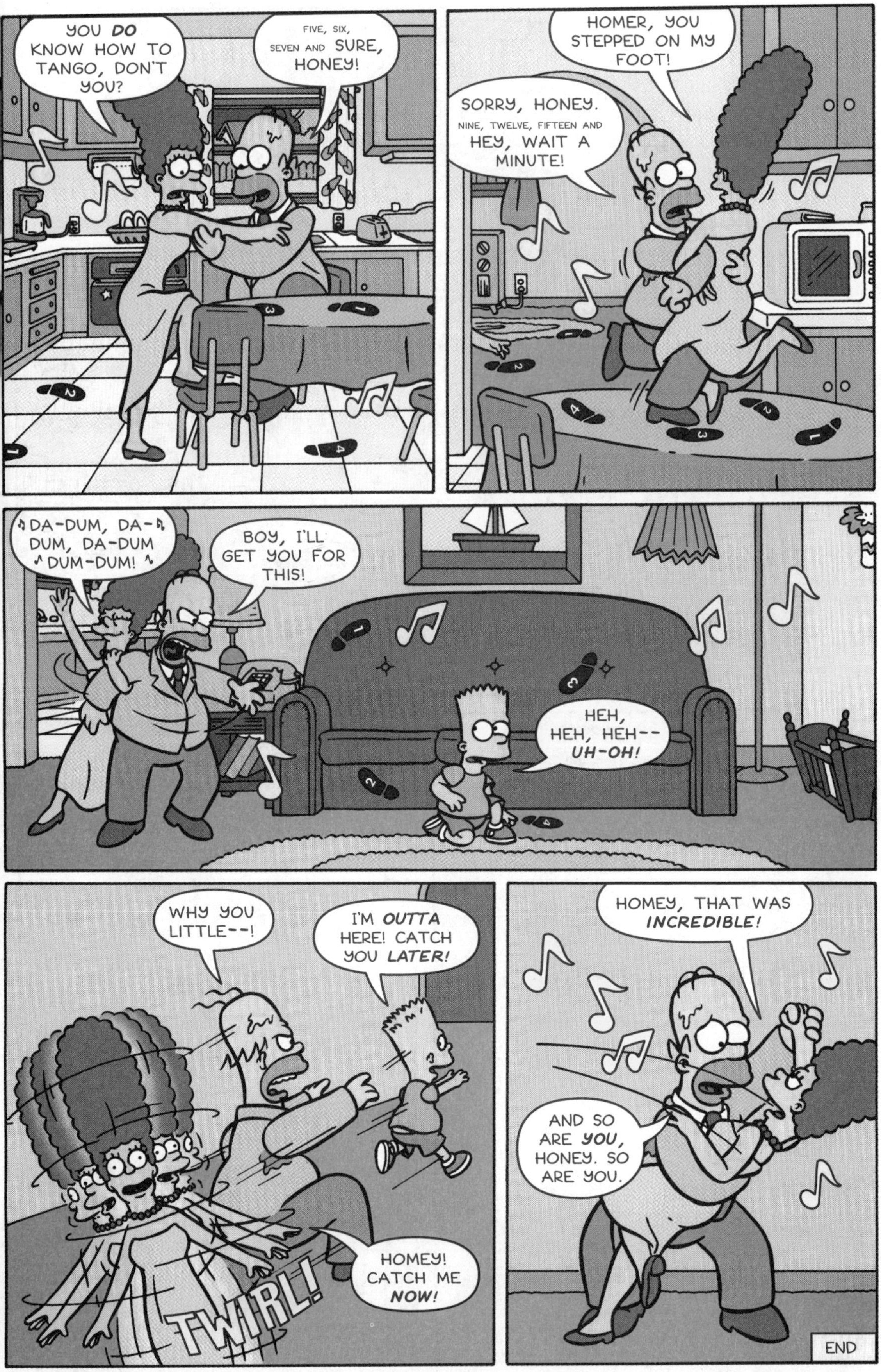
YOU *DO* KNOW HOW TO TANGO, DON'T YOU?
FIVE, SIX, SEVEN AND SURE, HONEY!
HOMER, YOU STEPPED ON MY FOOT!
SORRY, HONEY. NINE, TWELVE, FIFTEEN AND HEY, WAIT A MINUTE!
♪ DA-DUM, DA-DUM, DA-DUM ♪ DUM-DUM! ♪
BOY, I'LL GET YOU FOR THIS!
HEH, HEH, HEH-- *UH-OH!*
WHY YOU LITTLE--!
I'M *OUTTA* HERE! CATCH YOU *LATER!*
HOMEY! CATCH ME *NOW!*
TWIRL!
HOMEY, THAT WAS *INCREDIBLE!*
AND SO ARE *YOU*, HONEY. SO ARE YOU.
END

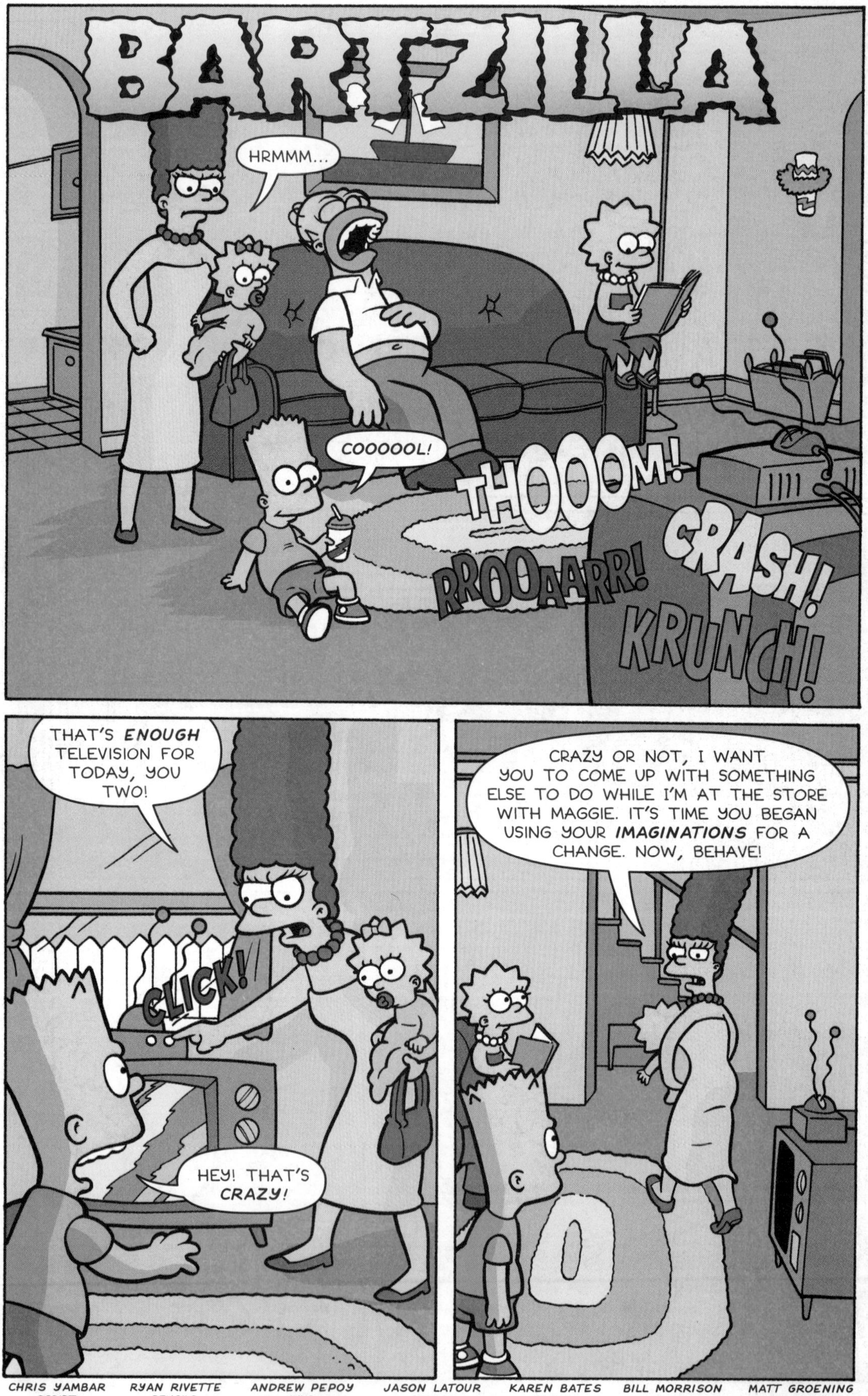
BARTZILLA
HRMMM...
COOOOOL!
THOOOM!
RROOAARR!
CRASH!
KRUNCH!
THAT'S ENOUGH TELEVISION FOR TODAY, YOU TWO!
CLICK!
HEY! THAT'S CRAZY!
CRAZY OR NOT, I WANT YOU TO COME UP WITH SOMETHING ELSE TO DO WHILE I'M AT THE STORE WITH MAGGIE. IT'S TIME YOU BEGAN USING YOUR IMAGINATIONS FOR A CHANGE. NOW, BEHAVE!

CHRIS YAMBAR SCRIPT · *RYAN RIVETTE* PENCILS · *ANDREW PEPOY* INKS · *JASON LATOUR* COLORS · *KAREN BATES* LETTERS · *BILL MORRISON* EDITOR · *MATT GROENING* KING OF KAIJU

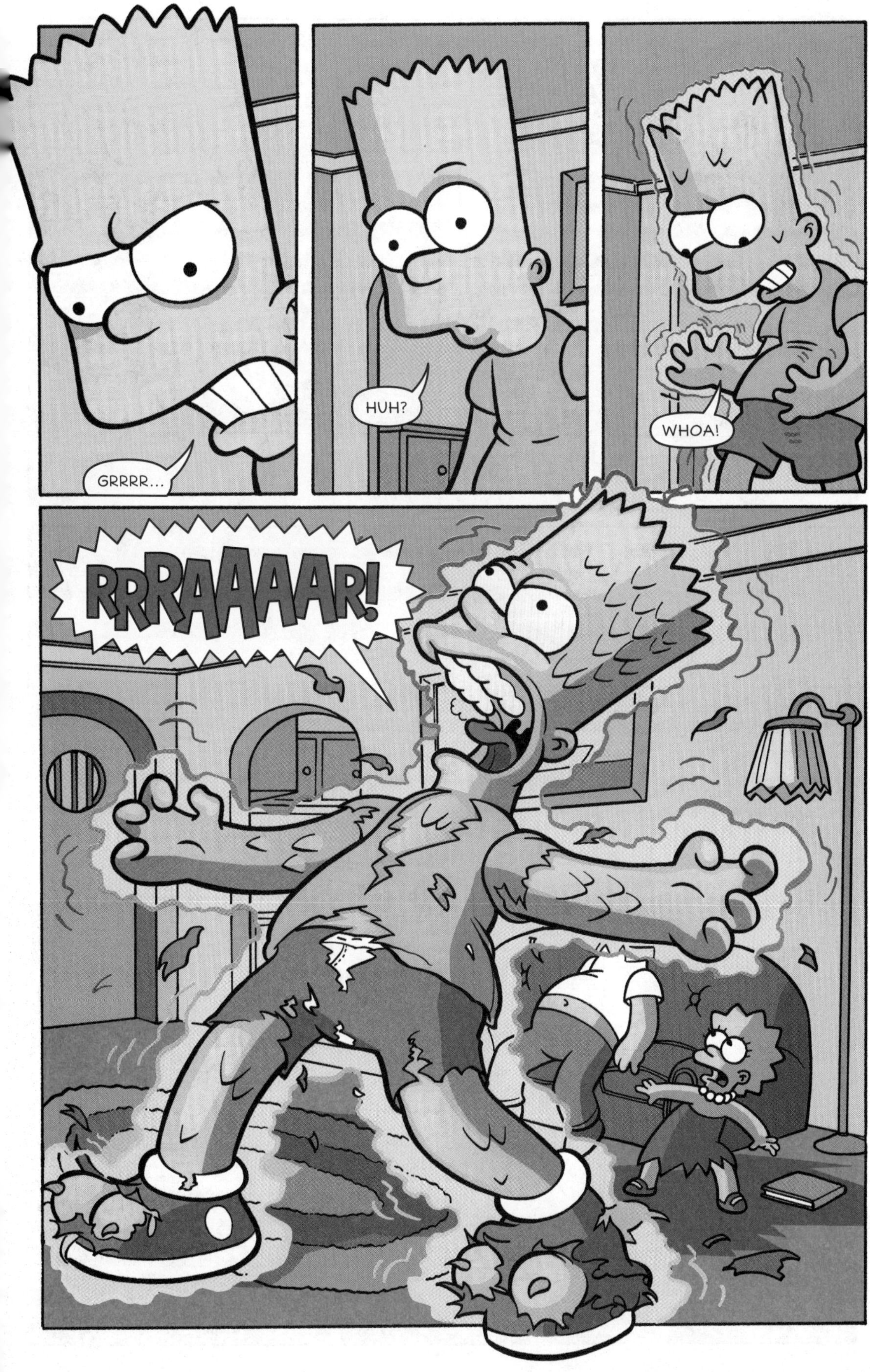
GRRRR...
HUH?
WHOA!
RRRAAAAR!

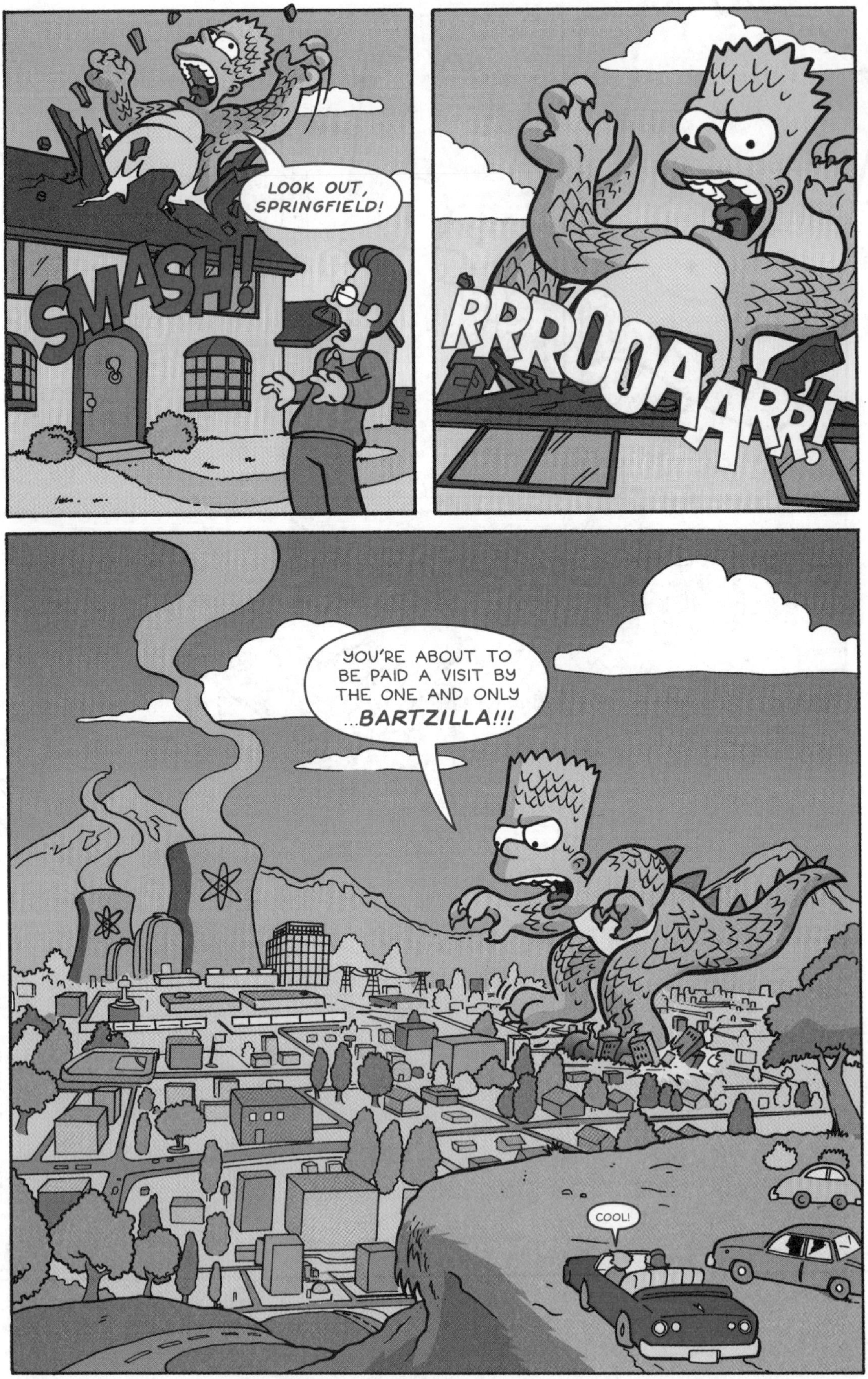
SMASH!
LOOK OUT, SPRINGFIELD!
RRROOAARR!
YOU'RE ABOUT TO BE PAID A VISIT BY THE ONE AND ONLY ...BARTZILLA!!!
COOL!

KAAH-THOOM!

MOE'S

NICE KITTY. :HIC!:

MOE'S

NOW, *THAT'S* ONE BIG TAD-POLE!

HOLD IT RIGHT THERE, YOUNG MAN! YOU'RE NOT TAKING ANOTHER STEP TOWARD THIS FINE ELEMENTARY SCHOOL!

IF YOU THINK YOU'RE GOING TO *DESTROY* THIS SCHOOL BY STEPPING ON IT, THEN YOU'RE FORGETTING THAT INSURANCE WILL HELP ME BUILD A *BIGGER* AND *BETTER* ONE IN ITS PLACE. WHAT DO YOU THINK OF *THAT*, LIZARD BOY?

FIELD NTARY CHOOL

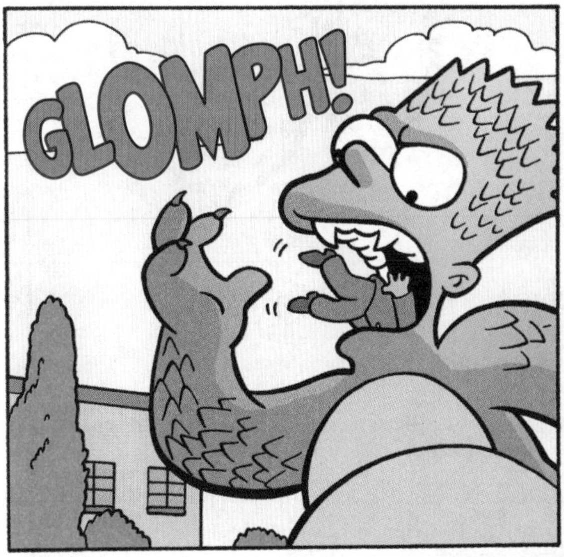
GLOMPH!

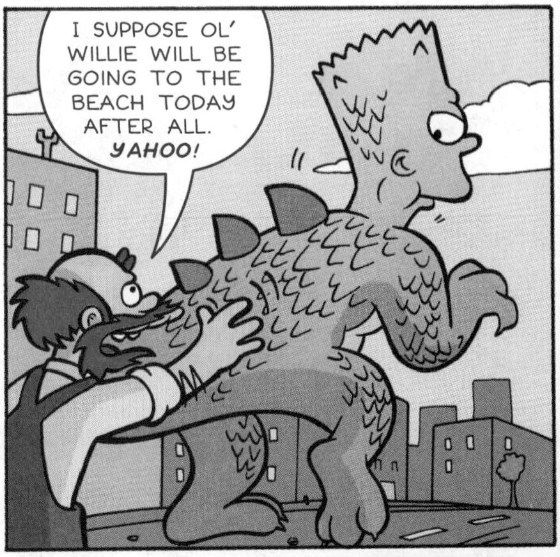
I SUPPOSE OL' WILLIE WILL BE GOING TO THE BEACH TODAY AFTER ALL. *YAHOO!*

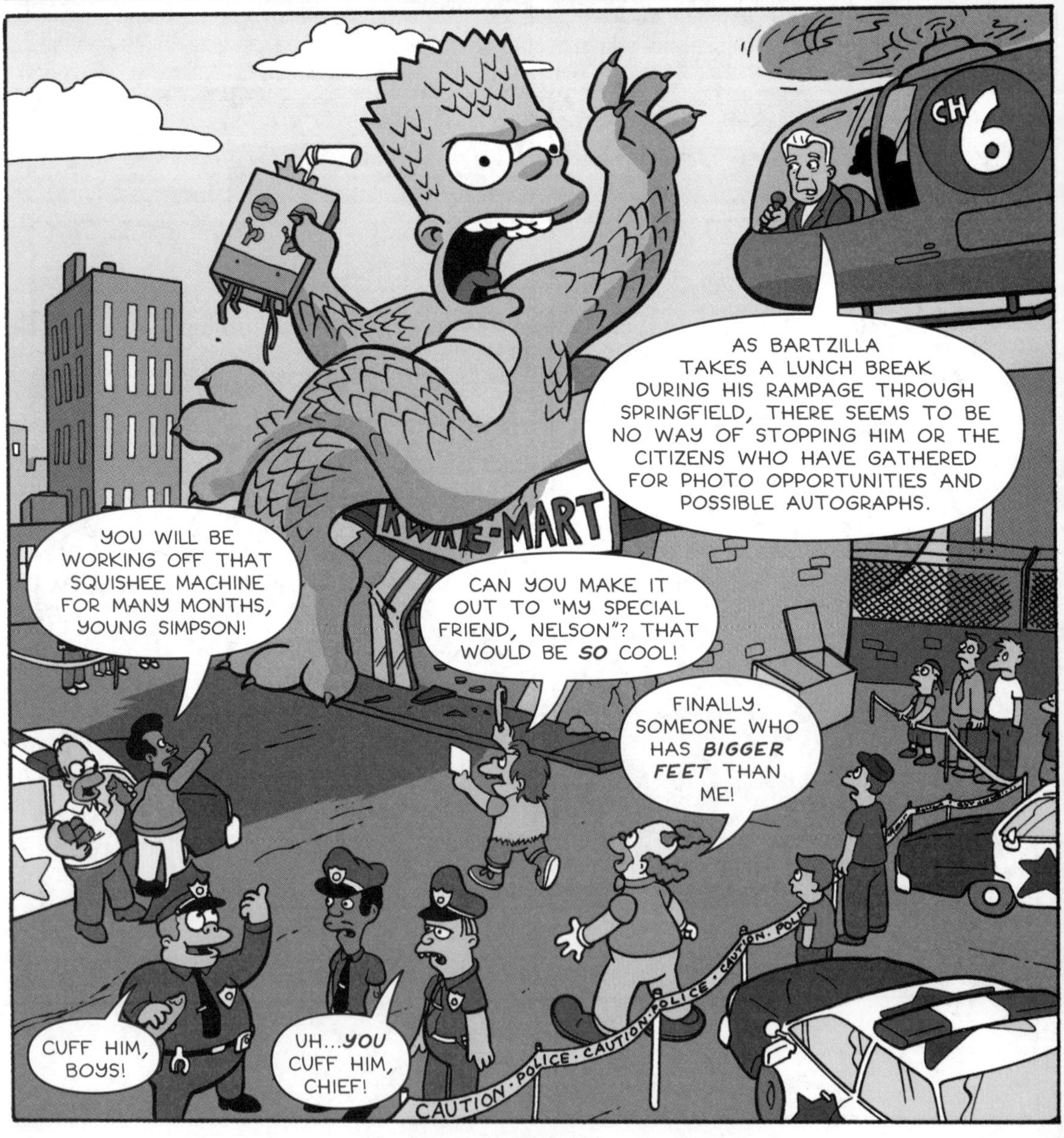
CH 6
AS BARTZILLA TAKES A LUNCH BREAK DURING HIS RAMPAGE THROUGH SPRINGFIELD, THERE SEEMS TO BE NO WAY OF STOPPING HIM OR THE CITIZENS WHO HAVE GATHERED FOR PHOTO OPPORTUNITIES AND POSSIBLE AUTOGRAPHS.
YOU WILL BE WORKING OFF THAT SQUISHEE MACHINE FOR MANY MONTHS, YOUNG SIMPSON!
CAN YOU MAKE IT OUT TO "MY SPECIAL FRIEND, NELSON"? THAT WOULD BE *SO* COOL!
FINALLY. SOMEONE WHO HAS ***BIGGER FEET*** THAN ME!
CUFF HIM, BOYS!
UH...*YOU* CUFF HIM, CHIEF!
CAUTION · POLICE · CAUTION · POLICE

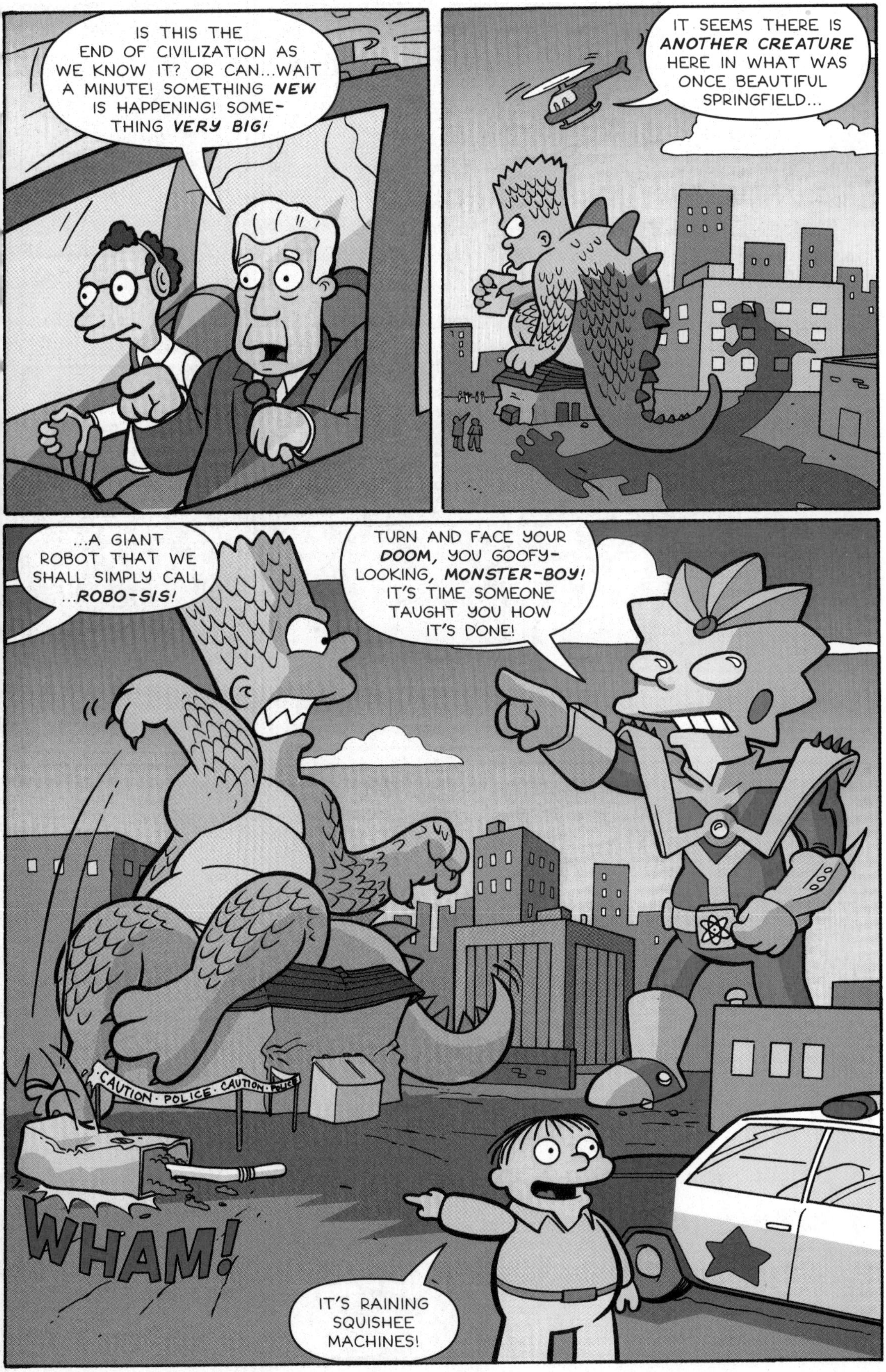
IS THIS THE END OF CIVILIZATION AS WE KNOW IT? OR CAN...WAIT A MINUTE! SOMETHING NEW IS HAPPENING! SOMETHING VERY BIG!
IT SEEMS THERE IS ANOTHER CREATURE HERE IN WHAT WAS ONCE BEAUTIFUL SPRINGFIELD...
...A GIANT ROBOT THAT WE SHALL SIMPLY CALL ...ROBO-SIS!
TURN AND FACE YOUR DOOM, YOU GOOFY-LOOKING, MONSTER-BOY! IT'S TIME SOMEONE TAUGHT YOU HOW IT'S DONE!
CAUTION · POLICE · CAUTION · POLICE
WHAM!
IT'S RAINING SQUISHEE MACHINES!

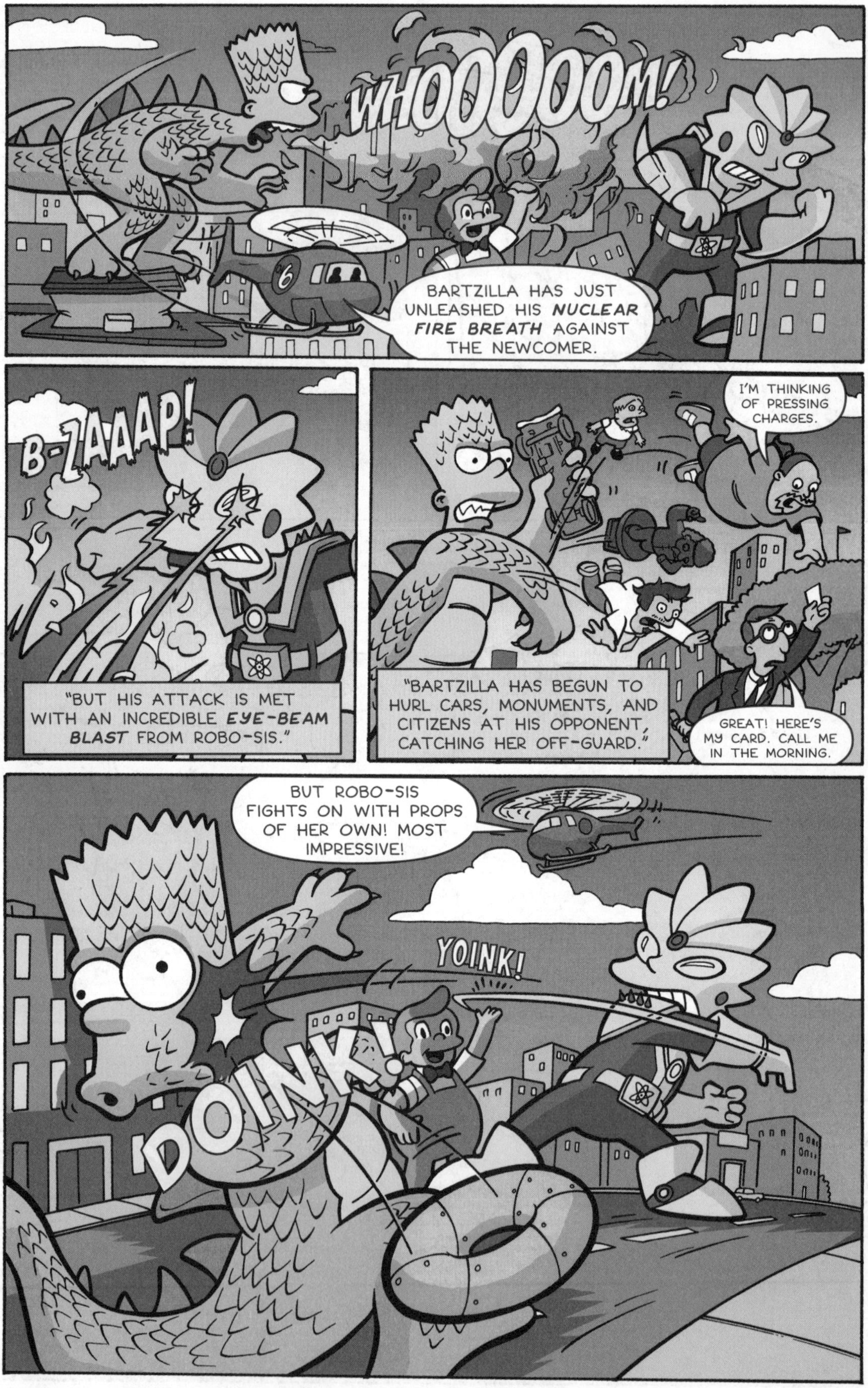
WHOOOOOOM!
BARTZILLA HAS JUST UNLEASHED HIS NUCLEAR FIRE BREATH AGAINST THE NEWCOMER.
B-ZAAAP!
"BUT HIS ATTACK IS MET WITH AN INCREDIBLE EYE-BEAM BLAST FROM ROBO-SIS."
I'M THINKING OF PRESSING CHARGES.
"BARTZILLA HAS BEGUN TO HURL CARS, MONUMENTS, AND CITIZENS AT HIS OPPONENT, CATCHING HER OFF-GUARD."
GREAT! HERE'S MY CARD. CALL ME IN THE MORNING.
BUT ROBO-SIS FIGHTS ON WITH PROPS OF HER OWN! MOST IMPRESSIVE!
YOINK!
DOINK!

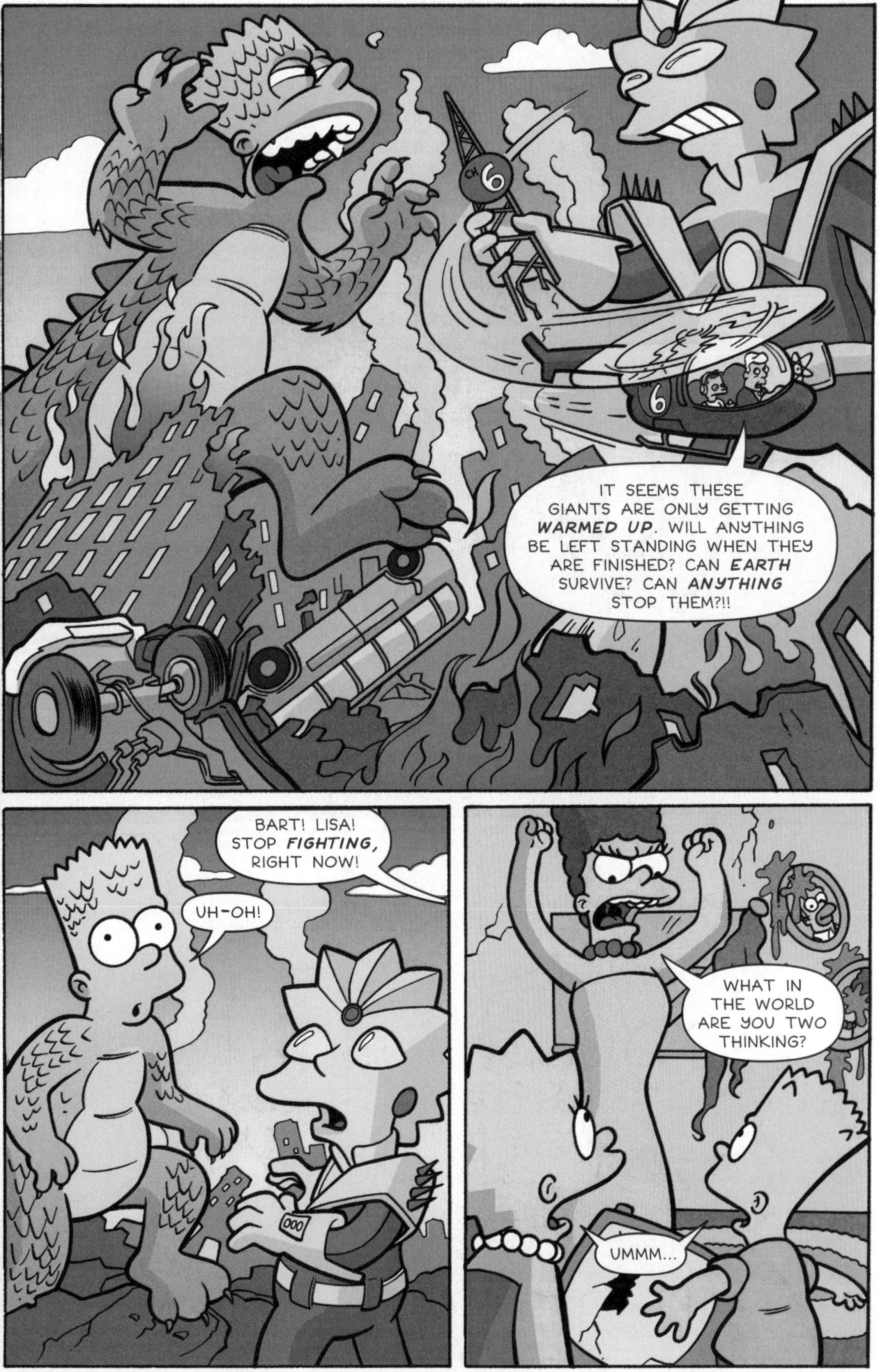
IT SEEMS THESE GIANTS ARE ONLY GETTING **WARMED UP**. WILL ANYTHING BE LEFT STANDING WHEN THEY ARE FINISHED? CAN **EARTH** SURVIVE? CAN **ANYTHING** STOP THEM?!!
BART! LISA! STOP **FIGHTING**, RIGHT NOW!
UH-OH!
WHAT IN THE WORLD ARE YOU TWO THINKING?
UMMM...

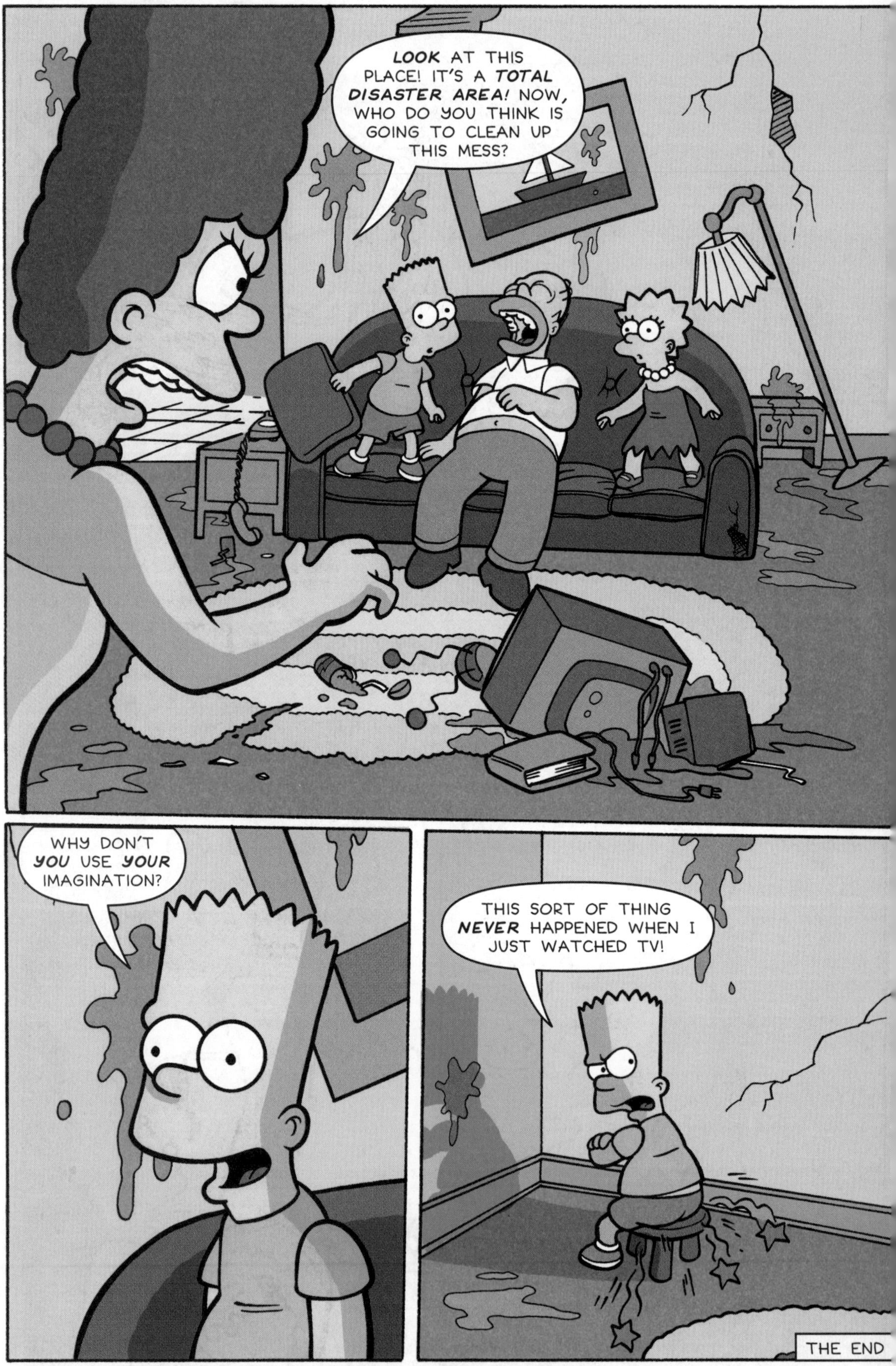
LOOK AT THIS PLACE! IT'S A TOTAL DISASTER AREA! NOW, WHO DO YOU THINK IS GOING TO CLEAN UP THIS MESS?
WHY DON'T YOU USE YOUR IMAGINATION?
THIS SORT OF THING NEVER HAPPENED WHEN I JUST WATCHED TV!
THE END

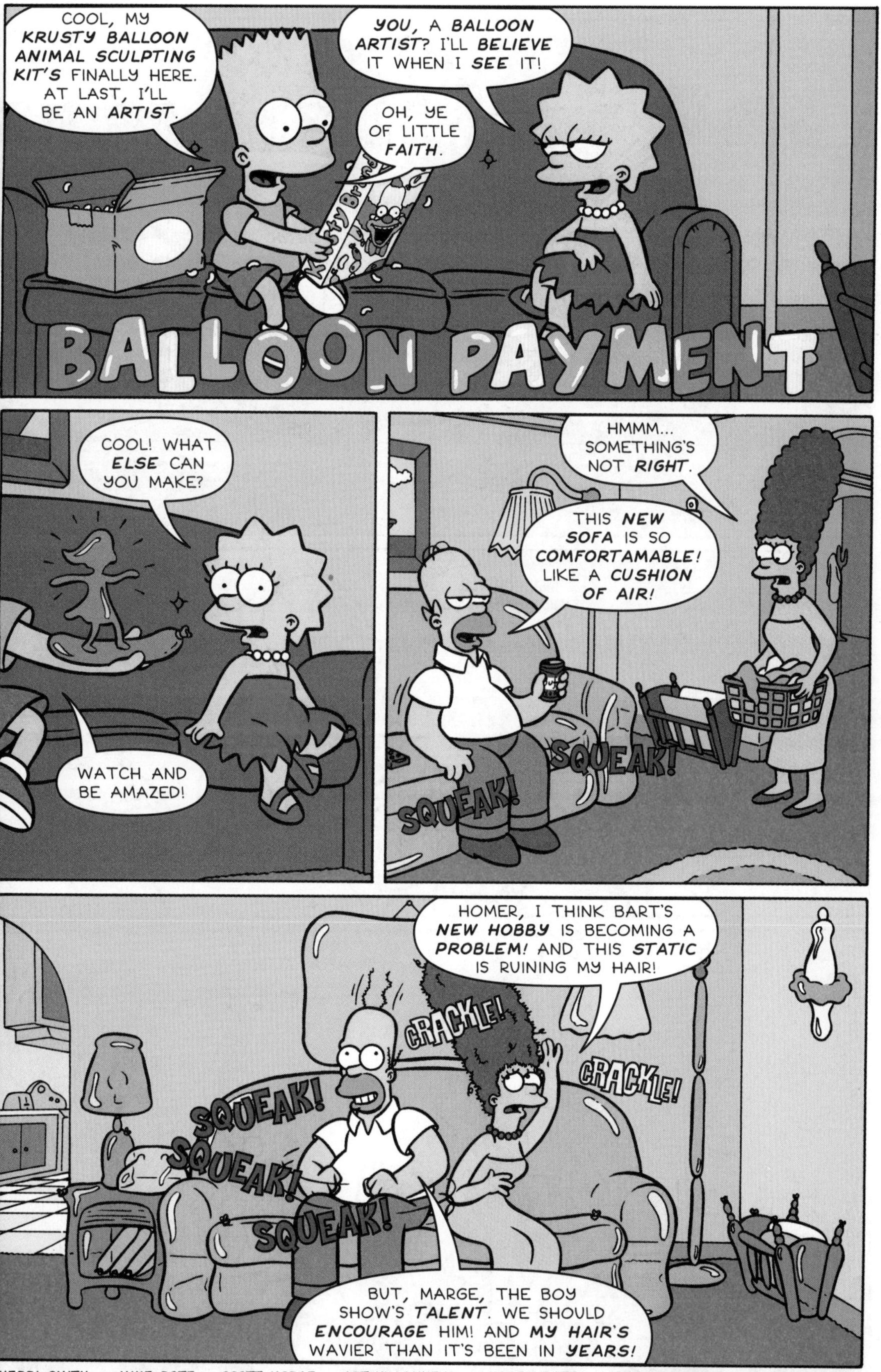
COOL, MY KRUSTY BALLOON ANIMAL SCULPTING KIT'S FINALLY HERE. AT LAST, I'LL BE AN ARTIST.
YOU, A BALLOON ARTIST? I'LL BELIEVE IT WHEN I SEE IT!
OH, YE OF LITTLE FAITH.
BALLOON PAYMENT
WATCH AND BE AMAZED!
COOL! WHAT ELSE CAN YOU MAKE?
HMMM... SOMETHING'S NOT RIGHT.
THIS NEW SOFA IS SO COMFORTAMABLE! LIKE A CUSHION OF AIR!
SQUEAK!
SQUEAK!
HOMER, I THINK BART'S NEW HOBBY IS BECOMING A PROBLEM! AND THIS STATIC IS RUINING MY HAIR!
CRACKLE!
CRACKLE!
SQUEAK!
SQUEAK!
SQUEAK!
BUT, MARGE, THE BOY SHOW'S TALENT. WE SHOULD ENCOURAGE HIM! AND MY HAIR'S WAVIER THAN IT'S BEEN IN YEARS!

HERRI SMITH SCRIPT · MIKE ROTE PENCILS · SCOTT MCRAE INKS · ART VILLANUEVA COLORS · KAREN BATES LETTERS · BILL MORRISON EDITS · MATT GROENING HOT AIR

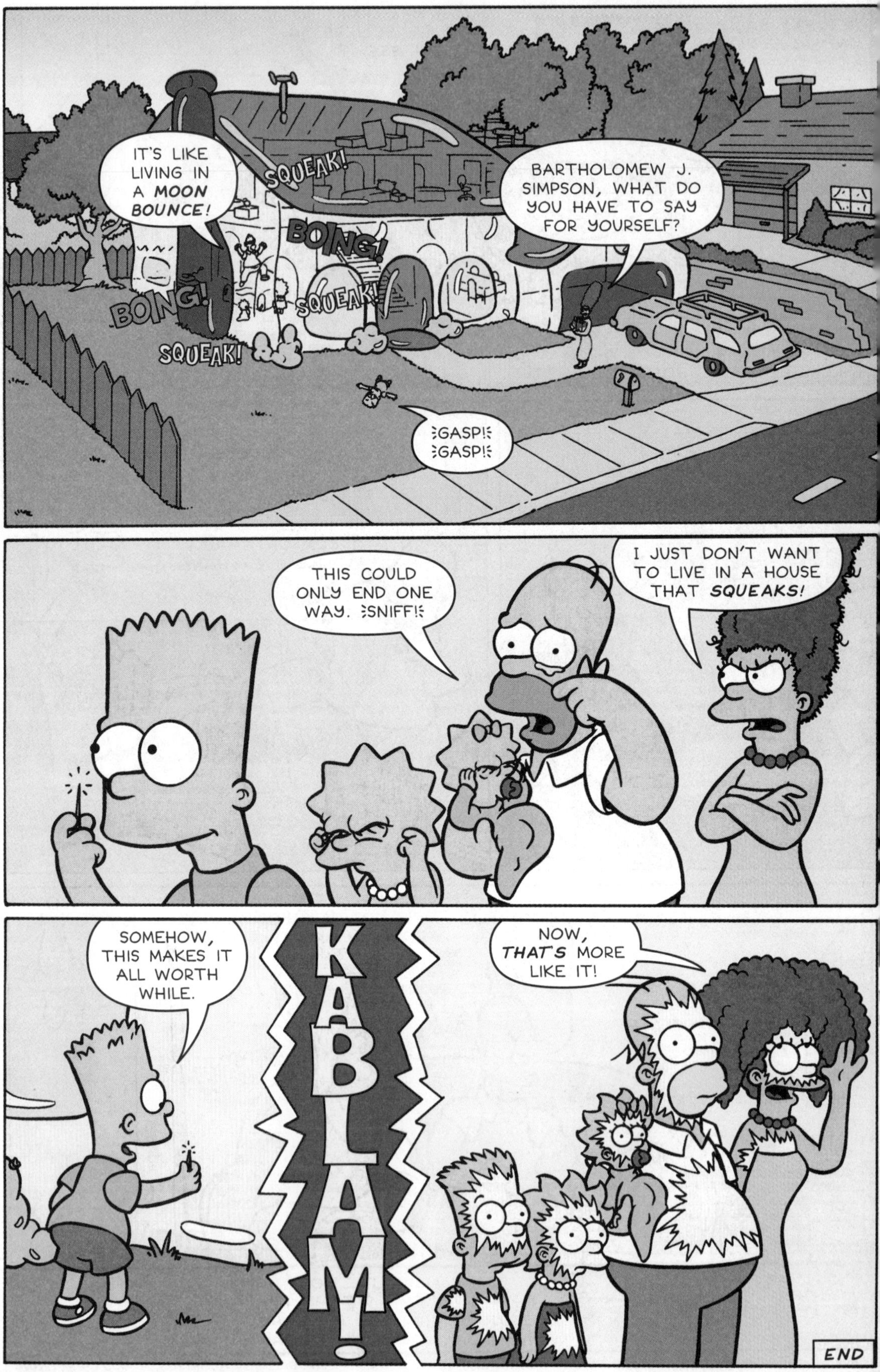
IT'S LIKE LIVING IN A MOON BOUNCE!
SQUEAK!
BOING!
BOING!
SQUEAK!
SQUEAK!
BARTHOLOMEW J. SIMPSON, WHAT DO YOU HAVE TO SAY FOR YOURSELF?
GASP! GASP!
THIS COULD ONLY END ONE WAY. SNIFF!
I JUST DON'T WANT TO LIVE IN A HOUSE THAT SQUEAKS!
SOMEHOW, THIS MAKES IT ALL WORTH WHILE.
KABLAM!
NOW, THAT'S MORE LIKE IT!
END

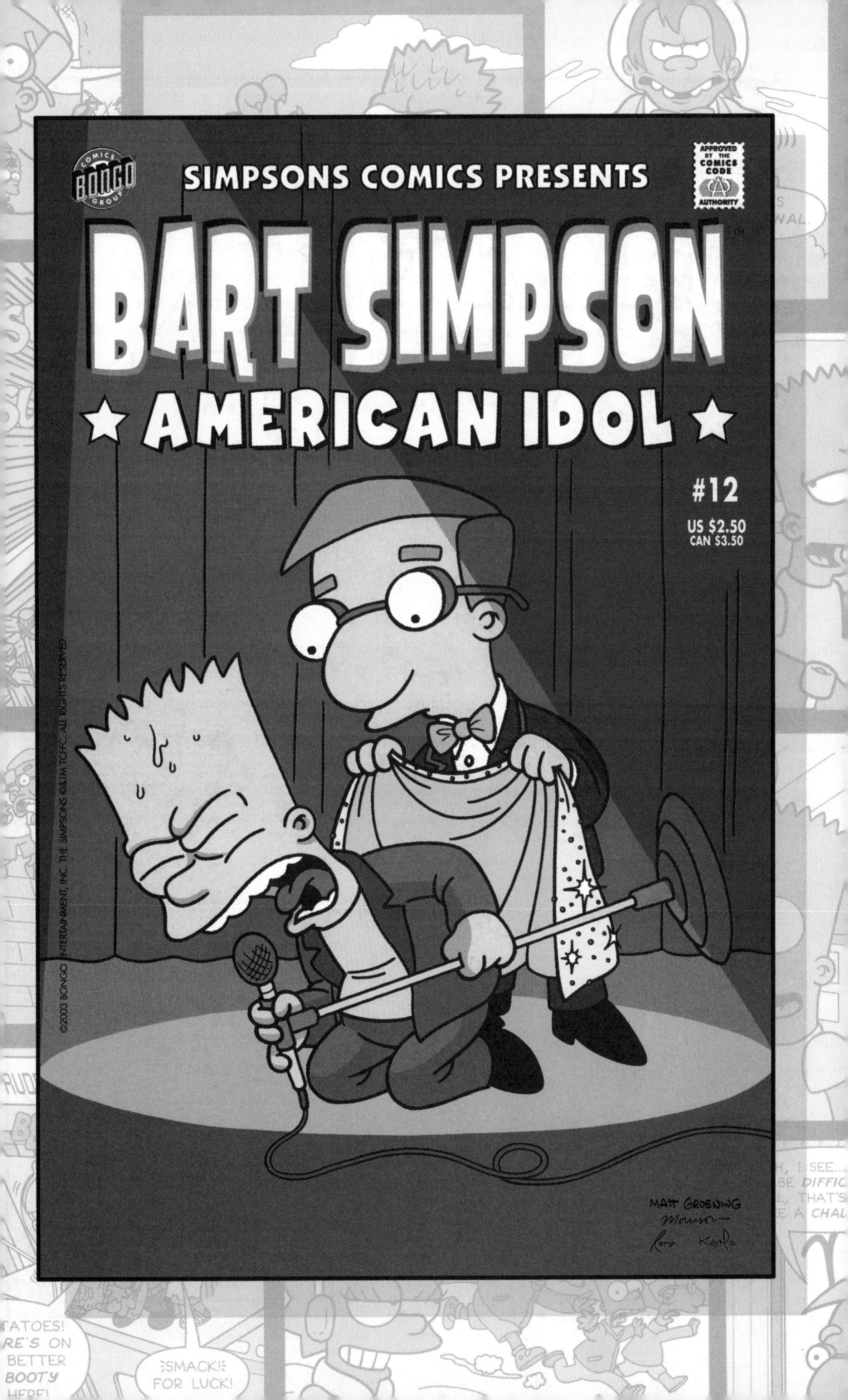
SIMPSONS COMICS PRESENTS
APPROVED BY THE COMICS CODE AUTHORITY
BART SIMPSON™
AMERICAN IDOL
#12
US $2.50
CAN $3.50
©2003 BONGO ENTERTAINMENT, INC. THE SIMPSONS ©&TM TCFFC. ALL RIGHTS RESERVED
MATT GROENING
SMACK!
FOR LUCK!

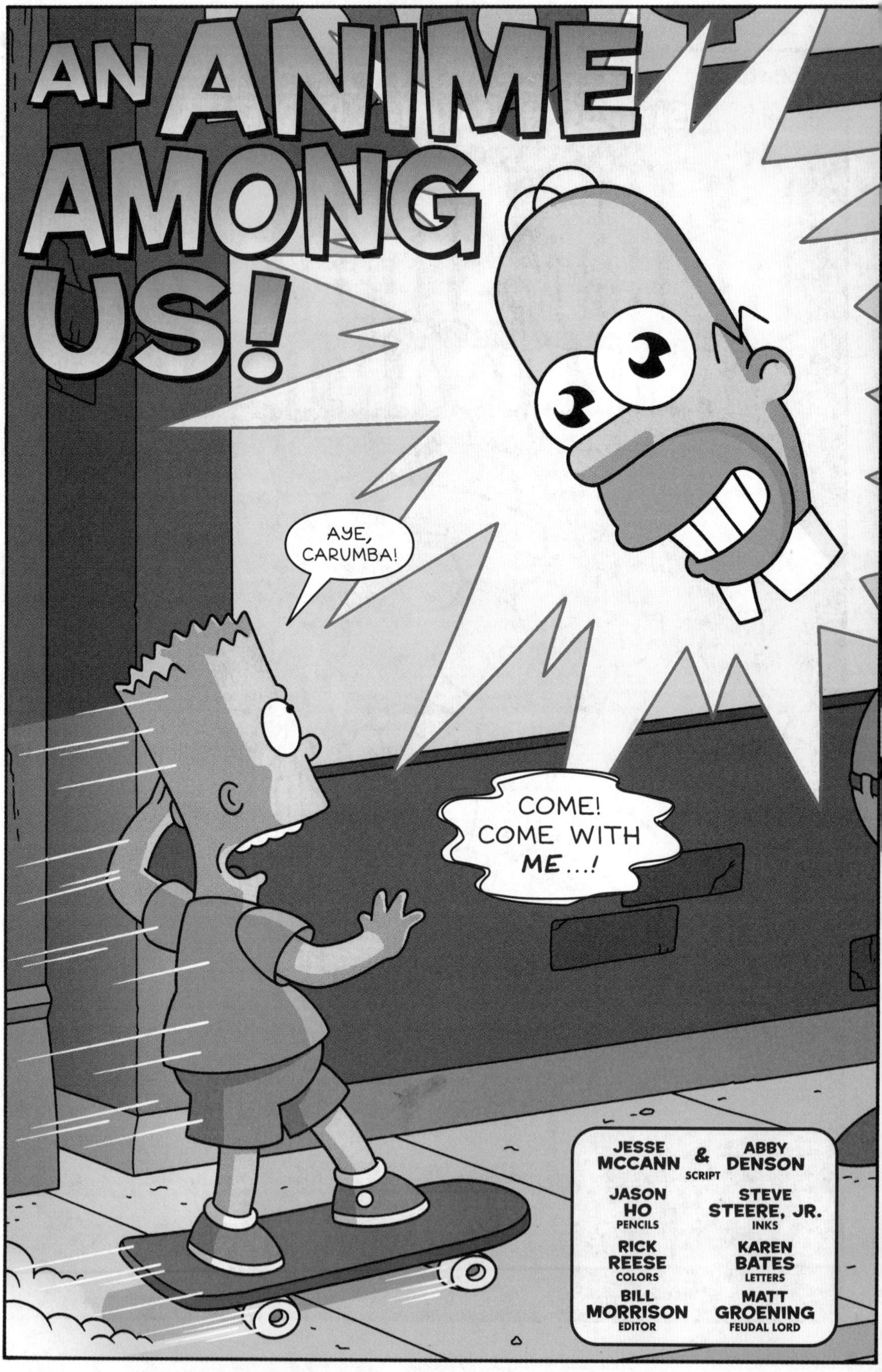
AN ANIME AMONG US!
AYE, CARUMBA!
COME! COME WITH ME...!
JESSE MCCANN & ABBY DENSON SCRIPT
JASON HO PENCILS
STEVE STEERE, JR. INKS
RICK REESE COLORS
KAREN BATES LETTERS
BILL MORRISON EDITOR
MATT GROENING FEUDAL LORD

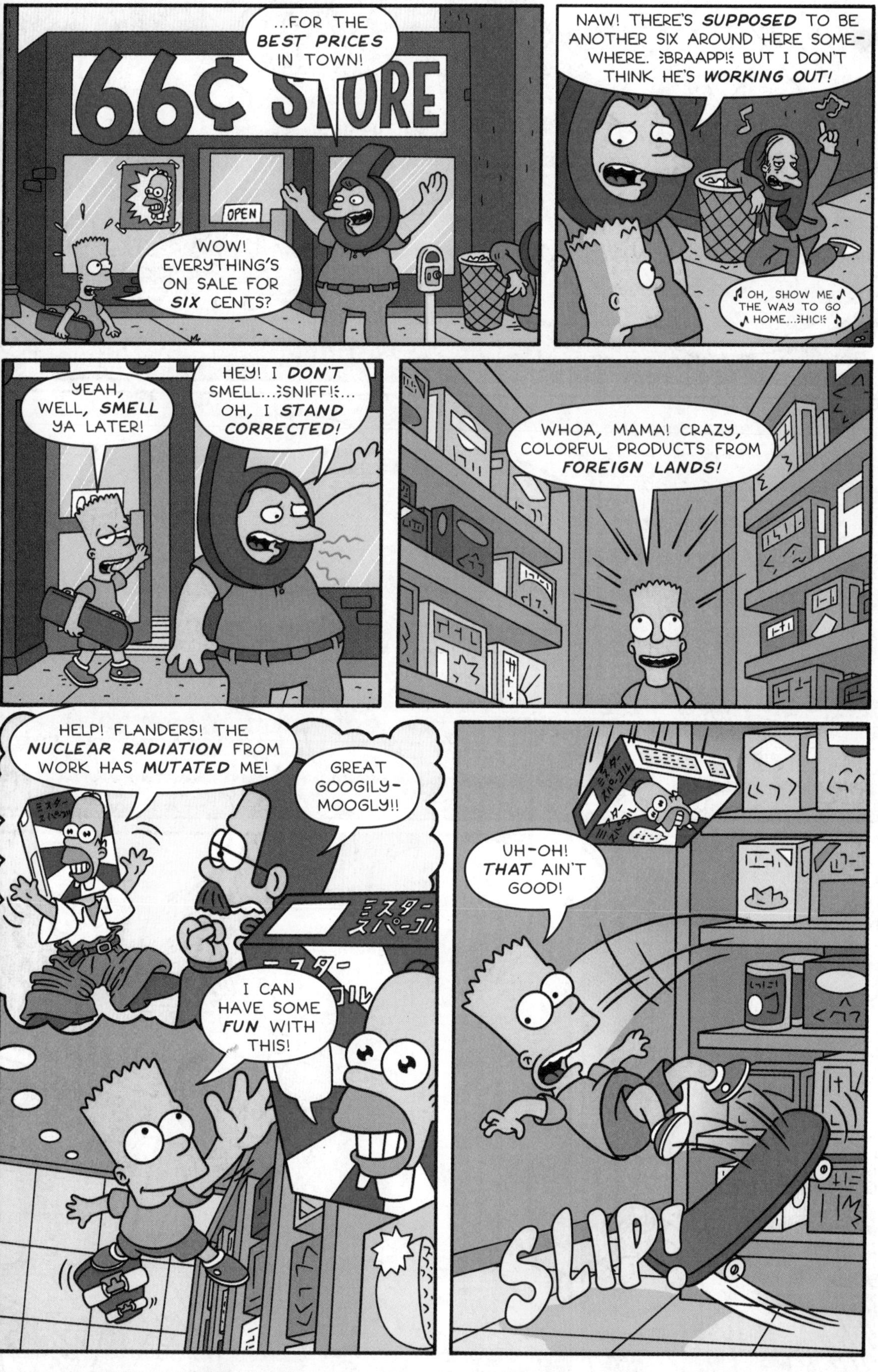
66¢ STORE
...FOR THE BEST PRICES IN TOWN!
OPEN
WOW! EVERYTHING'S ON SALE FOR SIX CENTS?
NAW! THERE'S SUPPOSED TO BE ANOTHER SIX AROUND HERE SOME-WHERE. :BRAAPP!: BUT I DON'T THINK HE'S WORKING OUT!
♪ OH, SHOW ME ♪ THE WAY TO GO ♪ HOME...:HIC!: ♪
YEAH, WELL, SMELL YA LATER!
HEY! I DON'T SMELL...:SNIFF!:... OH, I STAND CORRECTED!
WHOA, MAMA! CRAZY, COLORFUL PRODUCTS FROM FOREIGN LANDS!
HELP! FLANDERS! THE NUCLEAR RADIATION FROM WORK HAS MUTATED ME!
GREAT GOOGILY-MOOGLY!!
I CAN HAVE SOME FUN WITH THIS!
UH-OH! THAT AIN'T GOOD!
SLIP!

CLONNG!

ERF!

WHOA! WHAT'S HAPPENING?

THIS IS NO TIME TO BE *LYING DOWN* ON THE JOB!

C'MON, *SANTA-CHOO!* WE'VE GOT TO CATCH MORE *POCKET GOBLINS!* I'M GONNA BE THE BEST *POCKEGOB* TRAINER OF ALL!

SANTA! SANTA-CHOOO!

NOT SO FAST!

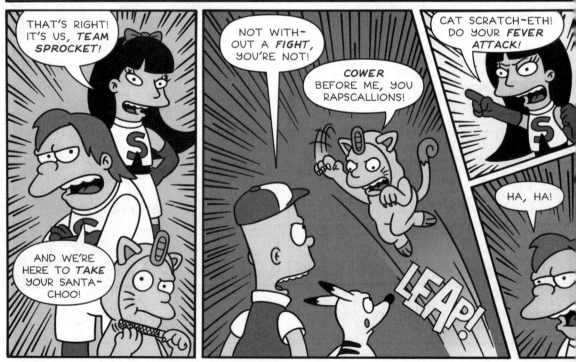

THAT'S RIGHT! IT'S US, *TEAM SPROCKET!*

AND WE'RE HERE TO *TAKE* YOUR SANTA-CHOO!

NOT WITH-OUT A *FIGHT*, YOU'RE NOT!

COWER BEFORE ME, YOU RAPSCALLIONS!

CAT SCRATCH-ETH! DO YOUR *FEVER ATTACK!*

HA, HA!

LEAP!

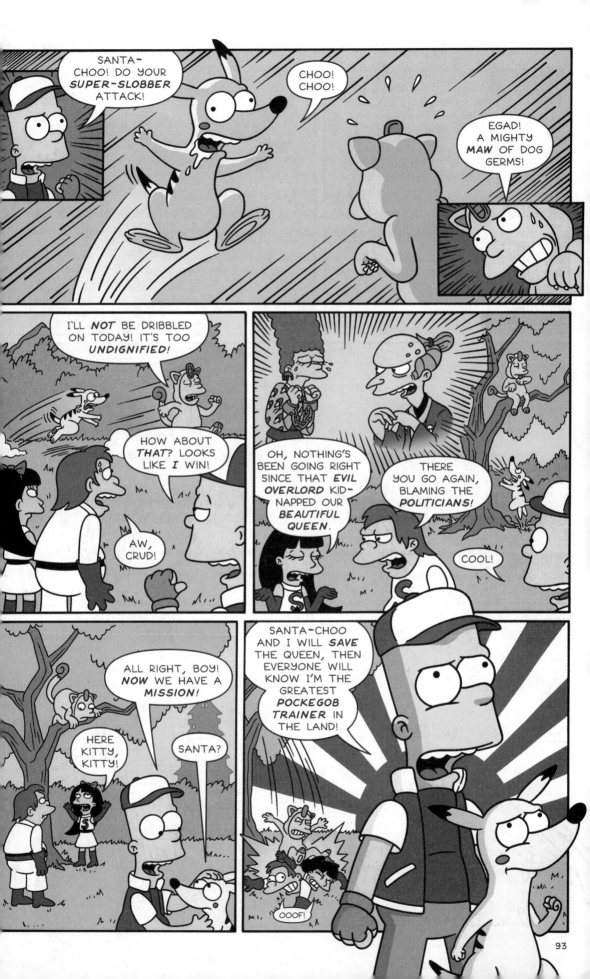

SANTA-CHOO! DO YOUR *SUPER-SLOBBER* ATTACK!

CHOO! CHOO!

EGAD! A MIGHTY *MAW* OF DOG GERMS!

I'LL *NOT* BE DRIBBLED ON TODAY! IT'S TOO *UNDIGNIFIED!*

HOW ABOUT *THAT*? LOOKS LIKE *I* WIN!

AW, CRUD!

OH, NOTHING'S BEEN GOING RIGHT SINCE THAT *EVIL OVERLORD* KID-NAPPED OUR *BEAUTIFUL QUEEN.*

THERE YOU GO AGAIN, BLAMING THE *POLITICIANS!*

COOL!

ALL RIGHT, BOY! *NOW* WE HAVE A *MISSION!*

HERE KITTY, KITTY!

SANTA?

SANTA-CHOO AND I WILL *SAVE* THE QUEEN, THEN EVERYONE WILL KNOW I'M THE GREATEST *POCKEGOB TRAINER* IN THE LAND!

OOOF!

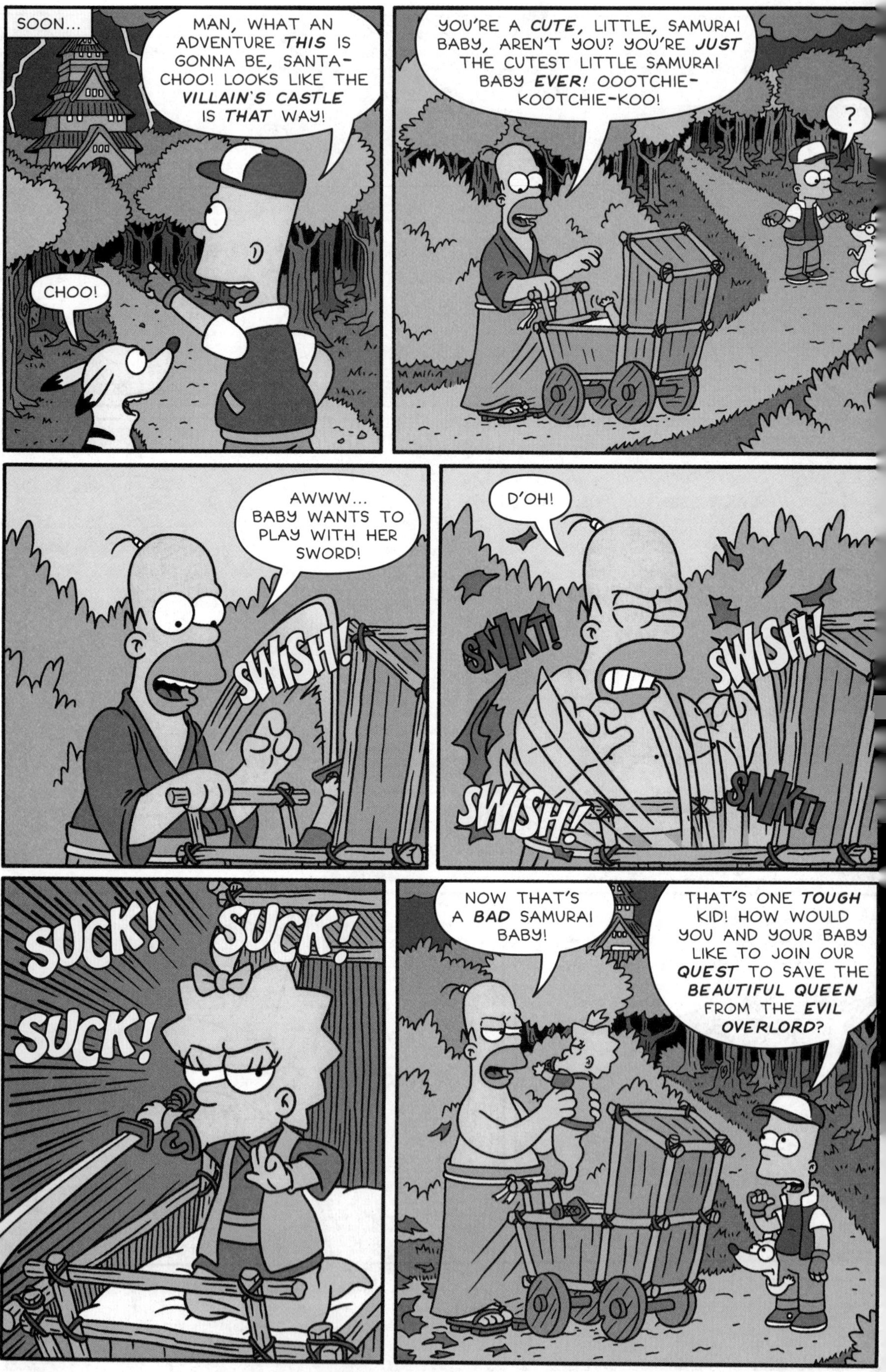
SOON...
MAN, WHAT AN ADVENTURE THIS IS GONNA BE, SANTA-CHOO! LOOKS LIKE THE VILLAIN'S CASTLE IS THAT WAY!
CHOO!
YOU'RE A CUTE, LITTLE, SAMURAI BABY, AREN'T YOU? YOU'RE JUST THE CUTEST LITTLE SAMURAI BABY EVER! OOOTCHIE-KOOTCHIE-KOO!
?
AWWW... BABY WANTS TO PLAY WITH HER SWORD!
SWISH!
D'OH!
SNIKT!
SWISH!
SWISH!
SNIKT!
SUCK!
SUCK!
SUCK!
NOW THAT'S A BAD SAMURAI BABY!
THAT'S ONE TOUGH KID! HOW WOULD YOU AND YOUR BABY LIKE TO JOIN OUR QUEST TO SAVE THE BEAUTIFUL QUEEN FROM THE EVIL OVERLORD?

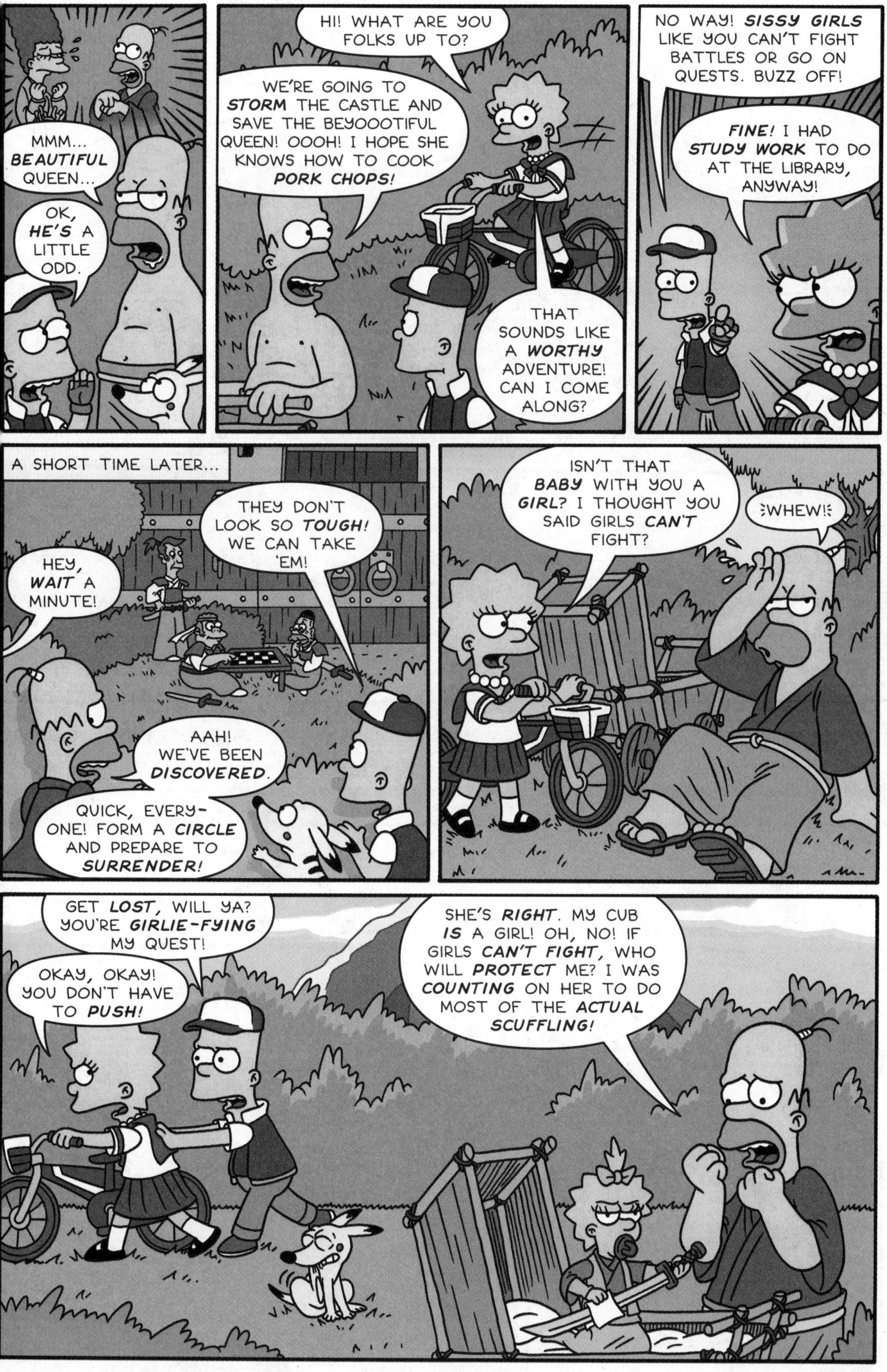
MMM... BEAUTIFUL QUEEN...
OK, HE'S A LITTLE ODD.
HI! WHAT ARE YOU FOLKS UP TO?
WE'RE GOING TO STORM THE CASTLE AND SAVE THE BEYOOOTIFUL QUEEN! OOOH! I HOPE SHE KNOWS HOW TO COOK PORK CHOPS!
THAT SOUNDS LIKE A WORTHY ADVENTURE! CAN I COME ALONG?
NO WAY! SISSY GIRLS LIKE YOU CAN'T FIGHT BATTLES OR GO ON QUESTS. BUZZ OFF!
FINE! I HAD STUDY WORK TO DO AT THE LIBRARY, ANYWAY!
A SHORT TIME LATER...
HEY, WAIT A MINUTE!
THEY DON'T LOOK SO TOUGH! WE CAN TAKE 'EM!
AAH! WE'VE BEEN DISCOVERED.
QUICK, EVERY-ONE! FORM A CIRCLE AND PREPARE TO SURRENDER!
ISN'T THAT BABY WITH YOU A GIRL? I THOUGHT YOU SAID GIRLS CAN'T FIGHT?
WHEW!
GET LOST, WILL YA? YOU'RE GIRLIE-FYING MY QUEST!
OKAY, OKAY! YOU DON'T HAVE TO PUSH!
SHE'S RIGHT. MY CUB IS A GIRL! OH, NO! IF GIRLS CAN'T FIGHT, WHO WILL PROTECT ME? I WAS COUNTING ON HER TO DO MOST OF THE ACTUAL SCUFFLING!

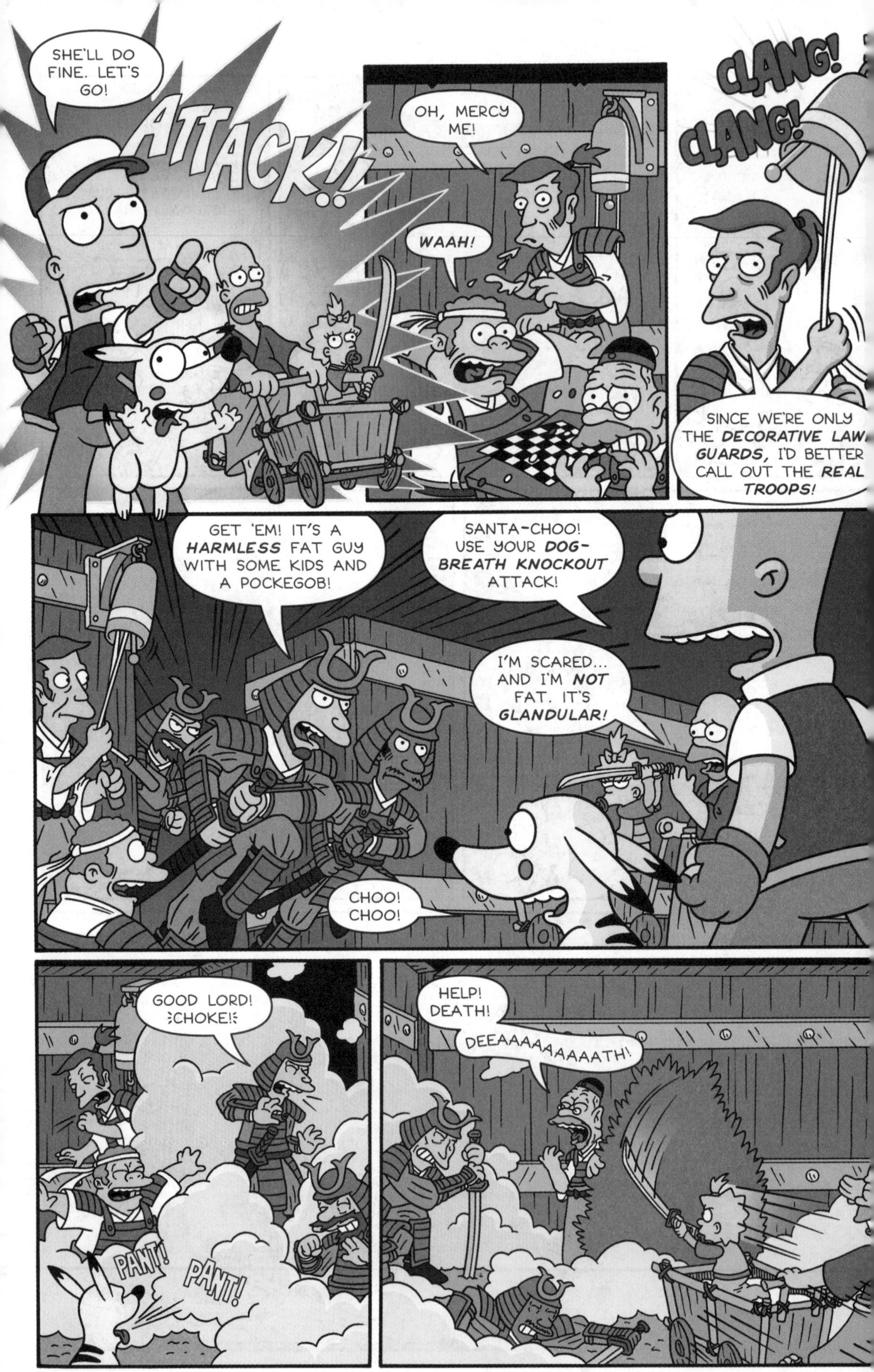
SHE'LL DO FINE. LET'S GO!
ATTACK!!
OH, MERCY ME!
WAAH!
CLANG!
CLANG!
SINCE WE'RE ONLY THE DECORATIVE LAW GUARDS, I'D BETTER CALL OUT THE REAL TROOPS!
GET 'EM! IT'S A HARMLESS FAT GUY WITH SOME KIDS AND A POCKEGOB!
SANTA-CHOO! USE YOUR DOG-BREATH KNOCKOUT ATTACK!
I'M SCARED... AND I'M NOT FAT. IT'S GLANDULAR!
CHOO! CHOO!
GOOD LORD! CHOKE!
PANT!
PANT!
HELP! DEATH!
DEEAAAAAAAAAATH!

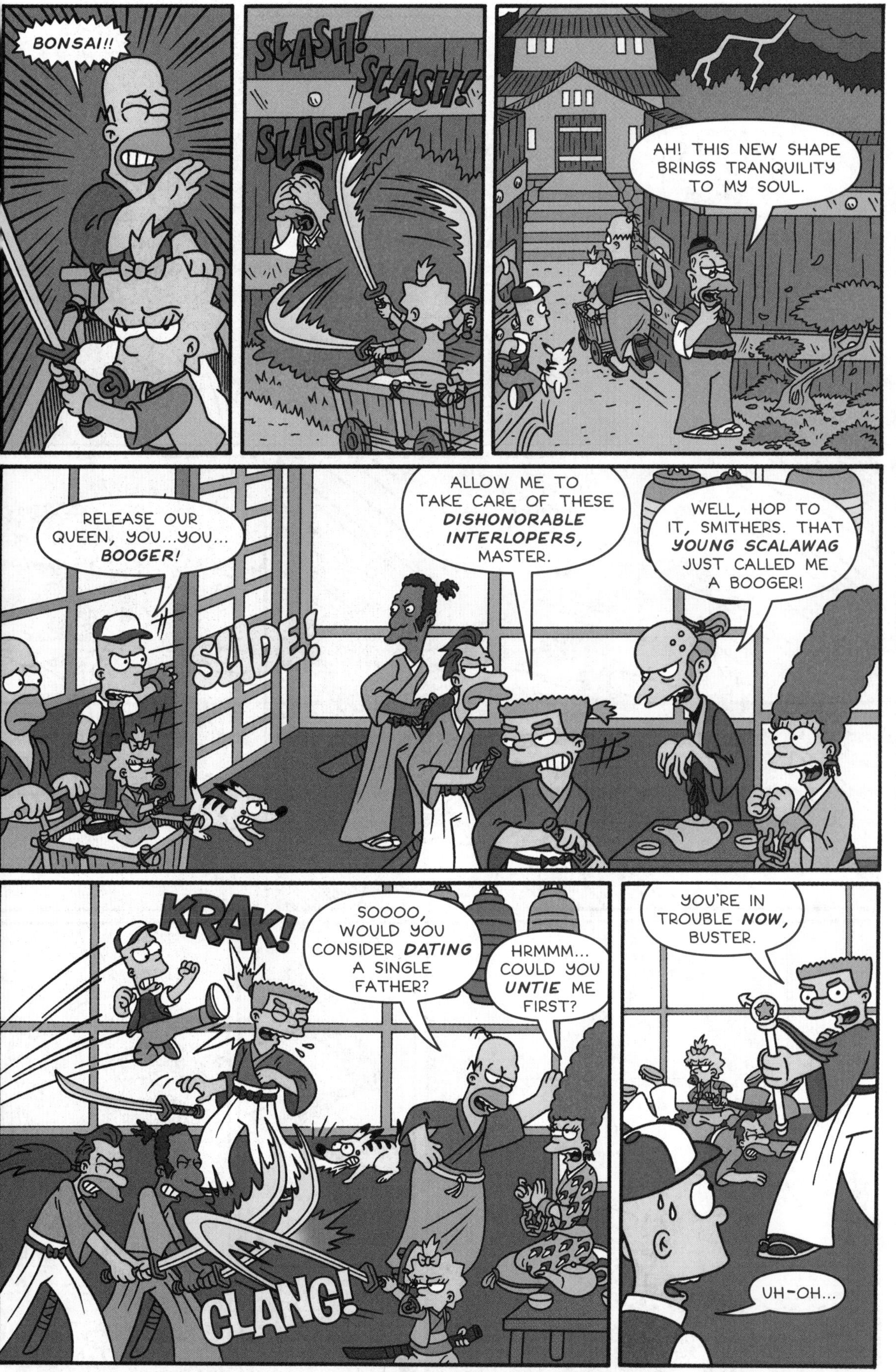
BONSAI!!
SLASH! SLASH!
SLASH!
AH! THIS NEW SHAPE BRINGS TRANQUILITY TO MY SOUL.
RELEASE OUR QUEEN, YOU...YOU... BOOGER!
SLIDE!
ALLOW ME TO TAKE CARE OF THESE DISHONORABLE INTERLOPERS, MASTER.
WELL, HOP TO IT, SMITHERS. THAT YOUNG SCALAWAG JUST CALLED ME A BOOGER!
KRAK!
SOOOO, WOULD YOU CONSIDER DATING A SINGLE FATHER?
HRMMM... COULD YOU UNTIE ME FIRST?
CLANG!
YOU'RE IN TROUBLE NOW, BUSTER.
UH-OH...

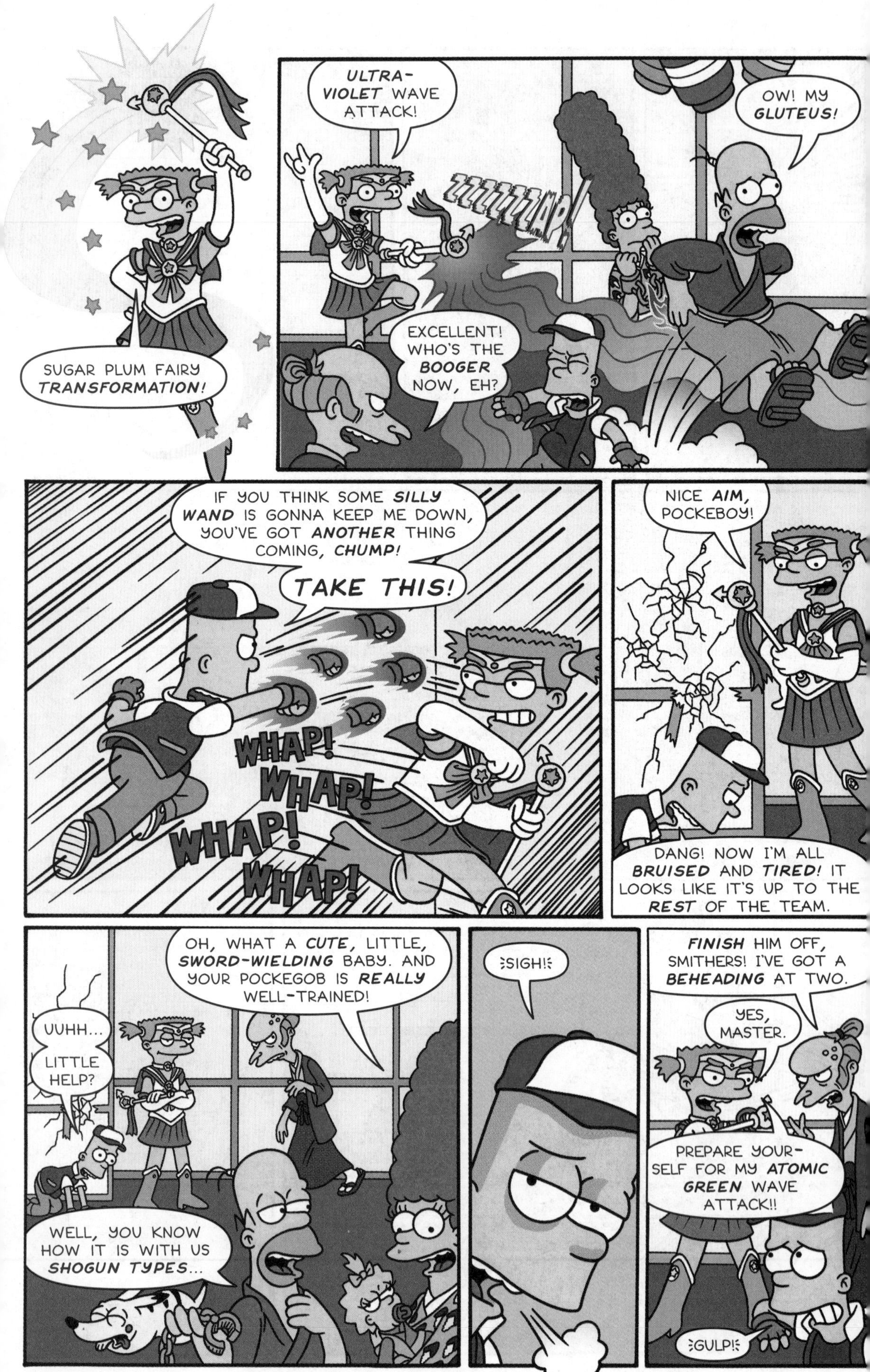
SUGAR PLUM FAIRY TRANSFORMATION!
ULTRA-VIOLET WAVE ATTACK!
ZZZZZZAP!
OW! MY GLUTEUS!
EXCELLENT! WHO'S THE BOOGER NOW, EH?
IF YOU THINK SOME SILLY WAND IS GONNA KEEP ME DOWN, YOU'VE GOT ANOTHER THING COMING, CHUMP!
TAKE THIS!
WHAP! WHAP! WHAP! WHAP!
NICE AIM, POCKEBOY!
DANG! NOW I'M ALL BRUISED AND TIRED! IT LOOKS LIKE IT'S UP TO THE REST OF THE TEAM.
OH, WHAT A CUTE, LITTLE, SWORD-WIELDING BABY. AND YOUR POCKEGOB IS REALLY WELL-TRAINED!
UUHH... LITTLE HELP?
WELL, YOU KNOW HOW IT IS WITH US SHOGUN TYPES...
SIGH!
FINISH HIM OFF, SMITHERS! I'VE GOT A BEHEADING AT TWO.
YES, MASTER.
PREPARE YOURSELF FOR MY ATOMIC GREEN WAVE ATTACK!!
GULP!

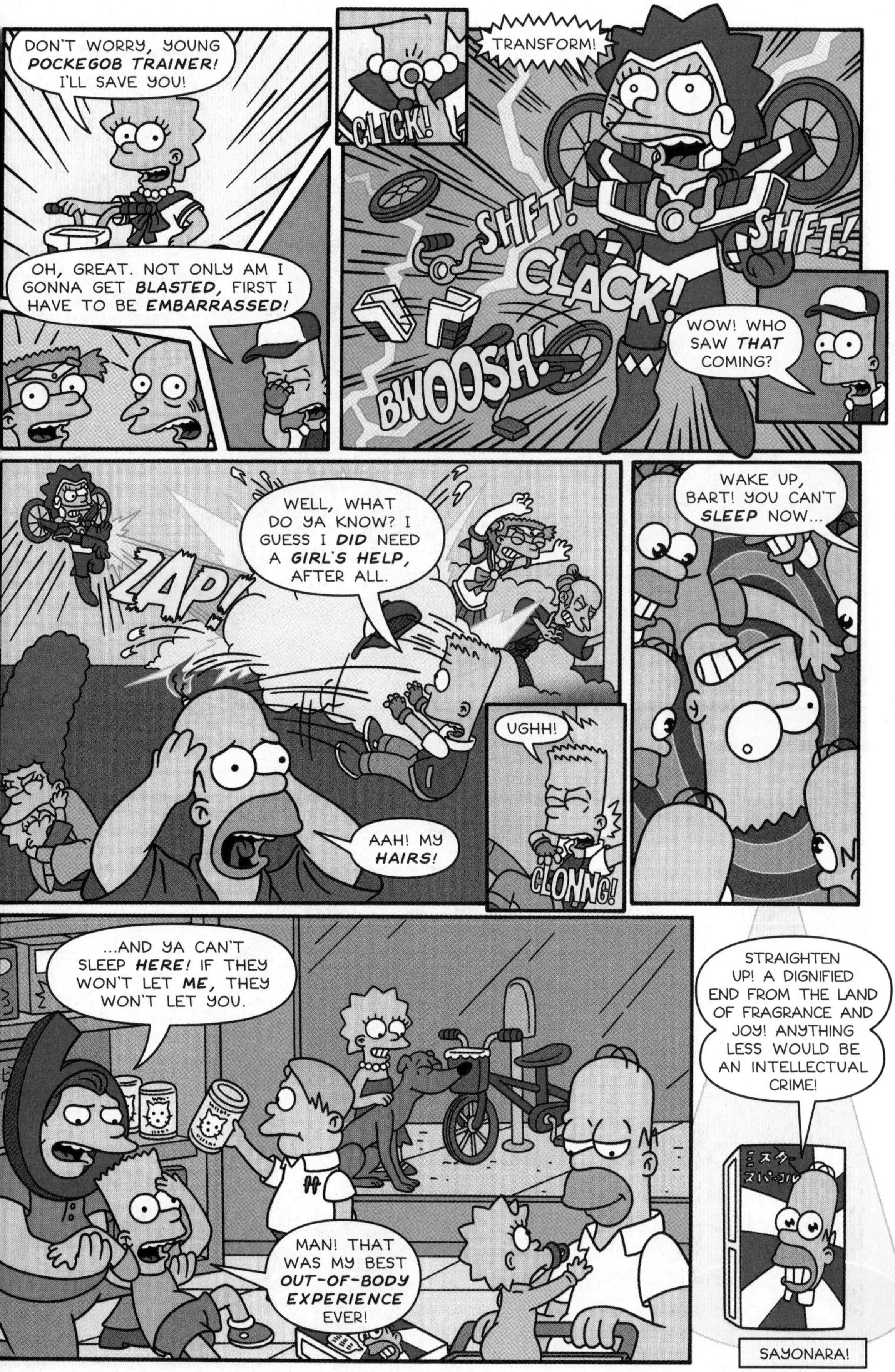
DON'T WORRY, YOUNG ***POCKEGOB TRAINER!*** I'LL SAVE YOU!
OH, GREAT. NOT ONLY AM I GONNA GET ***BLASTED,*** FIRST I HAVE TO BE ***EMBARRASSED!***
CLICK!
TRANSFORM!
SHFT!
CLACK!
SHFT!
BWOOSH!
WOW! WHO SAW ***THAT*** COMING?
ZAP!
WELL, WHAT DO YA KNOW? I GUESS I ***DID*** NEED A ***GIRL'S HELP,*** AFTER ALL.
AAH! MY ***HAIRS!***
UGHH!
CLONNG!
WAKE UP, BART! YOU CAN'T ***SLEEP*** NOW...
...AND YA CAN'T SLEEP ***HERE!*** IF THEY WON'T LET ***ME,*** THEY WON'T LET YOU.
MAN! THAT WAS MY BEST ***OUT-OF-BODY EXPERIENCE*** EVER!
STRAIGHTEN UP! A DIGNIFIED END FROM THE LAND OF FRAGRANCE AND JOY! ANYTHING LESS WOULD BE AN INTELLECTUAL CRIME!
ミスター スパーコル
SAYONARA!

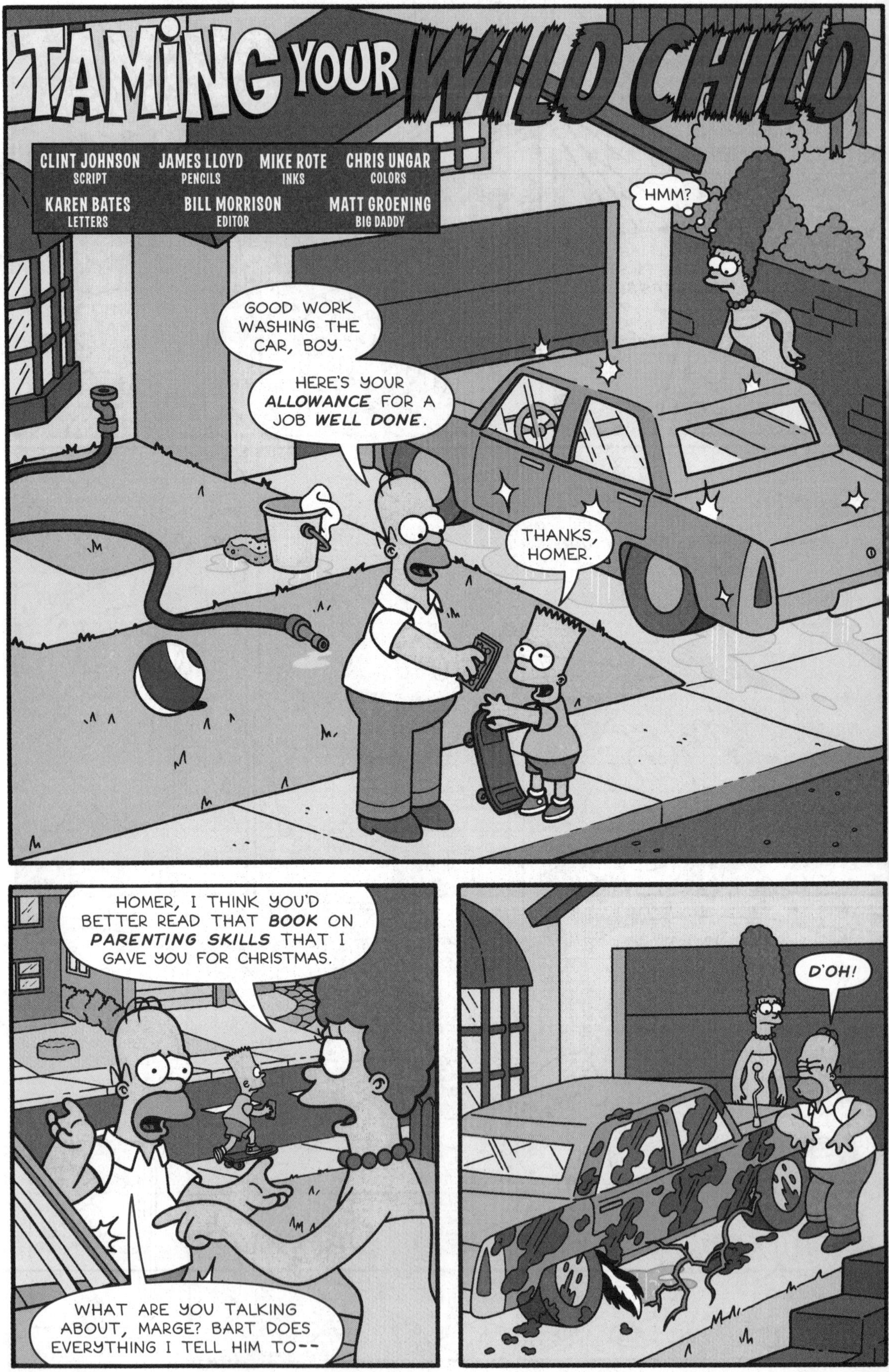
TAMING YOUR WILD CHILD
CLINT JOHNSON SCRIPT
JAMES LLOYD PENCILS
MIKE ROTE INKS
CHRIS UNGAR COLORS
KAREN BATES LETTERS
BILL MORRISON EDITOR
MATT GROENING BIG DADDY
HMM?
GOOD WORK WASHING THE CAR, BOY.
HERE'S YOUR ALLOWANCE FOR A JOB WELL DONE.
THANKS, HOMER.
HOMER, I THINK YOU'D BETTER READ THAT BOOK ON PARENTING SKILLS THAT I GAVE YOU FOR CHRISTMAS.
WHAT ARE YOU TALKING ABOUT, MARGE? BART DOES EVERYTHING I TELL HIM TO--
D'OH!

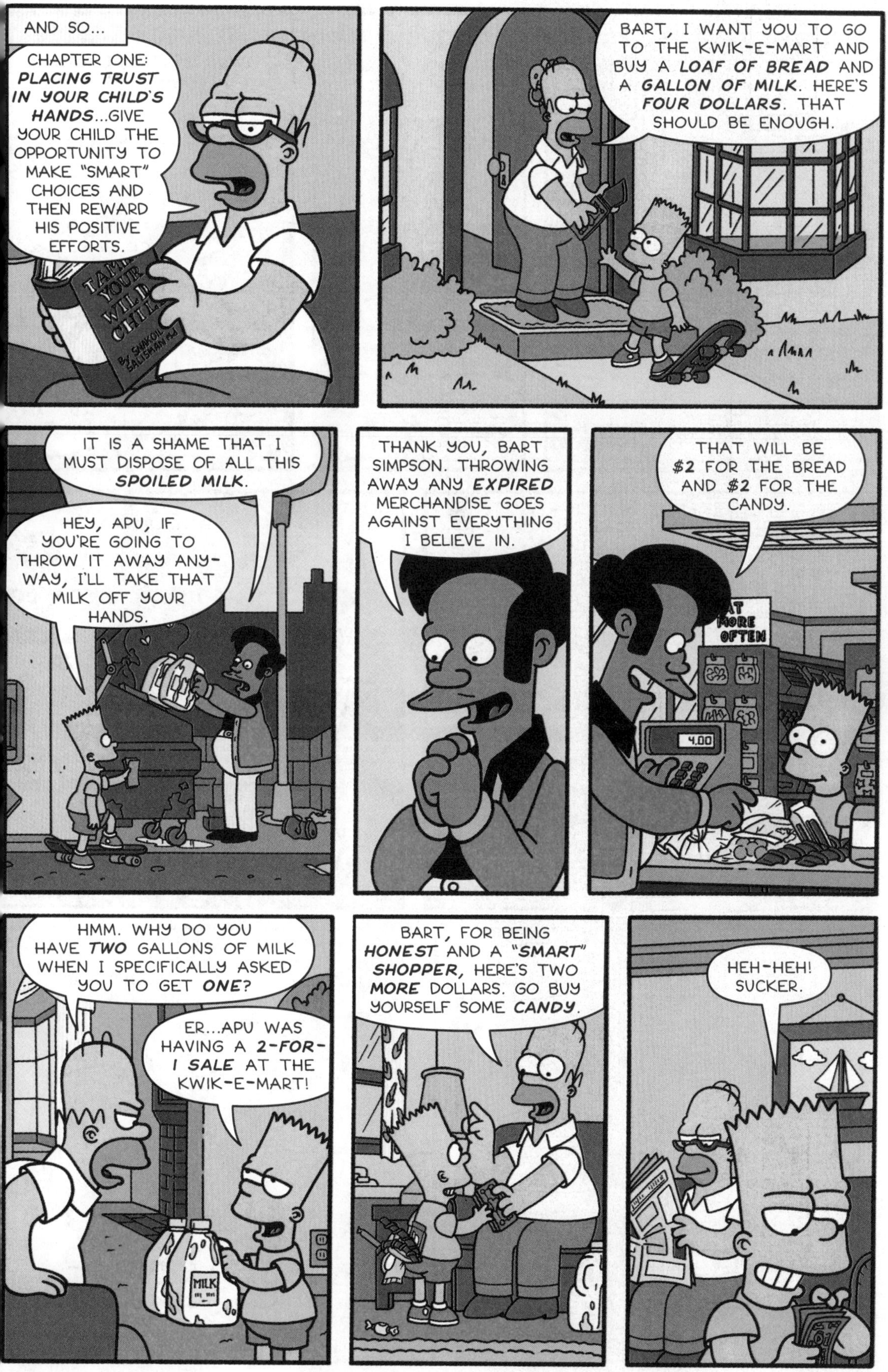
AND SO...
CHAPTER ONE: PLACING TRUST IN YOUR CHILD'S HANDS...GIVE YOUR CHILD THE OPPORTUNITY TO MAKE "SMART" CHOICES AND THEN REWARD HIS POSITIVE EFFORTS.
BART, I WANT YOU TO GO TO THE KWIK-E-MART AND BUY A LOAF OF BREAD AND A GALLON OF MILK. HERE'S FOUR DOLLARS. THAT SHOULD BE ENOUGH.
IT IS A SHAME THAT I MUST DISPOSE OF ALL THIS SPOILED MILK.
HEY, APU, IF YOU'RE GOING TO THROW IT AWAY ANY-WAY, I'LL TAKE THAT MILK OFF YOUR HANDS.
THANK YOU, BART SIMPSON. THROWING AWAY ANY EXPIRED MERCHANDISE GOES AGAINST EVERYTHING I BELIEVE IN.
THAT WILL BE $2 FOR THE BREAD AND $2 FOR THE CANDY.
HMM. WHY DO YOU HAVE TWO GALLONS OF MILK WHEN I SPECIFICALLY ASKED YOU TO GET ONE?
ER...APU WAS HAVING A 2-FOR-1 SALE AT THE KWIK-E-MART!
BART, FOR BEING HONEST AND A "SMART" SHOPPER, HERE'S TWO MORE DOLLARS. GO BUY YOURSELF SOME CANDY.
HEH-HEH! SUCKER.

"CHAPTER TWO: *USING REVERSE PSYCHOLOGY*...WHEN YOUR CHILD MAKES OUTLANDISH THREATS, GO ALONG WITH HIM AND HE WILL SOON GIVE UP THE CHARADE."

FOR THE LAST TIME, BART! WE ARE *NOT* GOING TO THE *CIRCUS*!

FINE, IF YOU WON'T TAKE ME, I'LL *RUN AWAY* AND *JOIN THE CIRCUS*!

I'LL HANDLE THIS! GO AHEAD AND JOIN THE CIRCUS, BART. I'LL EVEN *HELP* YOU!

WHA--!

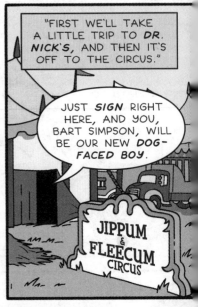

"FIRST WE'LL TAKE A LITTLE TRIP TO *DR. NICK'S*, AND THEN IT'S OFF TO THE CIRCUS."

JUST *SIGN* RIGHT HERE, AND YOU, BART SIMPSON, WILL BE OUR NEW *DOG-FACED BOY*.

JIPPUM & FLEECUM CIRCUS

EXCELLENT! YOU START *TOMORROW* AT 10 A.M. SHARP!

10 A.M.? I CAN'T, I...UH...ER...HAVE *SCHOOL*!

SCHOOL?! AREN'T YOU *OVER* 18?

NO.

DEWEY JIPPUM

THEN *YOU*, SIR, ARE RESPONSIBLE FOR THIS *LIFETIME CONTRACT*!

BUT...

DEWEY JIPPUM

HOWEVER, IF YOU BUY A LIFETIME *FAMILY MEMBERSHIP* TO THE JIPPUM & FLEECUM CIRCUS, I'LL *FORGIVE* THE TERMS OF THE CONTRACT.

LIFFTIM RACT

IT'S A *DEAL*!

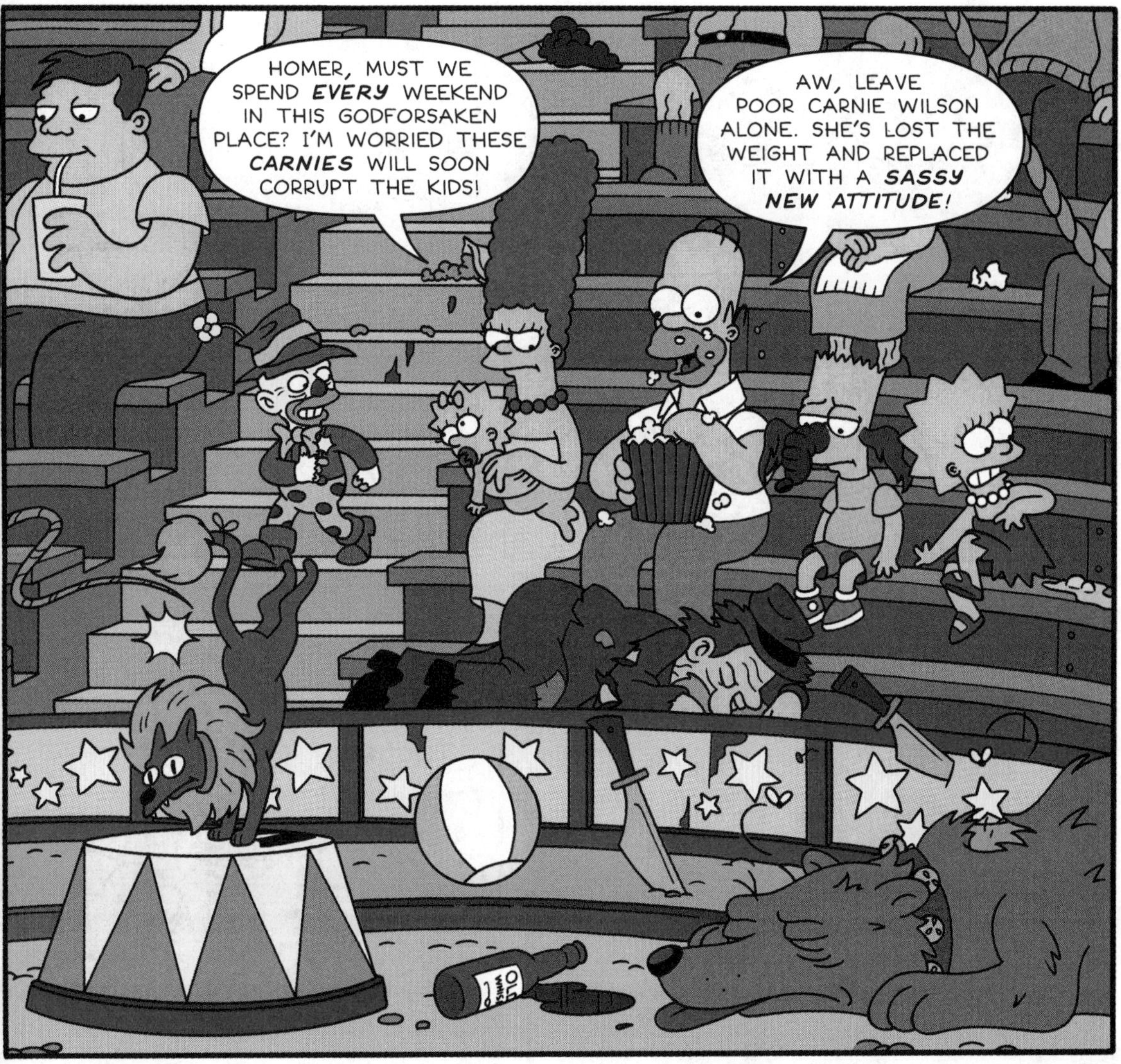
HOMER, MUST WE SPEND **EVERY** WEEKEND IN THIS GODFORSAKEN PLACE? I'M WORRIED THESE **CARNIES** WILL SOON CORRUPT THE KIDS!
AW, LEAVE POOR CARNIE WILSON ALONE. SHE'S LOST THE WEIGHT AND REPLACED IT WITH A ***SASSY NEW ATTITUDE!***

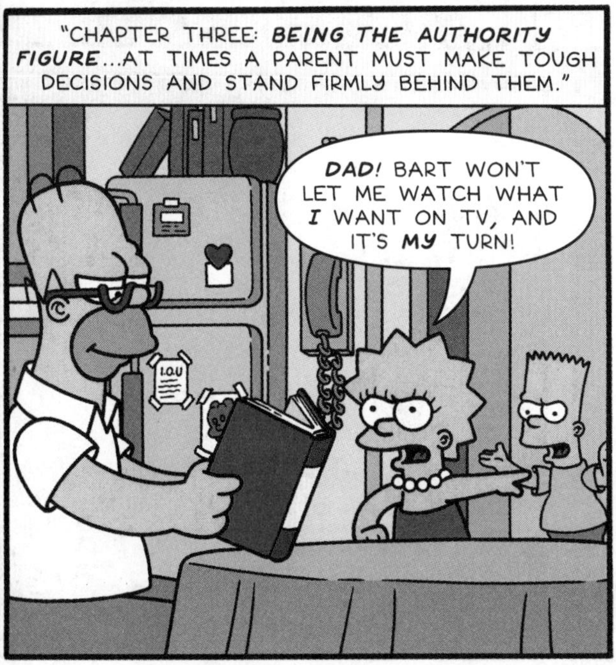
"CHAPTER THREE: ***BEING THE AUTHORITY FIGURE***...AT TIMES A PARENT MUST MAKE TOUGH DECISIONS AND STAND FIRMLY BEHIND THEM."
DAD! BART WON'T LET ME WATCH WHAT ***I*** WANT ON TV, AND IT'S ***MY*** TURN!

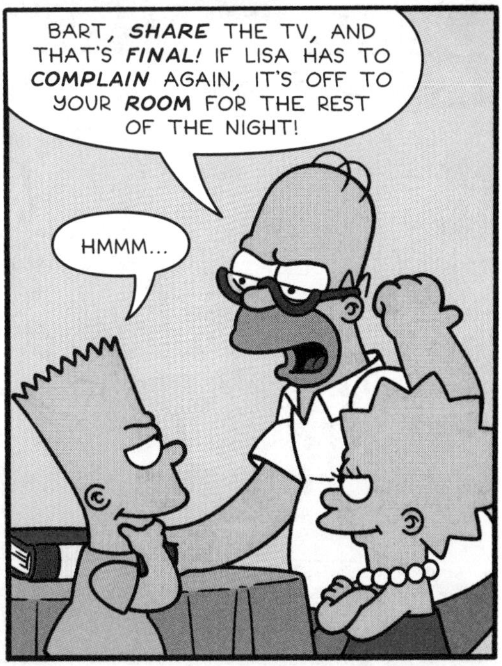
BART, ***SHARE*** THE TV, AND THAT'S ***FINAL!*** IF LISA HAS TO ***COMPLAIN*** AGAIN, IT'S OFF TO YOUR ***ROOM*** FOR THE REST OF THE NIGHT!
HMMM...

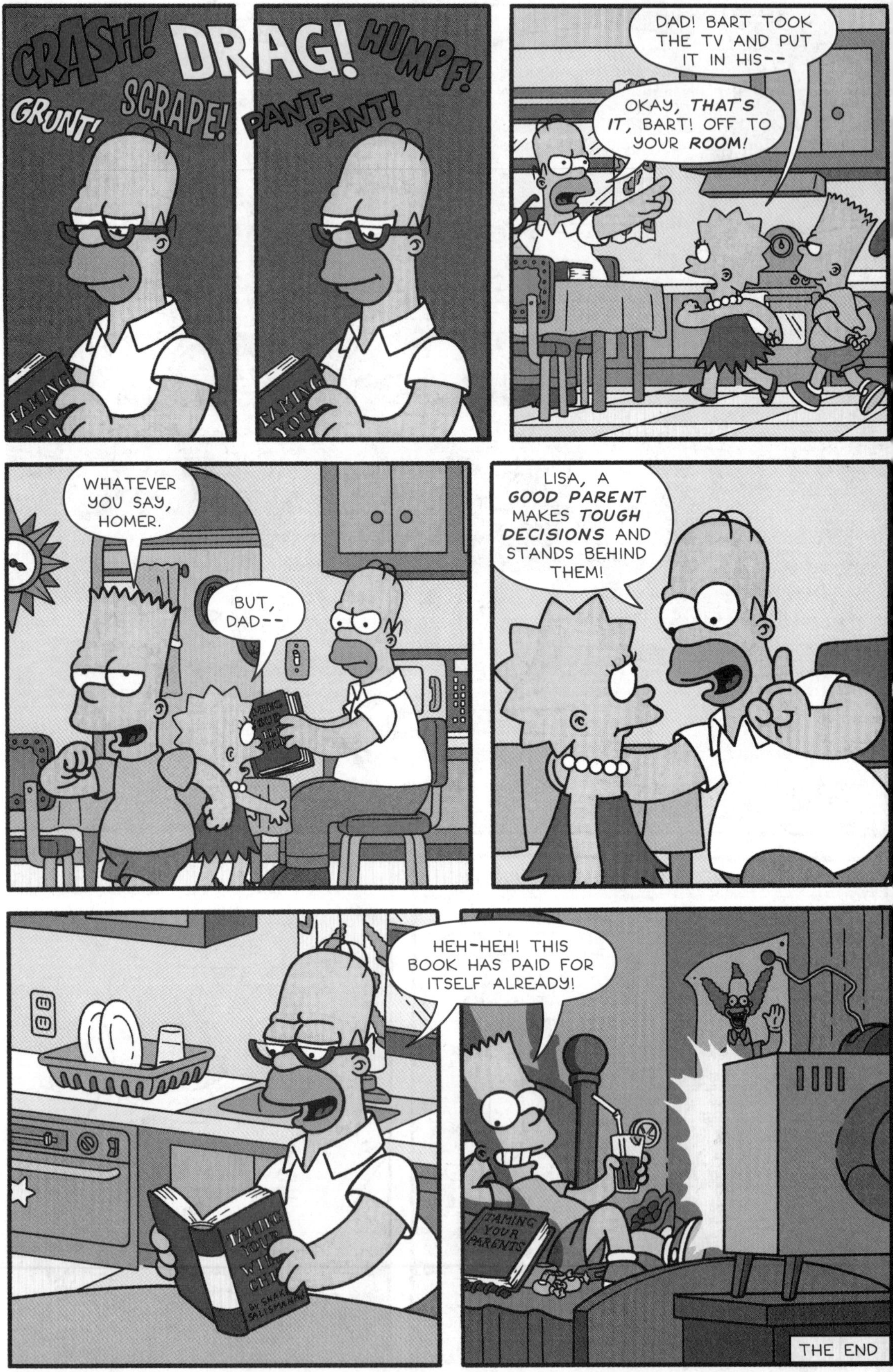
CRASH!
GRUNT!
SCRAPE!
DRAG!
HUMPF!
PANT-PANT!
DAD! BART TOOK THE TV AND PUT IT IN HIS--
OKAY, THAT'S IT, BART! OFF TO YOUR ROOM!
WHATEVER YOU SAY, HOMER.
BUT, DAD--
LISA, A GOOD PARENT MAKES TOUGH DECISIONS AND STANDS BEHIND THEM!
HEH-HEH! THIS BOOK HAS PAID FOR ITSELF ALREADY!
TAMING YOUR PARENTS
THE END

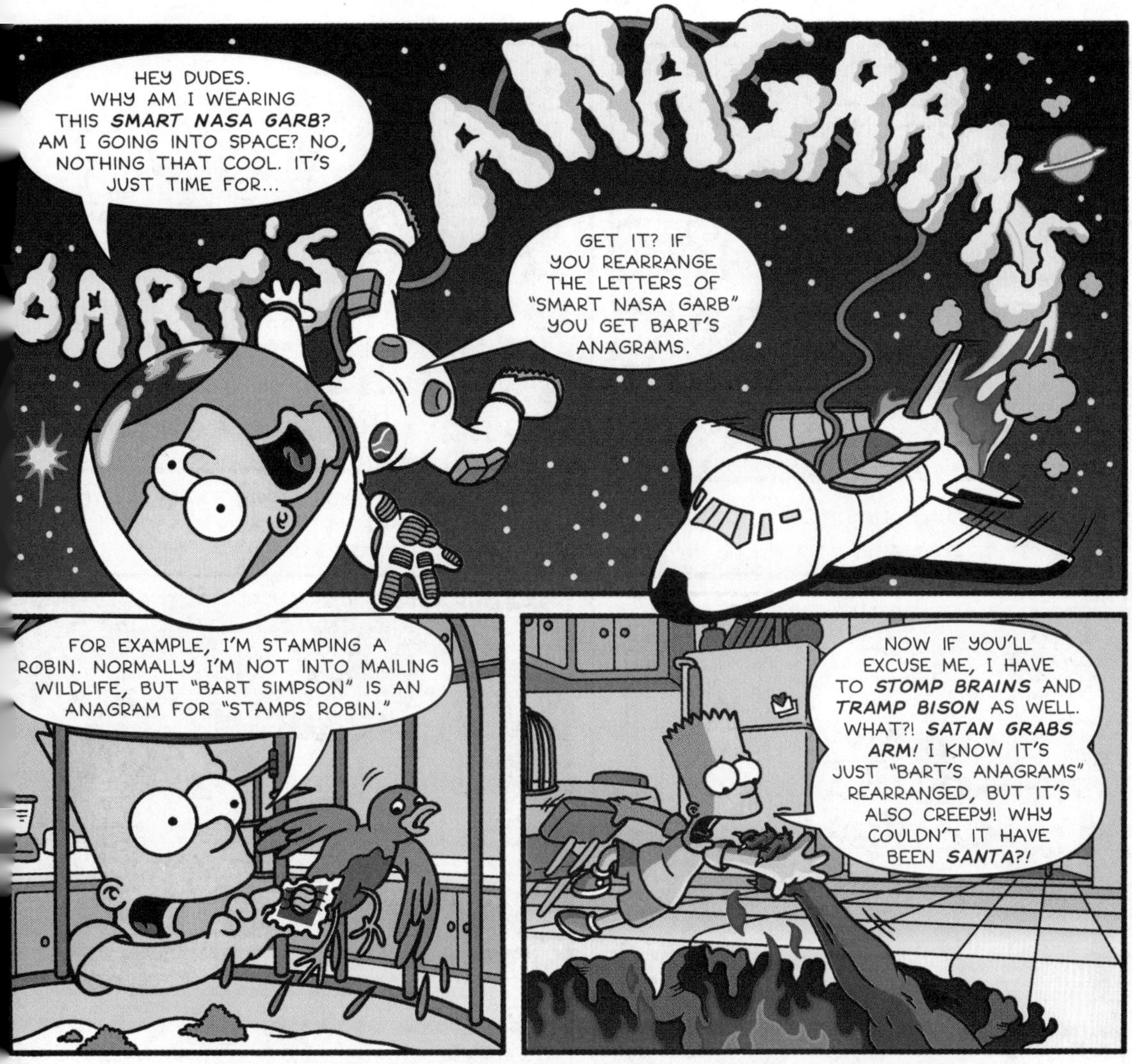

HEY DUDES. WHY AM I WEARING THIS SMART NASA GARB? AM I GOING INTO SPACE? NO, NOTHING THAT COOL. IT'S JUST TIME FOR...
BART'S ANAGRAMS
GET IT? IF YOU REARRANGE THE LETTERS OF "SMART NASA GARB" YOU GET BART'S ANAGRAMS.
FOR EXAMPLE, I'M STAMPING A ROBIN. NORMALLY I'M NOT INTO MAILING WILDLIFE, BUT "BART SIMPSON" IS AN ANAGRAM FOR "STAMPS ROBIN."
NOW IF YOU'LL EXCUSE ME, I HAVE TO STOMP BRAINS AND TRAMP BISON AS WELL. WHAT?! SATAN GRABS ARM! I KNOW IT'S JUST "BART'S ANAGRAMS" REARRANGED, BUT IT'S ALSO CREEPY! WHY COULDN'T IT HAVE BEEN SANTA?!

"HERE'S HOW IT WORKS: WITH EACH OF THE PICTURES BELOW, REARRANGE THE LETTERS OF THE PERSON'S NAME TO FIGURE OUT WHAT THEY'RE DOING."

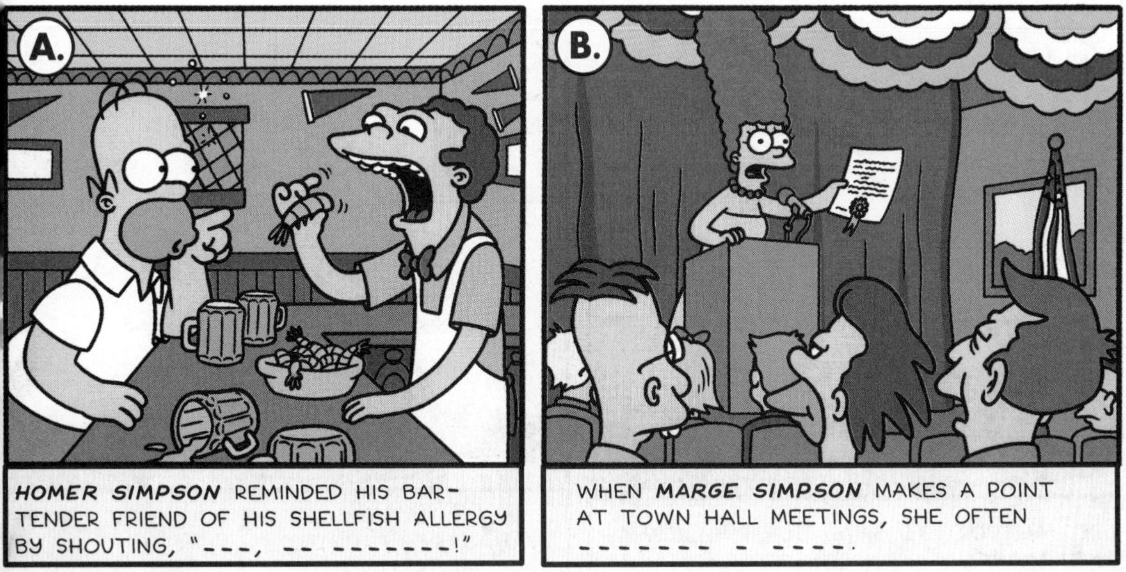

A.
HOMER SIMPSON REMINDED HIS BARTENDER FRIEND OF HIS SHELLFISH ALLERGY BY SHOUTING, "---, -- -------!"
B.
WHEN MARGE SIMPSON MAKES A POINT AT TOWN HALL MEETINGS, SHE OFTEN ------- - ----.

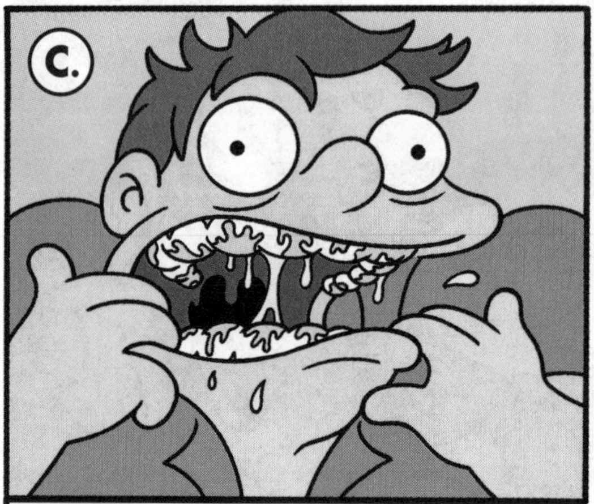
C.

BARNEY GUMBLE HAS TEETH COVERED IN ------ ------.

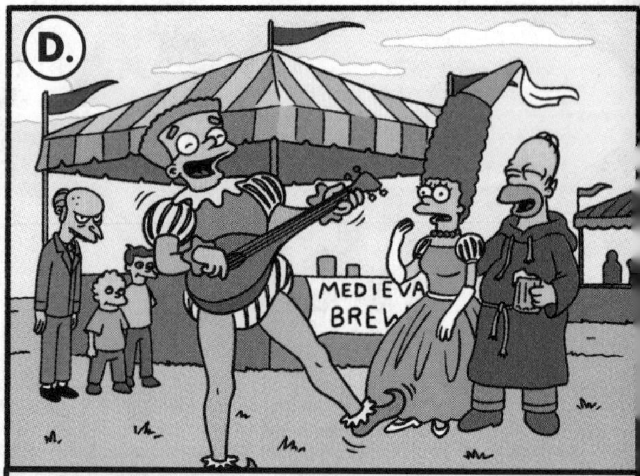
D.
MEDIEVA
BREW

AT THE SPRINGFIELDE RENAISSANCE FAIRE, ***WAYLON SMITHERS*** ALWAYS PLAYS - ----- --------.

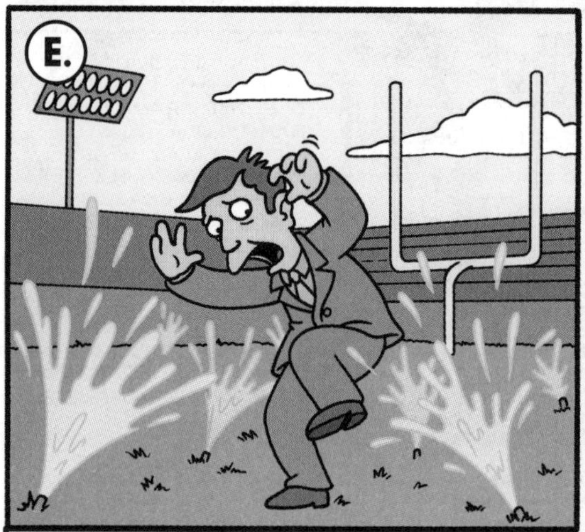
E.

PRINCIPAL SKINNER GOT CAUGHT ON THE FOOTBALL FIELD -- --------- -----.

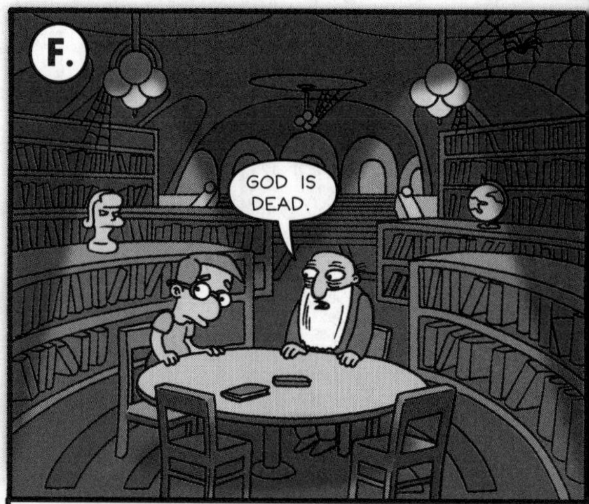
F.
GOD IS DEAD.

MILHOUSE VAN HOUTEN DID NOT ENJOY HIS ENCOUNTER WITH THE ---------- -------.

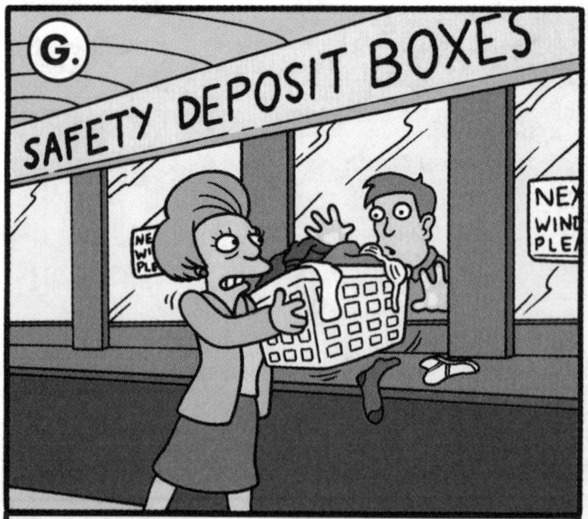
G.
SAFETY DEPOSIT BOXES

IN AN EFFORT TO SAVE CLOTHING, ***EDNA KRABAPPEL*** ------ -------.

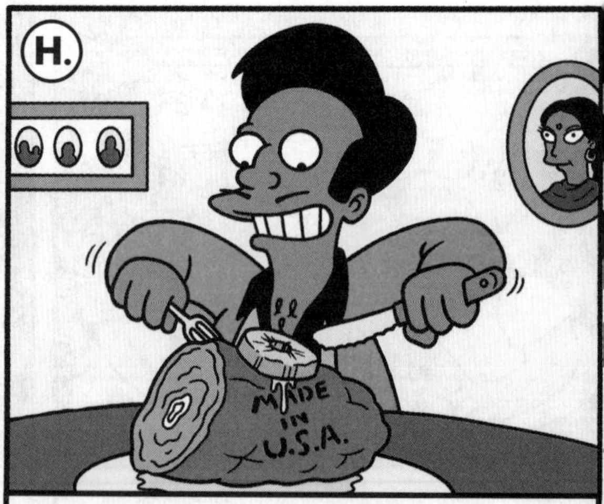
H.
MADE IN U.S.A.

LIKE ALL NATURALIZED CITIZENS, ***APU NAHASAPEEMAPETILON*** LIKES TO --- --------- -- - --- ---.

A. MOE, NO SHRIMPS!, B. SPRINGS A MEMO, C. GRUBBY ENAMEL, D. A SHOWY MINSTREL, E. IN SPRINKLER PANIC, F. VOLUMINOUS HEATHEN, G. BANKED APPAREL, H. EAT PINEAPPLE ON A USA HAM.

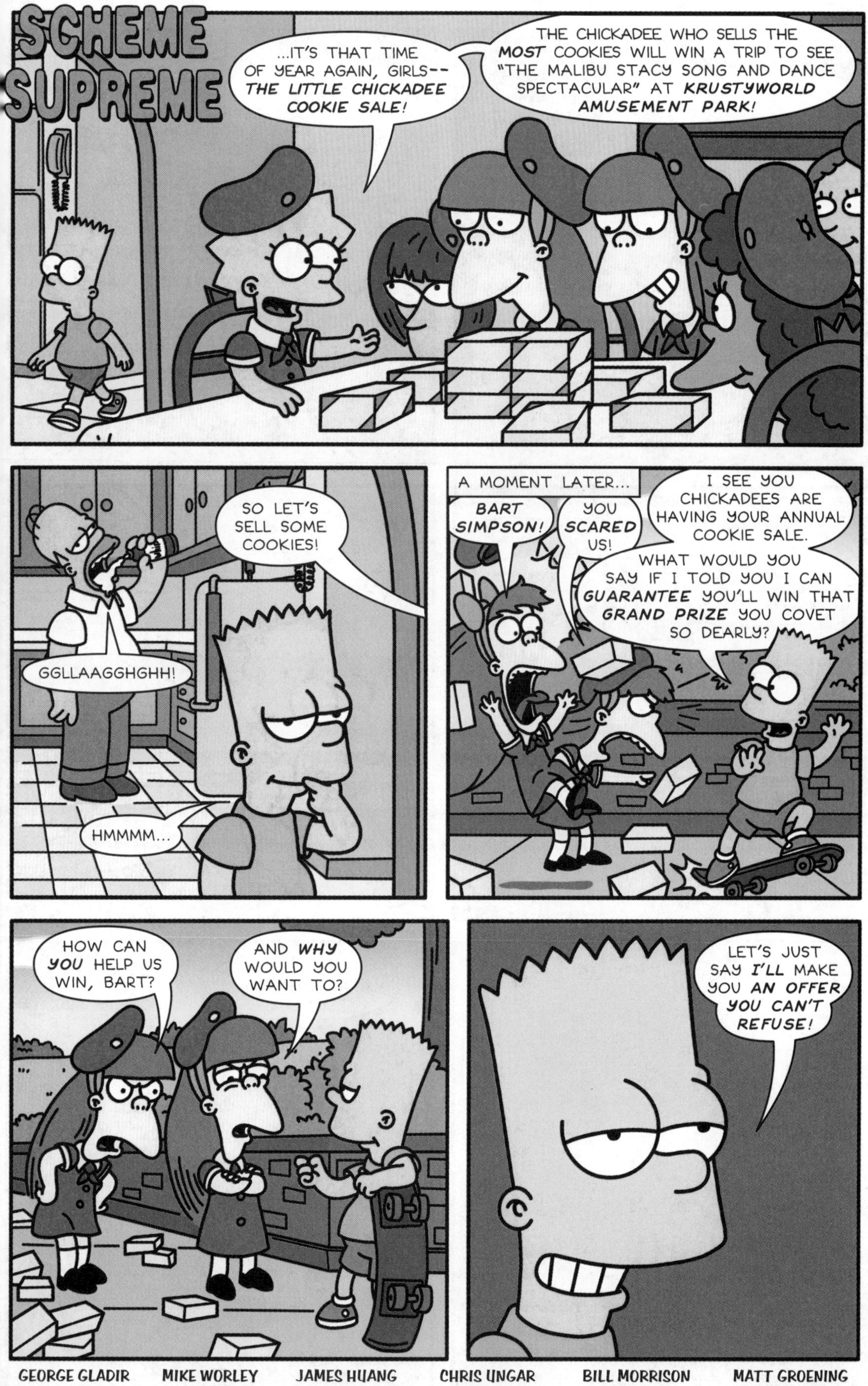
SCHEME SUPREME
...IT'S THAT TIME OF YEAR AGAIN, GIRLS-- THE LITTLE CHICKADEE COOKIE SALE!
THE CHICKADEE WHO SELLS THE MOST COOKIES WILL WIN A TRIP TO SEE "THE MALIBU STACY SONG AND DANCE SPECTACULAR" AT KRUSTYWORLD AMUSEMENT PARK!
SO LET'S SELL SOME COOKIES!
GGLLAAGGHGHH!
HMMMM...
A MOMENT LATER...
BART SIMPSON!
YOU SCARED US!
I SEE YOU CHICKADEES ARE HAVING YOUR ANNUAL COOKIE SALE.
WHAT WOULD YOU SAY IF I TOLD YOU I CAN GUARANTEE YOU'LL WIN THAT GRAND PRIZE YOU COVET SO DEARLY?
HOW CAN YOU HELP US WIN, BART?
AND WHY WOULD YOU WANT TO?
LET'S JUST SAY I'LL MAKE YOU AN OFFER YOU CAN'T REFUSE!

GEORGE GLADIR SCRIPT · MIKE WORLEY PENCILS · JAMES HUANG INKS · CHRIS UNGAR LETTERS/COLORS · BILL MORRISON EDITS · MATT GROENING THIN MINT ADDICT

THE NEXT DAY...

...AND WHY WOULD I LISTEN TO ANYTHING *YOU* HAVE TO SAY, BART?

BECAUSE I CAN SHOW YOU HOW TO WIN THAT COOKIE SALE CONTEST.

BUUUUT, IF YOU'D RATHER LET *SOMEONE ELSE* WIN...

NO! I'LL DO *ANYTHING* TO SEE THAT MALIBU STACY SHOW!

LET'S TALK TURKEY.

THAT AFTERNOON...

BUT WHY CAN'T YOU BUY ANY OF *MY* COOKIES, DAD? I WAS *COUNTING* ON YOU!

I'M *TAPPED OUT*, LISA!

I BOUGHT *EVERY LAST BOX* OF COOKIES FROM YOUR LITTLE CHICKADEE FRIENDS!

TOUGH LUCK THERE, LIS. I GUESS YOU SHOULD HAVE WORKED A LITTLE HARDER.

DING! DONG!

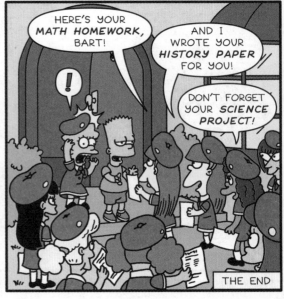

HERE'S YOUR *MATH HOMEWORK*, BART!

AND I WROTE YOUR *HISTORY PAPER* FOR YOU!

!

DON'T FORGET YOUR *SCIENCE PROJECT*!

THE END

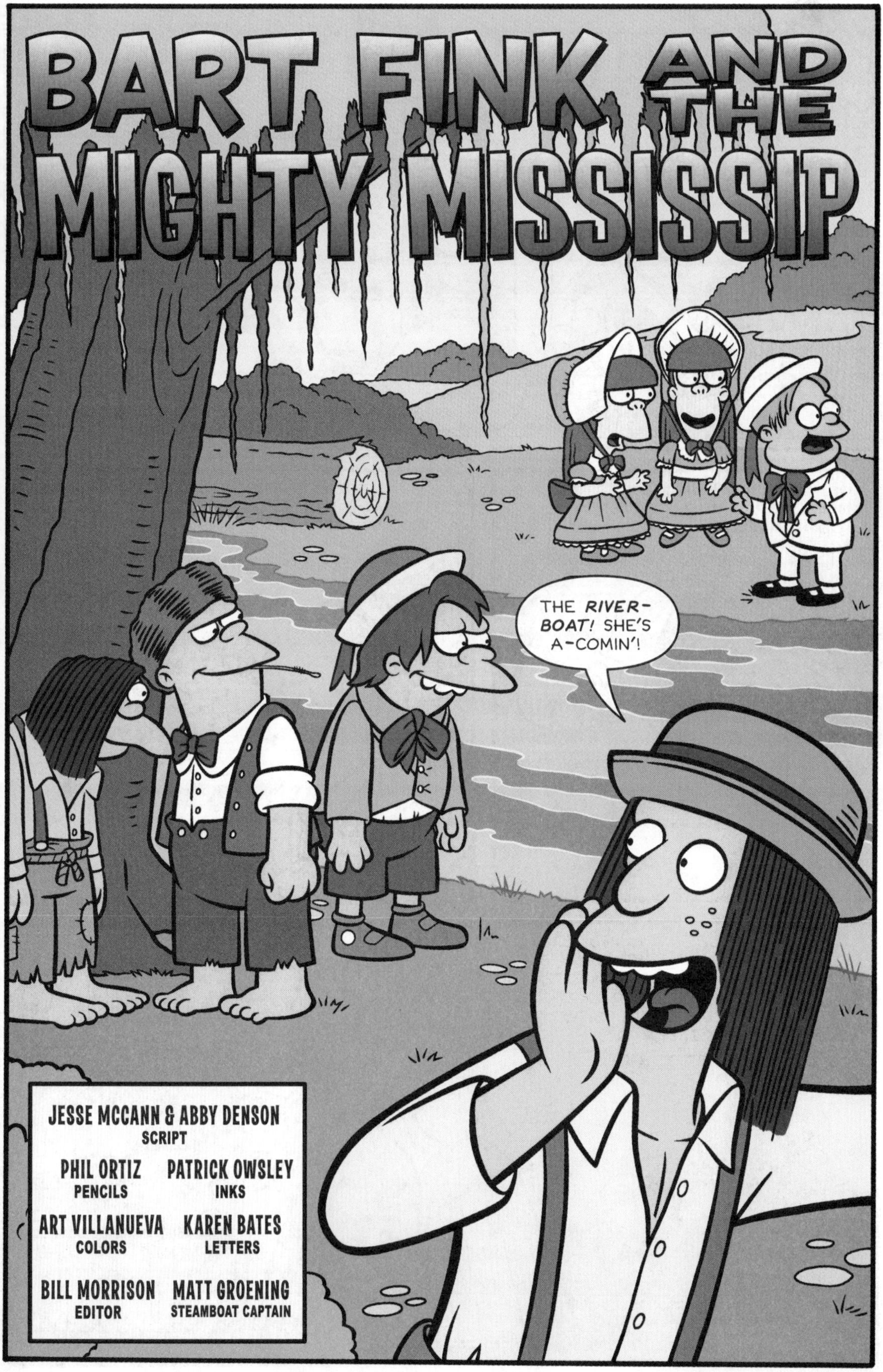
BART FINK AND THE MIGHTY MISSISSIP
THE RIVER-BOAT! SHE'S A-COMIN'!
JESSE MCCANN & ABBY DENSON
SCRIPT
PHIL ORTIZ
PENCILS
PATRICK OWSLEY
INKS
ART VILLANUEVA
COLORS
KAREN BATES
LETTERS
BILL MORRISON
EDITOR
MATT GROENING
STEAMBOAT CAPTAIN

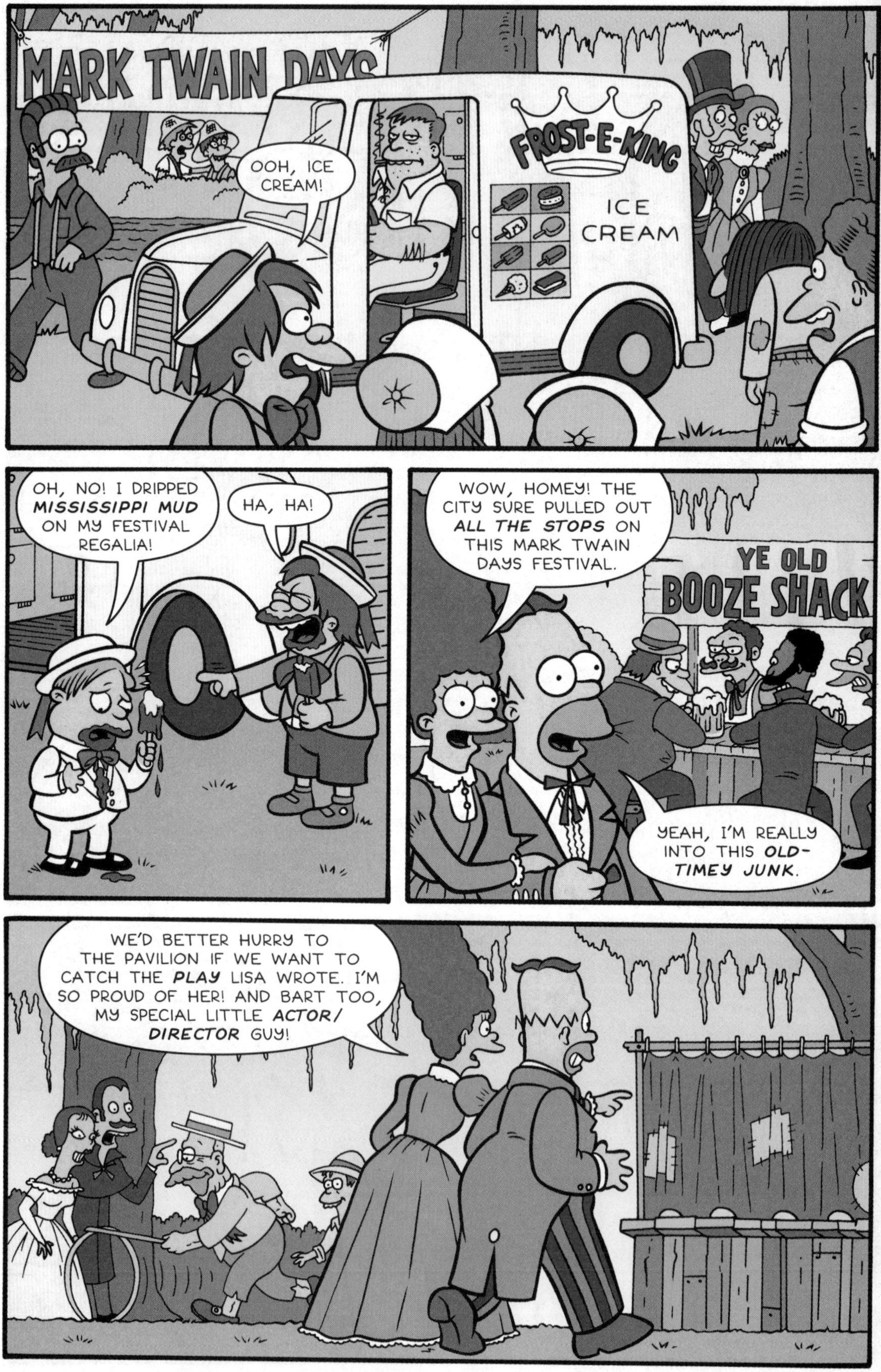
MARK TWAIN DAYS
FROST-E-KING
ICE CREAM
OOH, ICE CREAM!
OH, NO! I DRIPPED **MISSISSIPPI MUD** ON MY FESTIVAL REGALIA!
HA, HA!
WOW, HOMEY! THE CITY SURE PULLED OUT **ALL THE STOPS** ON THIS MARK TWAIN DAYS FESTIVAL.
YE OLD BOOZE SHACK
YEAH, I'M REALLY INTO THIS **OLD-TIMEY JUNK**.
WE'D BETTER HURRY TO THE PAVILION IF WE WANT TO CATCH THE **PLAY** LISA WROTE. I'M SO PROUD OF HER! AND BART TOO, MY SPECIAL LITTLE **ACTOR/ DIRECTOR** GUY!

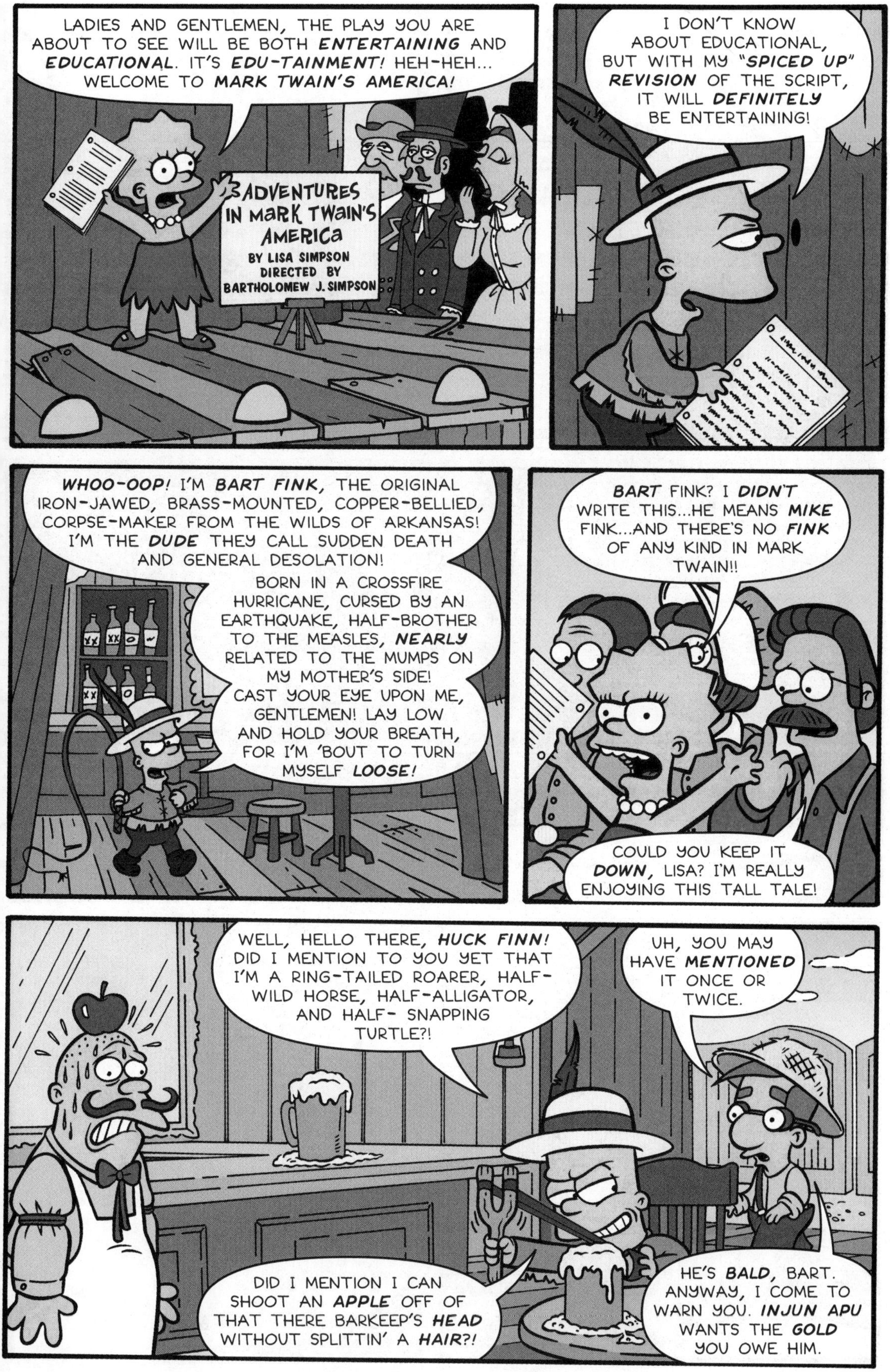
LADIES AND GENTLEMEN, THE PLAY YOU ARE ABOUT TO SEE WILL BE BOTH ENTERTAINING AND EDUCATIONAL. IT'S EDU-TAINMENT! HEH-HEH... WELCOME TO MARK TWAIN'S AMERICA!
ADVENTURES IN MARK TWAIN'S AMERICA BY LISA SIMPSON DIRECTED BY BARTHOLOMEW J. SIMPSON
I DON'T KNOW ABOUT EDUCATIONAL, BUT WITH MY "SPICED UP" REVISION OF THE SCRIPT, IT WILL DEFINITELY BE ENTERTAINING!
WHOO-OOP! I'M BART FINK, THE ORIGINAL IRON-JAWED, BRASS-MOUNTED, COPPER-BELLIED, CORPSE-MAKER FROM THE WILDS OF ARKANSAS! I'M THE DUDE THEY CALL SUDDEN DEATH AND GENERAL DESOLATION!
BORN IN A CROSSFIRE HURRICANE, CURSED BY AN EARTHQUAKE, HALF-BROTHER TO THE MEASLES, NEARLY RELATED TO THE MUMPS ON MY MOTHER'S SIDE! CAST YOUR EYE UPON ME, GENTLEMEN! LAY LOW AND HOLD YOUR BREATH, FOR I'M 'BOUT TO TURN MYSELF LOOSE!
BART FINK? I DIDN'T WRITE THIS...HE MEANS MIKE FINK...AND THERE'S NO FINK OF ANY KIND IN MARK TWAIN!!
COULD YOU KEEP IT DOWN, LISA? I'M REALLY ENJOYING THIS TALL TALE!
WELL, HELLO THERE, HUCK FINN! DID I MENTION TO YOU YET THAT I'M A RING-TAILED ROARER, HALF-WILD HORSE, HALF-ALLIGATOR, AND HALF- SNAPPING TURTLE?!
UH, YOU MAY HAVE MENTIONED IT ONCE OR TWICE.
DID I MENTION I CAN SHOOT AN APPLE OFF OF THAT THERE BARKEEP'S HEAD WITHOUT SPLITTIN' A HAIR?!
HE'S BALD, BART. ANYWAY, I COME TO WARN YOU. INJUN APU WANTS THE GOLD YOU OWE HIM.

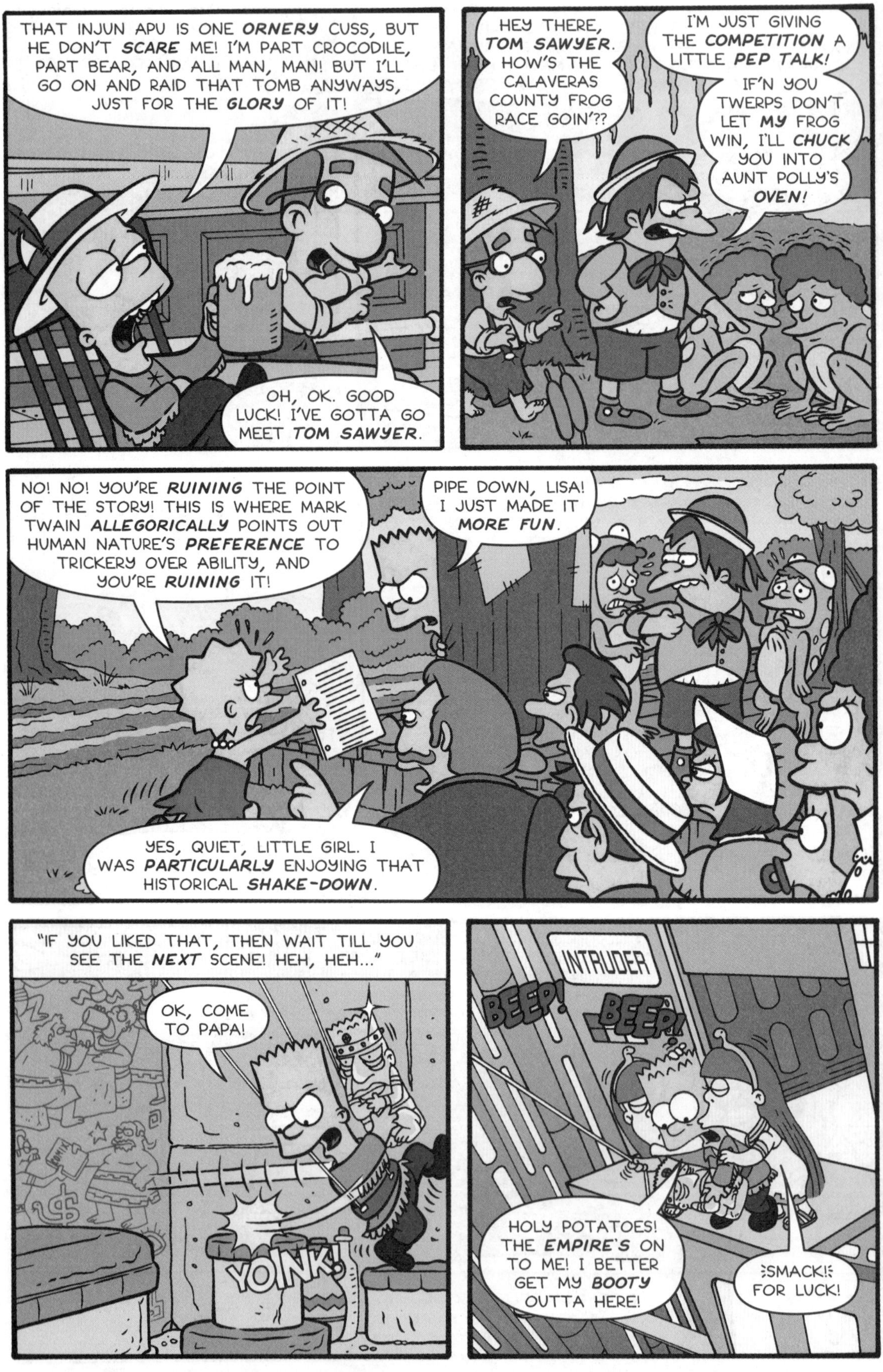
THAT INJUN APU IS ONE ORNERY CUSS, BUT HE DON'T SCARE ME! I'M PART CROCODILE, PART BEAR, AND ALL MAN, MAN! BUT I'LL GO ON AND RAID THAT TOMB ANYWAYS, JUST FOR THE GLORY OF IT!
OH, OK. GOOD LUCK! I'VE GOTTA GO MEET TOM SAWYER.
HEY THERE, TOM SAWYER. HOW'S THE CALAVERAS COUNTY FROG RACE GOIN'??
I'M JUST GIVING THE COMPETITION A LITTLE PEP TALK!
IF'N YOU TWERPS DON'T LET MY FROG WIN, I'LL CHUCK YOU INTO AUNT POLLY'S OVEN!
NO! NO! YOU'RE RUINING THE POINT OF THE STORY! THIS IS WHERE MARK TWAIN ALLEGORICALLY POINTS OUT HUMAN NATURE'S PREFERENCE TO TRICKERY OVER ABILITY, AND YOU'RE RUINING IT!
PIPE DOWN, LISA! I JUST MADE IT MORE FUN.
YES, QUIET, LITTLE GIRL. I WAS PARTICULARLY ENJOYING THAT HISTORICAL SHAKE-DOWN.
"IF YOU LIKED THAT, THEN WAIT TILL YOU SEE THE NEXT SCENE! HEH, HEH..."
OK, COME TO PAPA!
YOINK!
INTRUDER
BEEP! BEEP!
HOLY POTATOES! THE EMPIRE'S ON TO ME! I BETTER GET MY BOOTY OUTTA HERE!
SMACK! FOR LUCK!

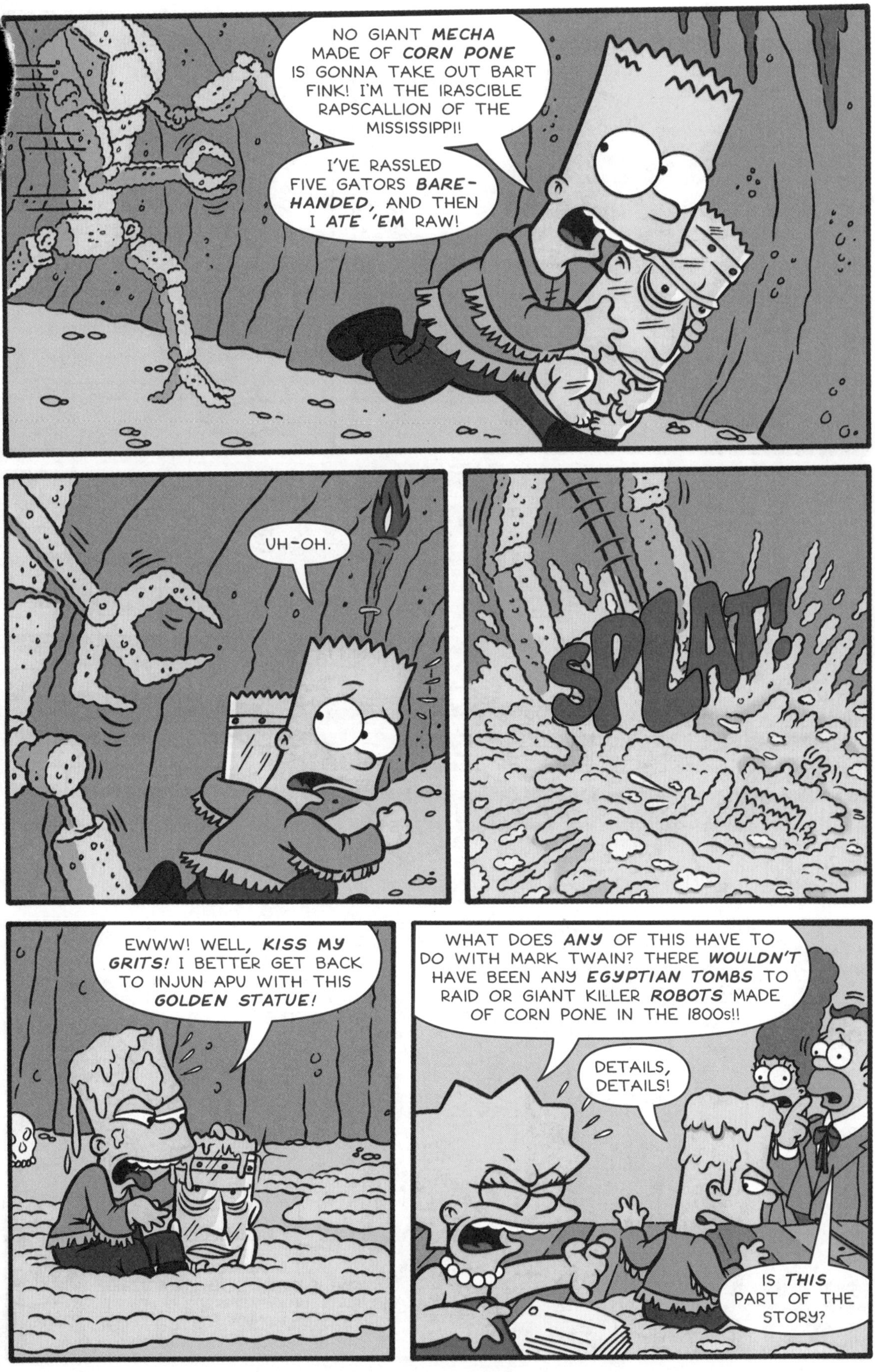
NO GIANT MECHA MADE OF CORN PONE IS GONNA TAKE OUT BART FINK! I'M THE IRASCIBLE RAPSCALLION OF THE MISSISSIPPI!
I'VE RASSLED FIVE GATORS BARE-HANDED, AND THEN I ATE 'EM RAW!
UH-OH.
SPLAT!
EWWW! WELL, KISS MY GRITS! I BETTER GET BACK TO INJUN APU WITH THIS GOLDEN STATUE!
WHAT DOES ANY OF THIS HAVE TO DO WITH MARK TWAIN? THERE WOULDN'T HAVE BEEN ANY EGYPTIAN TOMBS TO RAID OR GIANT KILLER ROBOTS MADE OF CORN PONE IN THE 1800s!!
DETAILS, DETAILS!
IS THIS PART OF THE STORY?

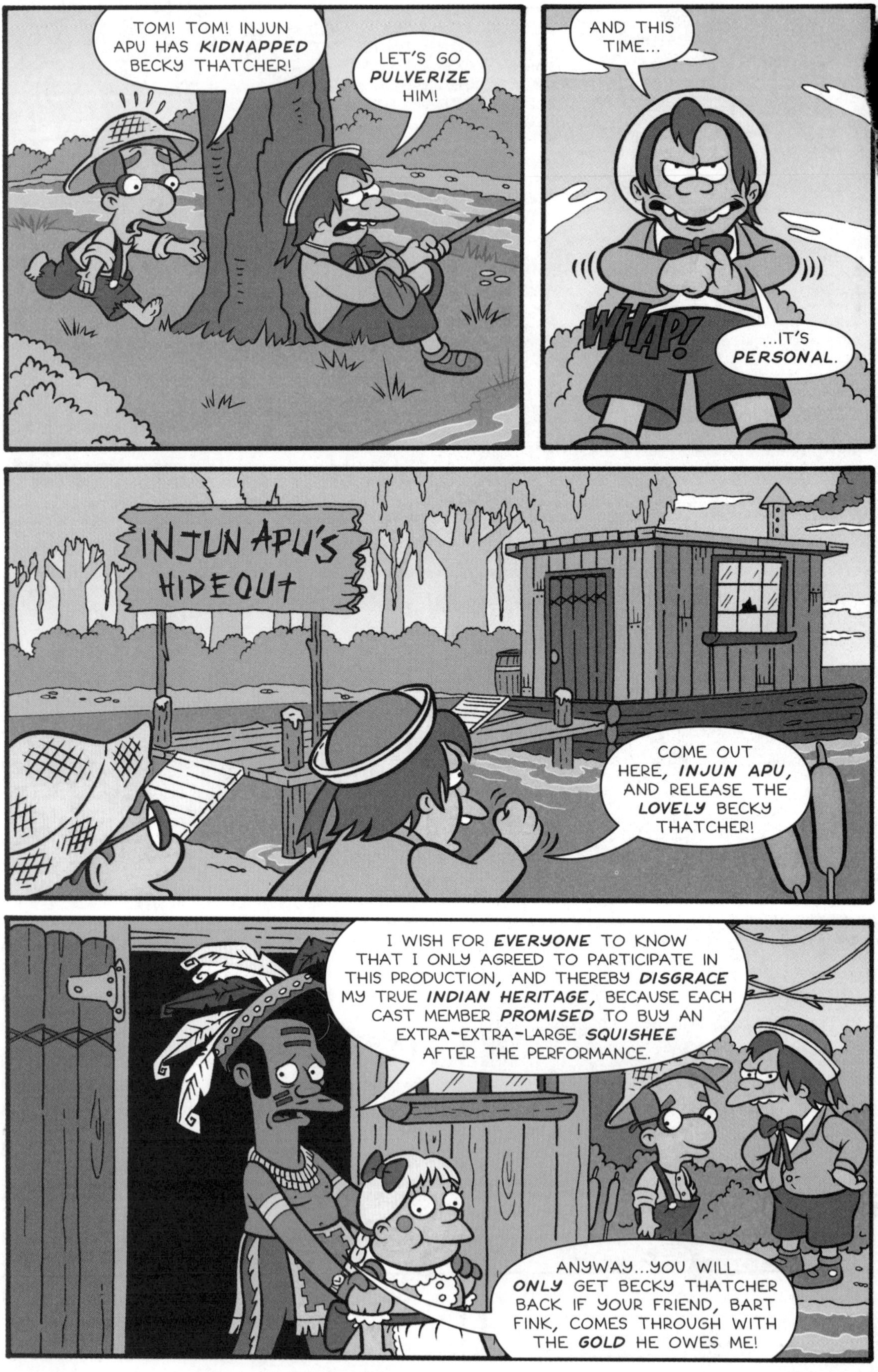
TOM! TOM! INJUN APU HAS KIDNAPPED BECKY THATCHER!
LET'S GO PULVERIZE HIM!
AND THIS TIME...
WHAP!
...IT'S PERSONAL.
INJUN APU'S HIDEOUT
COME OUT HERE, INJUN APU, AND RELEASE THE LOVELY BECKY THATCHER!
I WISH FOR EVERYONE TO KNOW THAT I ONLY AGREED TO PARTICIPATE IN THIS PRODUCTION, AND THEREBY DISGRACE MY TRUE INDIAN HERITAGE, BECAUSE EACH CAST MEMBER PROMISED TO BUY AN EXTRA-EXTRA-LARGE SQUISHEE AFTER THE PERFORMANCE.
ANYWAY...YOU WILL ONLY GET BECKY THATCHER BACK IF YOUR FRIEND, BART FINK, COMES THROUGH WITH THE GOLD HE OWES ME!

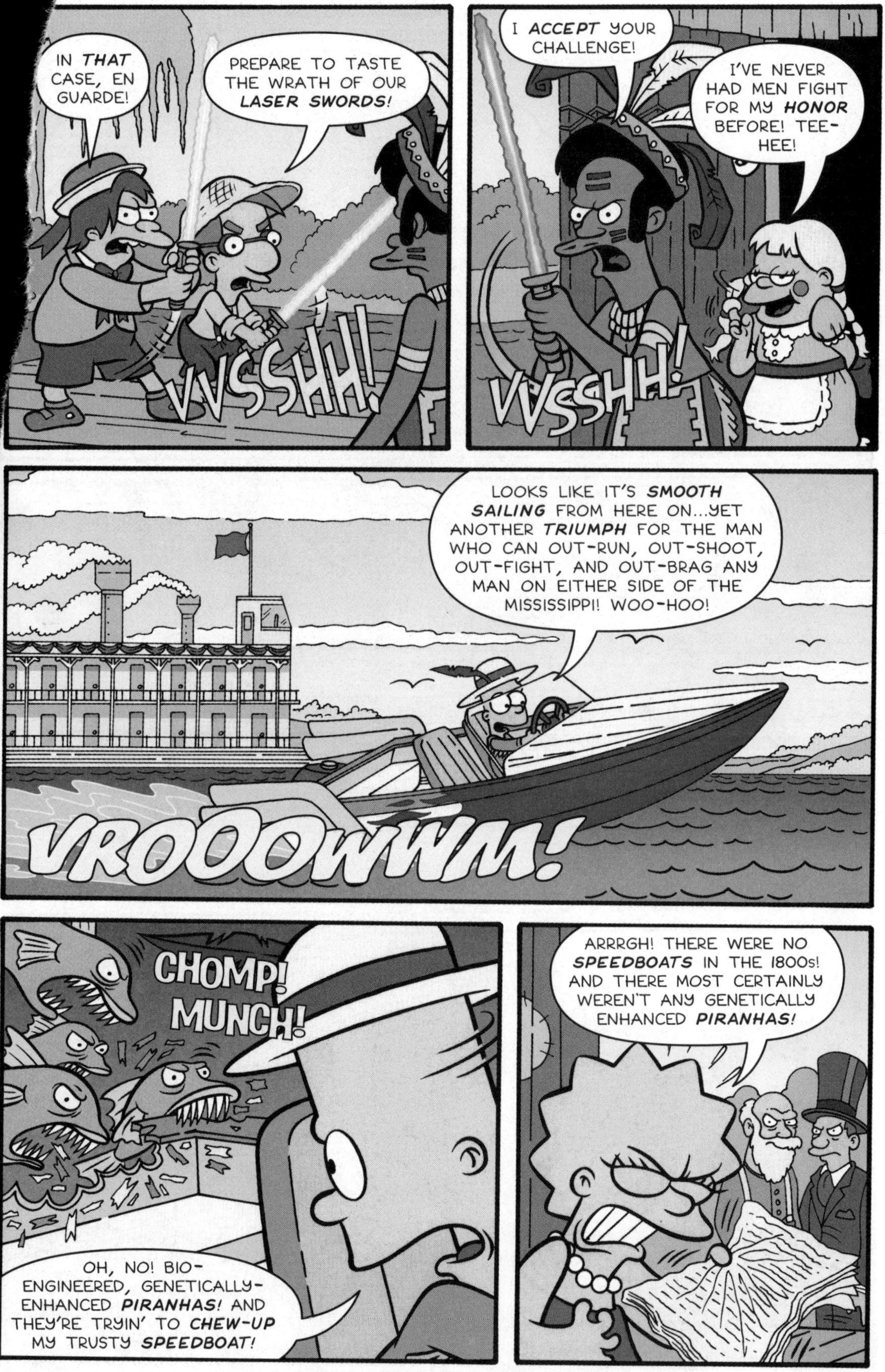

IN THAT CASE, EN GUARDE!
PREPARE TO TASTE THE WRATH OF OUR LASER SWORDS!
VVSSHH!
I ACCEPT YOUR CHALLENGE!
I'VE NEVER HAD MEN FIGHT FOR MY HONOR BEFORE! TEE-HEE!
VVSSHH!
LOOKS LIKE IT'S SMOOTH SAILING FROM HERE ON...YET ANOTHER TRIUMPH FOR THE MAN WHO CAN OUT-RUN, OUT-SHOOT, OUT-FIGHT, AND OUT-BRAG ANY MAN ON EITHER SIDE OF THE MISSISSIPPI! WOO-HOO!
VROOOWWM!
CHOMP! MUNCH!
OH, NO! BIO-ENGINEERED, GENETICALLY-ENHANCED PIRANHAS! AND THEY'RE TRYIN' TO CHEW-UP MY TRUSTY SPEEDBOAT!
ARRRGH! THERE WERE NO SPEEDBOATS IN THE 1800s! AND THERE MOST CERTAINLY WEREN'T ANY GENETICALLY ENHANCED PIRANHAS!

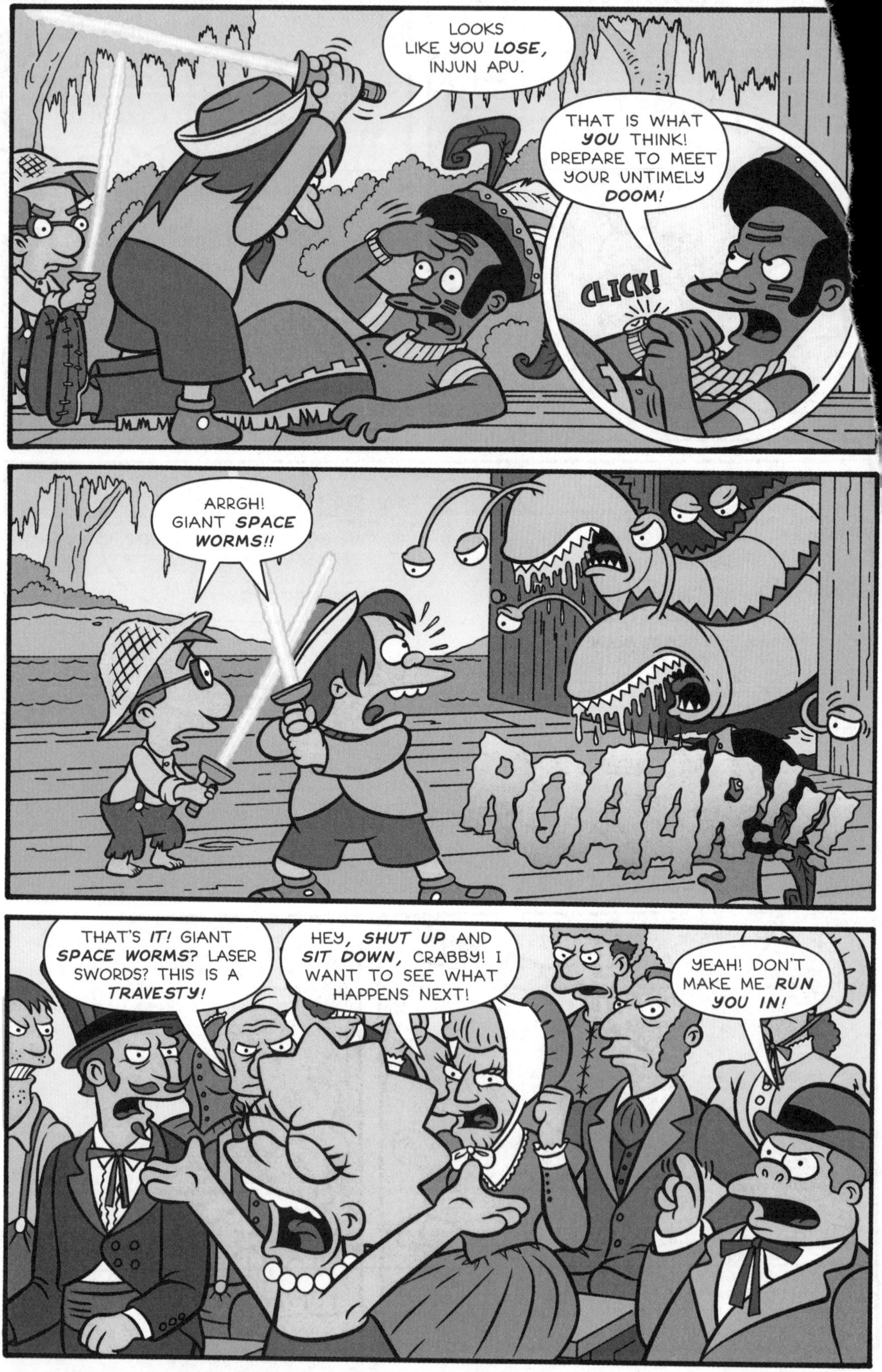
LOOKS LIKE YOU LOSE, INJUN APU.
THAT IS WHAT YOU THINK! PREPARE TO MEET YOUR UNTIMELY DOOM!
CLICK!
ARRGH! GIANT SPACE WORMS!!
ROAAR!!!
THAT'S IT! GIANT SPACE WORMS? LASER SWORDS? THIS IS A TRAVESTY!
HEY, SHUT UP AND SIT DOWN, CRABBY! I WANT TO SEE WHAT HAPPENS NEXT!
YEAH! DON'T MAKE ME RUN YOU IN!

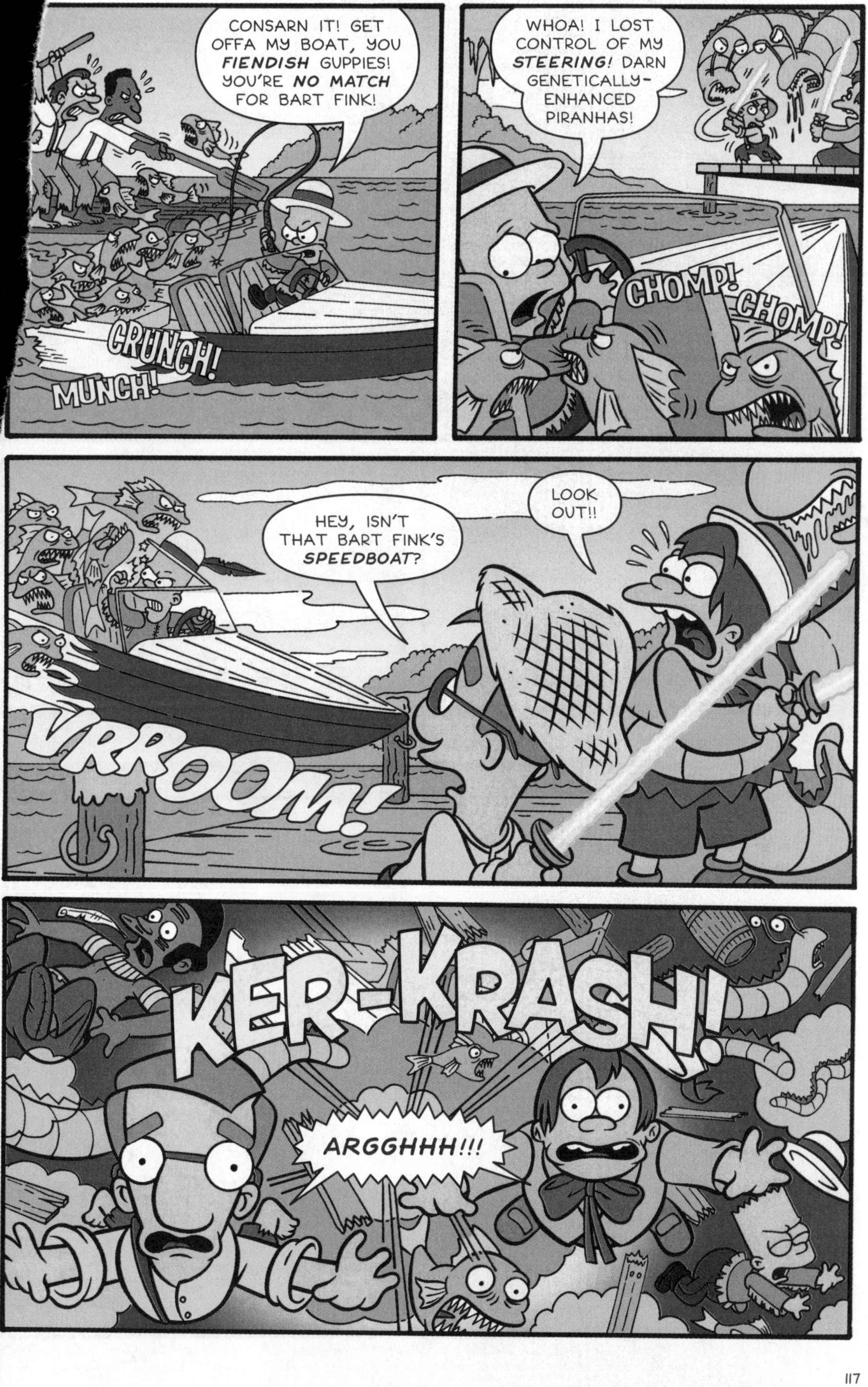
CONSARN IT! GET OFFA MY BOAT, YOU FIENDISH GUPPIES! YOU'RE NO MATCH FOR BART FINK!
CRUNCH!
MUNCH!
WHOA! I LOST CONTROL OF MY STEERING! DARN GENETICALLY-ENHANCED PIRANHAS!
CHOMP!
CHOMP!
HEY, ISN'T THAT BART FINK'S SPEEDBOAT?
LOOK OUT!!
VRROOM!
KER-KRASH!
ARGGHHH!!!

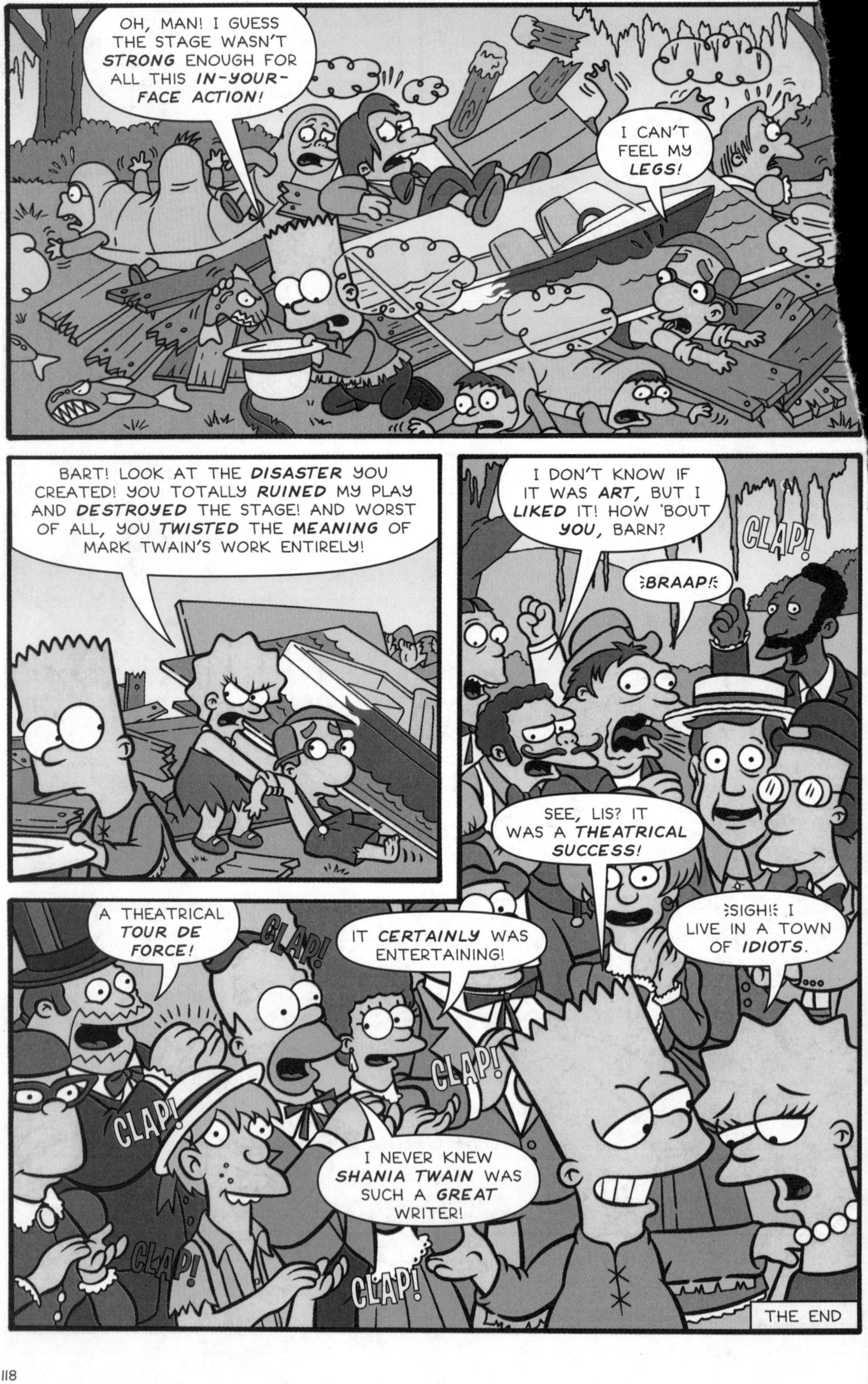
OH, MAN! I GUESS THE STAGE WASN'T STRONG ENOUGH FOR ALL THIS IN-YOUR-FACE ACTION!
I CAN'T FEEL MY LEGS!
BART! LOOK AT THE DISASTER YOU CREATED! YOU TOTALLY RUINED MY PLAY AND DESTROYED THE STAGE! AND WORST OF ALL, YOU TWISTED THE MEANING OF MARK TWAIN'S WORK ENTIRELY!
I DON'T KNOW IF IT WAS ART, BUT I LIKED IT! HOW 'BOUT YOU, BARN?
CLAP!
BRAAP!
SEE, LIS? IT WAS A THEATRICAL SUCCESS!
A THEATRICAL TOUR DE FORCE!
CLAP!
IT CERTAINLY WAS ENTERTAINING!
SIGH! I LIVE IN A TOWN OF IDIOTS.
CLAP!
CLAP!
I NEVER KNEW SHANIA TWAIN WAS SUCH A GREAT WRITER!
CLAP!
CLAP!
THE END

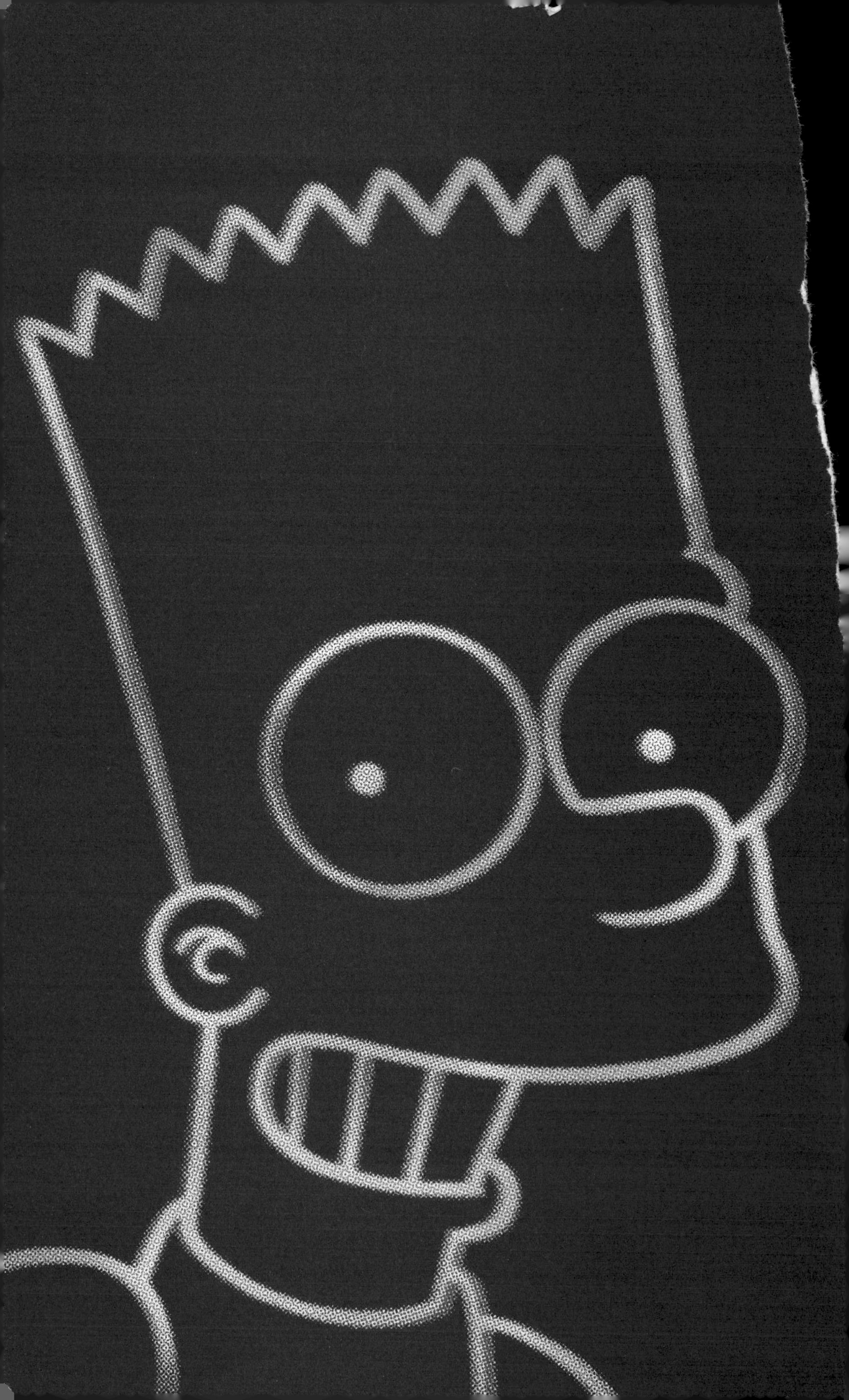